KENT AND ESSEX
SEA FISHERIES COMMITTEE.

REPORT

ON THE

SEA FISHERIES AND FISHING INDUSTRIES
OF THE THAMES ESTUARY.

(Prepared by Dr. JAMES MURIE.)

[ORDERED TO BE PRINTED AT MEETING OF THE KENT AND ESSEX
SEA FISHERIES COMMITTEE, 7th DEC., 1903.]

KENT & ESSEX SEA-FISHERIES DISTRICT.

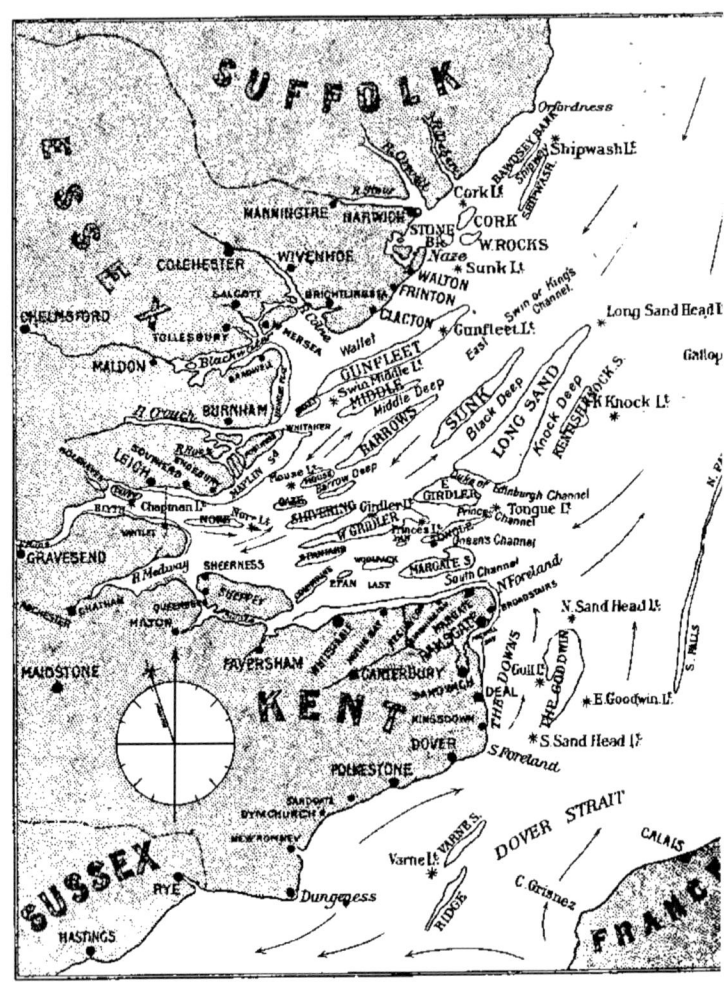

SKETCH MAP.

Diagrammatic Chart of the area comprising Kent and Essex Sea-Fisheries District, viz., Dungeness to Harwich (Dovercourt Lights). Sands and Shoals are enclosed in outlines (capitals), the Channels between (smaller lettering). Asterisks (*) denote Lights (Lightships and Lighthouses). Dots (●) mark Fishing Stations (save three inland towns). A Contour Line is added where extensive sands bound shore, *e.g.*, Maplins. Arrows indicate Tide Currents generally. The Thames Conservancy boundary, Crowstone (Leigh) to Yantlet, is shown by dotted line across river.

I. THE THAMES ESTUARY AND LEIGH-ON-SEA FISHERIES.

CONTENTS.

I. Purport of Report.
II. Thames Estuary and its Physical Formation.
III. Leigh as a Fishery Station.
IV. Whales, Food-fishes, Crustacea, Shell-fish, &c.
V. Fishing Grounds of the Leighmen.
VI. Special Estuarine Fisheries.
VII. The Leigh Fishermen.
VIII. Their Fishing Craft.
IX. Apparatus of Capture, Cooking, Transport, &c.
X. General Returns from Fisheries.
XI. Fish Product Manufacture.
XII. Economics of Fisheries.
XIII. Fishery Protection and Culture.
XIV. Summary and Recommendations.

I.—PURPORT OF REPORT.

THE Sub-Committee (composed of equal numbers of representatives from Kent and Essex) was appointed by your Committee on the motion of Captain Anderson—" To investigate the Fisheries, and recommend such steps as they may from time to time think best for their development."

The subject in question was amply discussed from various points of view. Among others, one fact was brought prominently into consideration, namely: that within our Sea Fisheries District there is included quite a variety of methods and conditions of fishing; notwithstanding a considerable amount of sameness and flatness of aspect in the greater part of the coast. For example, we have North Sea or Deep Sea Trawlers (Ramsgate, Dover, Folkestone and Brightlingsea) ; offshore and inshore fisheries (Harwich, Tollesbury, West Mersea, Margate, Deal, Dungeness, &c.); estuarine fisheries (Maldon, Sheerness, Queenborough, Southend and Leigh); besides the great shell-fish industries (Whitstable, Faversham, Burnham, &c.), so characteristic of the conjoint counties. Expressed otherwise there are in use, beam trawl and drift-net, long-line and hand-line, seine, bag or stow-net; Leigh shrimp-net, shove-net, dredge and kettle-net, crab and lobster pots, and, even to a limited degree, rod, leger-line and hoop-net may be included—altogether a very goodly array.

In short, it would seem that the interests involved, and thereby modes adopted, whether at the greater or lesser fishing centres, are to some extent occasionally antagonistic; speciality of fishery and peculiarity of method depending greatly on locality, its surroundings and prevalence of kinds of fish at certain seasons. It follows and becomes evident that difficulties beset any hard-and-fast lines of recommendation strictly applicable, and equally beneficial to all stations concerned.

Whilst one member of Sub-Committee submitted that the destruction of immature fish was the crying evil to be re-dressed, another supported the view that in our area the catch was plentiful enough with no diminution on the average, spite of supposed over-fishing; a third thought reduction of carriage and better markets were points worth inquiring into; a fourth held that it was essential, especially in the case of shell-fish, that a Government measure alone was the touchstone of improvement. But notwithstanding this seeming diversity of convictions, there was quite a consensus of opinion that deficiency of reliable information was the great drawback. Indeed, until such data are acquired, there can be no solid basis whereon to found recommendations, as to the fisheries development.

Of places which may be regarded as fishing stations there are about thirty; Kent and Essex having nearly equal numbers. Some are important centres, others quite the reverse. Of the latter out-of-the-way corners, however, all the more necessary is it that something further should be learned regarding them.

From the constitution of the Sea Fisheries Committees, whereof half the members are appointed by the County Council, the other by the Board of Trade, and the drawback that members' travelling expenses shall not be paid for them, there arises an acknowledged difficulty. It is this : that in nearly all the other Fisheries' Committees, as well as our own, attendance on the part of practical fishermen, who live at a distance, and who cannot afford to be present at the meetings, is consequently hindered. Hence, unfortunately, the fishermen class are not so thoroughly represented as they should be. This state of things seems incongruous, for the Sea Fisheries Act of 1888 was but an appendix to the Local Government Act of the same year, primarily to ensure the popular representation of the fishermen and "fishing interests "—so to say a mixed branch Committee of the County Council with limited jurisdiction and powers. Thus it is all the more clearly needful that positive information should be furnished as to the present actual status, the history, the prospects, and the requirements of every fishery locality within the bounds of the Fisheries District. Such at least was the view taken by a majority of the Sub-Committee.

The Sub-Committee further came to the determination— and it was unanimously resolved—that instead of merely outlining what should be the basis of the facts to be acquired at each special fishery station, the more business-like way of proceeding would be to present to your Committee data concerning a single locality. This, perhaps, varied with considerable abbreviations, according to circumstances, might serve as an example of the kind of thing they are inclined to recommend should be done in other instances. As to how this wider phase of the question may best be accomplished, and from what source the funds necessary are to be derived, these doubtless your Committee hereafter will take into consideration; meantime our colleague Dr. Murie has volunteered this contribution on the estuarine fishery station he represents.

Choice thus fell on Leigh :—(*a*) Its fishing grounds lie both in Kent and Essex waters ; (*b*) Besides flat and round fisheries, and its speciality of shrimping, it also combines oyster storing, cockling, and mussel and winkle beds ; (*c*) In certain aspects it offers material for study, and throws a side-light on the brood and undersized fish questions ; (*d*) Its history demonstrates the difficulties attendant on the rights of public *versus* private fisheries ; (*e*) In adjoining the Thames Conservancy and Rochester Corporation, the occasional friction of boundaries interests receives illustration ; (*f*) Data incident to changes in type, in methods of, and in apparatus can be traced pretty closely ; (*g*) Pollutions and other troublous matters furnish object lessons. Thus Leigh-on-Sea, so far, presents a kind of epitome of most of those topics affecting the working of the Sea Fisheries Districts generally—and which are so keenly discussed annually at the meetings of representatives of authorities under the Sea Fisheries Regulations Act, 1888.

A general Report on the entire District might result in statements, opinions or suggestions being somewhat modified.*

* Whilst upon your Sub-Committee, as a body, necessarily devolves the responsibility of this Report—which they have examined and freely criticised in MS. and printed proof—yet they desire to emphasize the fact that its conception and carrying out have vested solely with one of their members (Dr. Murie). They would here also express their combined thanks to the undermentioned individuals who have contributed such information, on local matters and otherwise, as has enabled the Report to be drawn up in its present form.

Fishermen.

Baxter, Barnard	Emery, George W., jun.	Meddle, Stephen
Bundock, Albert	„ Frederick	Murrel, Henry (?)
„ Beaumont	Gilson, George	„ William (?)
Bridge, Frederick	„ John	Noakes, Archer
Cotgrove, Henry	Harvey, John	Palmer, Charles
„ James	„ Robert	Partridge, Samuel
„ Nathan, sen.	„ William	Robinson, Abraham
„ Thomas	Johnson, Robert, sen.	Ritchie, Henry
„ William	„ Robert, jun.	Turnnidge, Samuel
Deal, Joe	Kirby, George	Tyrrel, James
Emery, Benjamin	„ Stephen	Wilder, Harry
„ George, sen.	Little, William	„ Mark

For much assistance, and quite a variety of communications and hints, among the above, R. Johnson, sen., and J. Tyrrel deserve special mention.

Old Residents, Officials, Boat Builders, Ship-Chandlers, &c.

Bradley, George	Dennis, Edward	Kirby, Frederick
Brown, Charles	(Station Master)	Partridge, Nathan
„ Walter	Epps, Albert	Thomson, Henry
(Fisherman's Agent)	Foster, William	„ Mrs. H.
Bundock, Thomas A.	Harris, John (?) (Custom	Tomlin, Thomas
„ Walter	House Officer, Southend)	„ Rev. Michael
Cotgrove, Arthur	Harrison, George, sen.	

II.—THAMES ESTUARY AND ITS PHYSICAL FORMATION.

On casual thought the connection between the physical formation of the Thames Estuary and its fisheries may not at once seem quite apparent. But on further inquiry and reflection on the subject, their intimate relationship becomes more manifest and appreciable.

1. Limits.—What are the precise limits of the Estuary? is a question easier asked than answered. As a matter of fact, there are no positive boundaries agreed on by authorities, and the discrepancies of the latter only show that convenience of purpose in view has been the sole guide. For instance, among others, this has been acknowledged by such a sound authority as Captain Tizard, R.N., in his extensive Hydrographical Surveys in the "Triton," 1882-9.*

He assumes and adopts as a western boundary a line drawn from Southend across to Sheerness; for an eastern line of demarcation the meridian of the Kentish Knock Light-vessel; for the south, Kent [to N. Foreland]; and for a northern limit the coast of Essex. This area contains some 800 square nautical miles, and is crowded with sandbanks. Viewed from a hydrographical standpoint, Tizard's eastern boundary may be accepted; but his western is merely an arbitrary or nominal one, chosen possibly as including Sheerness and naval interests.

The Thames Conservancy's limit (Crowstone to Yantlet) is merely a formal divisionary line, serving to define sharply where their and the Trinity Board's jurisdiction abut, irrespective of estuarine demarcation. Notwithstanding it has a certain historic importance, not only as concerns the ancient septennial water pageants of the Corporation of the City of London, but likewise as denoting the Isle of Grain's exemption from the City's jurisdiction.†

---

* Summarised in his paper on "The Thames Estuary" [its channel changes], "Nature," 1890.
† Consult Fletcher, Jour. Statist. Soc., Vol. IV. (1841) —"Ancient Prescriptive Jurisdictions over the Thames possessed by the Corporation of London."

From the aspect of geography and physics, probably the west end of the estuary might best be regarded as the head of Sea Reach, or as it merges into the Lower Hope near the boundary stone of the Watermen's Company. Hereabouts the shores more decidedly narrow, and this is where brackish water becomes more sensibly evident, even at half-ebb. Thus the change in temperature through the tidal mixture of fresh and salt water here most truly denotes an estuarine character. Moreover, the interests of estuary fishermen (notably those of Leigh and Southend) extend thus far; so practically for sea-fishery purposes the natural west extension of the Thames Estuary to the Lower Hope is preferable to that of Tizard or of the Conservancy's limit.

If the same principle of the physical geography with refer-ence to the salinity and temperature of the water be taken into account, then the eastern section of the Thames' mouth—say from the Nore or, perhaps, the Mouse Light, due south, might be considered under the denomination of a firth,[*] as holds good in the Forth, the Clyde and other northern rivers. But, on the other hand, the term "Thames Estuary," *par excel-lence*, has been applied for centuries by navigators, fishermen, Government and other authorities to the area stretching from between the North Foreland towards Harwich, and embracing the exit of the rivers Medway, Crouch, Blackwater, Colne, Stour and Orwell. Hence we may abide by the common defi-nition Thames Estuary, irrespective of the scientific distinction betwixt an estuary and a firth, or the minor inflowing rivers above-mentioned.

2. **Estuary Origin.**—To obtain a retrospective view of this estuarine question and its bearings on fisheries, a glance at the geological evidence is instructive. In long past ages Kent joined the continent of Europe, for then there were no Straits of Dover. Most of the southern part of the North Sea was low, flat, dry land. Through this ran a great river which drained

---

[*] *See* Mill, "On River Entrances," Brit. Assoc. Rep. for 1886, and 6th Ann. Rep. Fishery Board, Scotland, for 1886.

mid-Europe northwards—a precursor of the modern Rhine. Towards its embouchure it received a western tributary, namely, what may be regarded as an ancient Thames. This latter took a sharp N.E. bend (where now is the estuary) before joining its waters with the more voluminous continental river. Thus it coursed somewhat in the direction of the present Black Deep or the Swin, and quite possibly formed a sort of delta among the then low-lying marshy land there. It is interesting, therefore, to note that this ancient Thames river's sweep foreshadowed the present main or north channel of the later-formed Thames Estuary.

As geological time rolled on there was a gradual subsidence of the "North-Sea-Land," a pouring in of the North Atlantic, and, consequently, steady formation of the present North Sea. At the period in question there was another great sea inlet, entering, however, from the west—an equivalent of the existing English Channel; but its eastern end probably did not reach further than where the Ridge and Varne shoals are now situate. Whether, in consequence of the gradual land depression, as aforesaid, or erosion of the chalk barrier—most probably by a combination of these forces—the northern and western arms of these seas met, forming what constitutes the Straits of Dover. At all events, from this sea-junction dates the physical configuration and concomitant phenomena belonging to the present area of our Fisheries District. (*See* diagrammatic chart.)

Captain Tizard (*loc. cit.*) has assumed that the sands are upwards of 60 feet thick; indeed, he states that borings have proved the Goodwins to be 80 feet in vertical depth. He points out that with the exception of deposits of shingle off Whitstable and Garrison Point, the banks are mainly composed of sand intermixed with shells. When dry the banks are firm; but partake of the nature of quicksands on other occasions, as some members of our Committee can substantiate from personal experience.

Thus, though the sands undoubtedly constitute the expansive groundwork of the estuarine area, yet the occurrence of the chalk at Margate, London clay at Sheppey and Leigh, and old river gravels, &c., elsewhere, give variety to the marine life and fish-food. (*See* Sect. V., Fishing Grounds.)

3. **Tides and Winds.**—The unusual states of the tides at the Straits of Dover are troublesome both to fishermen and mariners, as, unfortunately, is too well known to them. Now the explanation of the apparent erratic tide movements there has to be sought for in the physiography of the District and its antecedent derivation as given above. The rationale seems to be that the area of the sea-bottom of the ancient land, with its declivity northwards, still exerts an influence on current and tidal phenomena. Thus, from our southernmost station, Dungeness, a line drawn thence to Capo Gris-nez, or say Boulogne, and another from the North Foreland towards Dunkerque, enclose what may be termed a neutral zone. Within this, besides a see-saw direction of the northerly (North Sea) and southerly (English Channel) streams, the tides are rotary, with scarcely an interval of slack water (Pilot's Handbook). There is a heaping up of the water in the Strait, which temporarily swerves any excess of North Sea flood-wave into the Thames Estuary. About high tide the Channel stream has pressed towards Dover or even somewhat beyond; as ebb begins it retires in favour of the North Sea stream, which follows to about opposite Beachy Head. Here commences a sharp parting; one stream continues its westerly course, the other runs back into the North Sea.

Whence blows the wind! has a further effect on the Thames Estuary. If it blows from the S.W., veers to the W., and quickly changes to strong N.W. gales, extraordinary high tides prevail in the river—as happened on the memorable 29th November, 1897.

On that occasion the flood reached the ancient high-water level at Leigh, and there was sad destruction on the North Kent shores. The phenomena of these excessive tides, then, is accounted for by the wind first driving the stream up the

English Channel to its narrow eastern end; whilst the Gulf-
Stream immediately thereafter forces the current round the
north of Scotland, and carries the mass of the North Sea waters
along the English east coast towards the Kentish promontory,
where, blocked, it rushes in volume up river.

4. **Fish and North Sea Currents.**—How these marine currents
and aerial perturbations affect the South-east Anglian fisheries receives elucidation from various sources. Though the
North Sea has been fished for centuries, yet it is only 30 years ago
since its hydrography and biology have been systematically
studied as bearing on fishery questions; but there is still much
to learn. The German Fish Commission (1872-73) led the
way, and other exploring expeditions followed, in which
Norway, Sweden, Denmark and Britain have taken part.

The Fishery Board for Scotland instituted a series of experiments to ascertain the direction taken by some thousands
of drift-bottles thrown into various parts of the North Sea.
From the data thus furnished, Dr. Fulton[*] goes on to show that
the surface water of the North Atlantic in the neighbourhood of
the Orkneys veers southwards along the Scotch and English
coasts to as far as the Wash. Thence it trends across towards
the north of Holland, where it once more changes its course
northwards along the coasts of Denmark and Norway.

In brief, these drift-bottles demonstrated a U-shaped
circulation of the surface water in the North Sea. Only on
one occasion during a long spell of S.E. winds did the drifters
show a tendency to reversal of direction. It is further worthy
of remark that none of the drift-bottles crossed southwards of
the supposed limits of the ancient "delta-land" as heretofore
defined.

Mr. Garstang[†] has made similar experiments to test the
direction of the English Channel currents, starting the floats

[*] "The Currents of the North Sea and their relations to Fisheries," 15th Ann.
Rep. for 1896, and 14th Rep., 1895. About the same time Prof. Herdman, of Liverpool,
also made investigations of like kind in the Irish Sea, which yielded interesting
results, but here these need not be further referred to. (*See* Lancashire S.F. Reports,
issued 1895 and 1896); also Fulton, "Additional Note, &c.," 18thAnn. Rep. S.F.B. for 1899.
[†] "Report on the Surface Drift of the English Channel and neighbouring Seas
during 1897," Jour. Mar. Biolog. Assoc., Vol. V., 1898.

from the neighbourhood of the Eddystone. Some bottles went west, even rounding the Land's End. The majority passed along the English coast, or grounded at various points. Some again, about opposite Dungeness, swerved to the French coast, between Calais and Boulogne. A solitary one got to near Ramsgate, and a number passed the Straits of Dover and were eventually stranded on the continental coasts from Holland to Norway. These last show that under certain states of the tide, with westerly wind, a surface drift leads into the east side of the Dover Strait. Yet the normal tidal streams of the Channel (Pilot's Handbook) are to a certain degree circulatory as in the North Sea: to wit, the ancient barrier still has a sway.

Reverting to another aspect of the question, viz. :—Have the currents on the east British coast any influence on the migration of food fish or on the location of the spawning grounds? These points have likewise received elucidation from the Scotch Fishery Board.*

The general results are to the following effect:—That the important food-fish whose eggs float, such as the cod, haddock, plaice, sole, lemon-sole, turbot and halibut, *do not spawn* within the east coast territorial waters, whilst sprat and flounder *do spawn*, chiefly within the three-mile limit. Others, again, whiting, dab and gurnard *hover within the limits*, or spawn *further off-shore*, as the case may be. Then, again, the investigations show that the buoyant eggs, often hatching *en route*, are swept by the currents *south* and *inshore*. There also seems to be in different species a relation in length of time in egg development, according to temperature and the distance the eggs are floated. Where carried into estuaries the post-larval fish there congregate in "nurseries" in immense numbers. As a rule, the young fish mainly take a course up the estuary towards the *south shore;* while the fuller grown and more adult

---

* Fulton. " Migration and Rate of Growth of Food Fishes," 15th Ann. Rep. for 1892; also " Relation of Marine Currents to Off-shore Spawning Areas and Inshore Nurseries," 13th Ann. Rep. for 1894; and 17th Ann. Rep. for 1898. *See* likewise Cunningham, " Marketable Marine Fishes, 1895 "; and McIntosh & Masterman, " British Marine Food Fishes, 1897."

fish leave in a *northern* direction and ultimately hie back towards their original spawning-ground.

Now these data of migration, spawning and otherwise, do not apply alone to one locality, but are equally applicable to a wide east coast range. *Cæteris paribus*, they accord with what has been observed in the great bight of the Moray Firth, in the Tay and St. Andrew's Bay, the Forth and the Humber. Nay, in spite of the easterly deviation of North Sea surface current, as mentioned above, we have evidence in favour of the same phenomena being partially applicable to the estuary of the Thames, even though in the latter the ebb tide, by addition of pent-up river water, flows longer and stronger than the flood.

5. **Efflux.**—The Thames and the Medway of a certainty carry down an immense quantity of detritus mud and floating débris. Part of the mud is deposited on the shores and shoals, or reaches the creeks; but of the lighter particles an immeasurable amount is swept outwards and northwards by the very strong ebb tides. This is markedly evident at the slack and turn of the tide, say at the edge of the Maplins, the Mouse Light and the Oaze. Then, as the undercurrent begins to creep up-stream, if the more stationary surface water is examined, it will be found grumly, crowded with buoyant material, and often alive with animal forms feeding thereon. Doubtless the Crouch, the Roach, the Colne and the Blackwater contribute their share of river mixtures. But these are indeed scant in proportion to the bulk transported by the Thames and Medway, where towns, riparian factories and enormous river traffic concur to augment their quota of effluent towards the estuary mouth.

It may incidentally be remarked that this mud and supernatant stuff is not altogether an unmixed evil so far as the fish themselves and the fisheries are concerned. (*See* Sects. IV. and XIV.) Also it is remarkable how relatively little mud there seems to remain on the usual fishing grounds from the Nore seawards. The heaviest particles would seem to intermingle completely with the sands, which are nearly everywhere predominant.

6. General Results.—Taking into consideration what precedes, it seems a legitimate inference that the present conditions of the whole coast of our Sea-Fisheries District amply bear witness to a permanent influence of former times, notwithstanding the wondrous changes which have occurred during the lapse of ages.

Seeing that the English Channel is the near cut of ocean route to the Thames Estuary, one would expect its influence paramount. Instead, the Atlantic gulf-stream, with its contingent of colder Arctic water, comes by the long route round Scotland and swoops into the North Sea. A funnel-shaped offset of the North Sea current, or perhaps flood tide-wave, presses the water along the Suffolk and Essex coasts, terminating in the Thames Estuary and adjoining rivers. The ebb-tide of stronger and longer duration returns in the same course. Thus it is that the surface-floating lower organisms ("Plankton" of science) and fish-food, at times swarming in myriads, are almost all of the types or allied to northern forms, as are the great majority of the fish.*

Then this bight of the southern section of the North Sea, comparatively shallow (save in a narrow middle strip of some 20 to 30 fathoms depth) shorewards, harbours mussels, cockles and worms in plenty, with crustaceans varied and numerous; all these furnishing the bulk of the flat-fish food. Again, the many sand-banks offshore (*see* chart diagram) are doubtless, with exceptions, the chief spawning-grounds and rendezvous of certain of the mature fish whose floating spawn and brood crowd the inner estuary in due season.

Lastly, as is well known, the North Kent and the Essex shores are famous for their oysters and other edible shell-fish. This is greatly dependent on the physical formation of the district. The shallow waters conduce towards a congenial temperature. Then their salinity just hits the happy medium,

---

* Consult Cunningham and Holt's "North Sea Investigations," and especially the former's "Physical and Biological Conditions in the North Sea," where species entering from north and south are discussed. Jour. Mar. Biol. Assoc., Vols. II., III., IV. (1891-7).

varied by occasional freshets from the rivers. But the great factor of the oysters thriving and breeding so well in the Thames Estuary, and the creeks and waters connected therewith, is the abundance of diatoms, foraminifera and such like microscopic plants and animals. On the muddy clay, when dry at ebb, there is everywhere a coating of olive-brown, slimy looking material, otherwise a delicate film of diatoms of various species. Now nothing equals the unctuous blue London clay—locally known as "clyte"—together with brackish water, for the fostering of these lowly organized algæ. Add to this a substratum of gravel and shelly sand, with just sufficient superficial deposit, teeming as it does with microscopic life, and you have a choice home[*] for the sedentary oyster and its molluscan fraternity, &c.

Take Whitstable, for example, which is peculiarly and happily situated. This, inasmuch as the neighbouring Isle of Sheppey (a mass of London clay constantly tumbling from the cliffs), aided by a slight south-easterly ebb current, regularly bring abundant supply of oyster-food. The Whitstable grounds, moreover, are so placed as to miss the full force of the North Sea flood-current, which passes in a somewhat south-westerly direction from the Swin and Deeps round the opposite Essex coast up-river. The Kentish Flats area, again, lie to a certain extent in a comparatively neutral tidal zone, or, rather, sea-eddy; for there is a perceptible volume of the warmer Dover Strait ebb-wave pressed round the North Foreland partially along the North Kent shore. Therefore, freely bathed alternately with copious supply of sea and brackish water, with plenitude of "culch" derived from centuries of oyster growth, constant cleaning of the grounds, &c., all the conditions of healthy, successful oyster culture are present.

Other nooks in Essex, with degrees in variation of conditions, fully sustain the reputation for edible shell-fish rearing and culture which our Sea-Fisheries District bears.

---

[*] *Vide* Winslow's Description of Natural Beds, Rep. Oyster Beds, James River, Virginia, 1881 ; also Anson & Willett, "Oyster Culture," Lond., 1884.

As a corollary to this section it may be sustained:—(*a*) That the physical geography of our Fisheries District is of primary importance; (*b*) that meteorological conditions, *i.e.*, weather as affecting winds and tides, &c., play a not less secondary part; (*c*) that one season, say either with severe frost or long continued intense heat and sunshine, or of gloomy, wet, stormy weather, has depressing or elevating effects accordingly on the sensitive minute marine life, and the disastrous or successful sequel of which is only appreciable the following season or seasons; (*d*) that paucity or abundance of fish is indissolubly linked with the less appreciable presence or otherwise of the minor (often microscopic) life extant—not, therefore, as frequently emphasized, solely owing to objectionable instruments or methods of capture.

III.—LEIGH AS A FISHING STATION.

Early History.—In the Domesday Book (1086) we learn* that at Leigh there were five " Bordarii," or what corresponded to cottar-fishermen families. They possessed no land for cultivation, and were, in fact, poor free fishermen in their position and ways. These Bordars, truly speaking, represented the nucleus or were the forerunners of the later fishing community of Leigh. It was well-nigh a century and a half after that Henry III. (*circa* 1220) granted the right of a several fishery in Hadleigh Ray to his great Justiciar, Hubert de Burgh, builder of Hadleigh Castle. Here commences the Leigh fisheries record, which has continued without intermission to the present day.

The fisheries, &c., frequently reverting to the Crown are heard of in the reign of Edward I. (1280) by his minister furnishing fishery accounts, and in 1303 payments for " Kidell " apparatus. Quite a string of dukes and earls possessed the

---

* *See* " History of the Rochford Hundred," by the late Philip Benton.

patrimony, even to the Queen of Edward IV. (*circa* 1460). Henry VIII.'s wives held the fishery as pin money; his last spouse, Catherine Parr, in a plan drawn by her own hands, added the words, " *Nostra Piscaria in dominio Hadleigh* " (1547 ?). But a few years later (1551) Edward VI. presented the fishery to Lord Rich, who in 1555 successfully sued a William Gillett for taking mussels. On descending to the Earl of Warwick he leased "all that is fishing and liberty of fishing " to Anne Brand and others from 1649. There occurred an important departure in oyster laying about 1700, by a lessee under Sir Francis St. John. (*See* Oyster Industry, sect. VI.)

Between the close of the previous up to the middle of the 19th century the fishery was the property of Sir John Bernard and Lady Olivia Bernard Sparrow—the latter a most bountiful patron to the Leigh fishermen in many ways. From these by both lease and purchase it passed to several parties, among others Messrs. Hainidge, Alston, Plumb, Hilton, Baxter, Foster, Tabor, Hammond, Wright, and finally the Salvation Army. Thus from Royalty to the "Submerged Tenth " has been the fate of this old fishery. From first to last it has been a continual conflict between the Leigh fishermen insisting upon their supposed rights of free fishery, and the defence of the claims of private ownership; as the late Baron Pollock tersely remarked on the Bench in the Foster *versus* Frost case, he "feared that the fishery had gone to feed the lawyers."[*]

What first Fisheries.—From the preceding remarks it is obvious that Leigh as a station commenced with fisheries in general, though after a while and for a period shell-fish—oysters, mussels and winkles—were the most marked feature. The fisheries, however, were by no means confined to this branch, for among the earliest intimations we find (*supra*) the very sovereigns paid their quota towards "Kidells " in the adjoining Ray—said instruments being weir-nets for capture of flat-fish, salmon and other round fish.

---

[*] *See* paragraph in (London) " Standard," 29th January, 1887; but for circumstantial reports of the case and full evidence of witnesses, &c., consult the "Southend Standard," issues 12th June and 31st July, 1885; likewise 3rd February, 1887.

That at a comparatively early time there were boats and fisheries of some consequence at Leigh the subjoined document verifies, and points out that the London headquarters had an eye to their doings.

"A true copy* of a notice to the Craft owners in Leigh, "Mr. Wm. Pateridge." . . . . . . "You are hereby "required to be and appear at a Court of Assistants of the "Company of Free Fishermen of the River of Thames on "Thursday being the 17th Day of Feby. 1725 by Ten of the "Clock in the George Office the George in Lee, to bind your "Servants, pay your Quarteridge, number your Craft, and "qualify yourself in every respect, As the Act of Parliament "and Bye-Laws of the said Company direct. Or in default "thereof you will be prosecuted according to Law."

"St. John Gates, Cl."

The same Company about this period in a petition to Parliament urge that :—"The fishery of the River Thames, especially for salmon fish, hath been in times past justly reputed the best and most plentifully stocked of any fishery in Europe, but the same is now wholly destroyed." That this could not be quite the truth is known, inasmuch as 50 years after the salmon fishing was in force on the Thames, even at London itself.

Smugglers and Coastguard.—That Leigh should have had its smugglers' roost is not to be wondered at, seeing that every creek, &c., on the whole coast of Essex was the resort of boats devoted to little else.

On the old "Peter Boat" public-house, High Street, Leigh (dating beyond 1695), being burnt down in 1892, a large unsuspected underground room with waterside entrance was discovered, and relics of its contraband use brought to light. This adjoined the Alley Dock, and a narrow path once upon a time led thence up hill and across country, a branch running towards Dawes Heath. This last place was a notorious ren-

---

* This is in possession of a Leigh fisherman (Abraham Wilder), to whom we are indebted for the use hereof.

dezvous of highwaymen, and report sayeth many a cask of Geneva and brandy and packets of tobacco, &c., found their way there by the connivance of the Leigh fishing community.

John Loten, collector of customs at Leigh (*circa* 1786) according to Benton,* was aware of some ten vessels of from 10 to 13 tons which, under guise of coasters and fishing craft, carried on illicit traffic in the creeks seawards of this station. A place of evil repute for the temporary deposition of spirits was " Gantlebor," a solitary spot near the Yantlet.

James Baxter, sen., now a number of years deceased, told one of his nephews that when an officer in the Leigh Custom House, the beginning of the 19th century, he made seizures *every day* in July, 1802. This clearly shews something more than fishery supported a section of the Leigh men.

There still lives at Leigh one hale, hearty, but very old fisherman, who acknowledges that he used to go alone in a small boat far down the estuary of the Thames (at times towards France), where, after boarding foreign vessels, he returned by stealth in the darkness to Leigh with his contraband. He was strongly suspected and watched, but he managed never-theless to elude the search officers, though, as report goes, it was sometimes by a narrow shave.

The Coastguard station, we learn, was introduced at Leigh some 60 years ago or thereabouts. Their old watchhouse, a square wooden erection, was only lately demolished, on the formation of the Railway goods' station.

Early aspects as Fishing Village.—Originally some of the fishers' dwellings on the beach must have been little better than shanties; for men now living remember some of the old wooden houses, not only on the ground floor, but sunk in the ground, so that two or three steps had to be descended to their entrance, and they had no upper storeys. One by one they disappeared—a mere remnant of these low-roof dwellings attesting their former prevalence—and now many comfortable fishers' cottages are on the hill away from the water-side.

---

* *Op. cit.* Vol. II., p. 442.

In those pre-railway days Leigh was a market town. The market-place was a large open space extending from the foot of the hill, opposite the Ship Inn, across to the High Street and right on to the beach. The area in question has since been, bit by bit, encroached on. First by the railway running through it—where now is the cart crossing, new railway bridge, signal box and adjoining ground, and portion of the down platform—and afterwards by erection of houses facing the beach.

At the first census taken in 1801 the entire population consisted of 570 individuals. Possibly two-thirds of these were fishermen and families. or others connected with maritime pursuits. Census 1891 gives 2.108 population, with about one-third fishermen and families.*

The Harbour.—The inner creek-harbour and embayment out to the Leigh Road during the decade— end of thirties to end of forties—presented a different aspect to subsequent years. To as far as " Clam-shell gut " there was plenty of water at all states of the tide. The fishing boats, chiefly " Pink-sterns," with very few " Square-sterns," were remarkably small craft, the largest no more than four tons. They lay well together moored—anchored fore and aft—close alongside the quays, and as a rule used " legs " or struts to keep them upright when the tide was out. They had no small boats with them to land when tide was up. Each craft paid a weekly sum to a party (Mr. Sam. Johnson) who kept a small flat punt for taking the crews aboard and ashore each fishing trip.

Biggish vessels, traders, coasting schooners and such like, along with Alston's deep-sea oyster dredging fleet of smacks, anchored at " Clam-shell gut," where the water enabled them to swing freely with the tide. None of the then small fishing craft anchored outside in the Ray as is now the case, and yachts and yachtsmen were an unknown quantity. Instead, there strutted in *the* street or loafed round the publicans' doors the declining remnants of Norden and Camden's " lusty seamen." †

---

* Now doubled within the last 9 years.   † Magna Britannia, 1720.

Catch : How sent to market,—Till about 1820, or not long after, the main catch of the Leigh fishermen had to be sent to Billingsgate by boat, or occasionally by a cart, according to old Mr. Gilson. London was the chief market, probably Sheerness and Chatham received a small share. Thereafter a Mr. James Cook commenced to run vans nightly from Leigh to London.

These vans were large, four-wheeled, open vehicles, wherein were placed the shrimp "pads,"—viz., oblong lidded baskets— and bags of oysters or other fish as the case might be. Each "pad" would hold from eight to ten gallons of shrimps, and they were packed one above another, a tarpaulin covering the lot, and the driver perched on a high seat in front. The vans started from the "Billet" Wharf between six and seven p.m., occasionally later even to nine o'clock. With considerable excitement they were driven four-horsed up the steep hill of the village, then two or three horses took on the load, according to its weight or condition of the roads. They went by Wickford and Shenfield. At the latter they changed horses, and, again starting, arrived at Billingsgate between four and five next morning.

Mr. Cook, accidentally falling from his van, broke his neck and died. A Mr. W. R. Hay bought the vans, &c., and continued the business as heretofore. The vans were licensed to carry passengers, so fishermen occasionally paid a visit to Billingsgate to ascertain how business went, and otherwise have a day's town enjoyment. Before long Hay had a rival firm for the fish traffic in Messrs. Ab. Surridge and Sam Hong. The latter soon, though, left the opposition firm, and Hay and Surridge became partners. Hay ran between Leigh and Shenfield, and Surridge from Shenfield to London.

Next came the railway to Leigh (1855-56 ?), when Hay split partnership and became contractor to the railway, carrying the fish, &c., from the City Goods Station to Billingsgate. Surridge for a short time unsuccessfully attempted competition with the Railway Company, and since then the Railway Company have been the sole fish carriers; though, mark! the van rates have never been reduced.

Changes in Typical Fisheries.—Taken as a whole, Leigh Fishery Station has passed through successive stages of rise and decline of certain fisheries. Here suffice to say that stake-nets or stop-nets in the creeks for several sorts of fish, "banding" a modification for "trotting" for flat fish, the long-lining for cod, &c., the English Channel dredging for oysters, and several other fisheries, each having its predominant influence for the time being at the Leigh centre, have either passed entirely away or declined to a nonentity (consult sect. VI., Special Fisheries). Those fisheries for which Leigh as a fisheries station is now best known—viz., shrimping, whitebaiting, and cockling—belong to the 19th century and relatively are of modern growth, particularly cockling, whose rise is quite recent. Neither is shrimping the oldest fishery, as Dr. Laver* says:— "Of late years, however, they have been forced to go much farther out to sea than they were wont to do, in consequence of the great increase of impurities in the water, and the disturb-ance caused by the passing up and down of large numbers of steamships bound to and from the Port of London." A ten-dency to the very reverse is the case, the Leigh men rather grumbling at the restrictions to their passing up-river. Still less is it a fact, as the same writer mentions, that:—"Another section of the Leigh fishermen spends many weeks and months trawling for fish in the North Sea." Possibly the allusion is here meant to apply to the Leigh pink-shrimpers who make Harwich a summer rendezvous; but even these, as we hereafter shew, leave and return daily to port. Again, their fishing grounds there are either inshore or slightly offshore—*i.e.*, from the Gunfleet and East Swin northwards by the Sunk and Cork towards Orfordness. The above therefore enforce the practical lesson how necessary further information is desirable on the

---

* "The Mammals, Reptiles and Fishes of Essex." The latest of the Essex Field Club Special Memoirs. Vol. III. Introduction, p. 13. (Chelmsford and London, 1898.)

history, changes and actual state of facts bearing on the Fisheries Stations of our District. (*Antea, Sect. I.*)

Drawbacks and wherefore.—As a Fisheries Station, Leigh has a most serious drawback to prosperity, to wit, a shallow creek, whose depth of water, unfortunately, steadily decreases. According to tradition, the "Slade," near the Southend Pier, was the only entrance to the Swatchway and the Ray. After a time a tendency was noticed by the fishers of the steady shallowing of the Swatch, the Leigh Creek and the Ray. The current notion has been that the mussel culture in Hadleigh Ray has partly been the cause of its silting. During 1883-4 (?) a narrow deep channel with bar entrance opened up rather suddenly across the marsh-end sand—the so called " Low-way " —about 100 yards below a previous Low-way gut. The " Low-way " is now the only entrance to Leigh and Benfleet, for during low tide the Swatch is nearly dry, yet 20 years ago the fishing smacks used regularly to beat up the Swatchway at three-quarter ebb, where now they cannot sail except at high water.

The fishers further say that the elder Mr. Alston, oyster merchant, blocked up an original cross gut—viz., one in a line with the Pottery, and that he cut another new cross gut almost facing the " Crow Stone." This latter is that which at present is used by row-boat to get into the Leigh Creek during low tide.

In an Admiralty chart, " From Gravesend to Sheerness," containing data between 1856-70, we find the fishermen's state-ments borne out, all excepting the " Low-way " entrance, which had not then existence.

Accompanying the " Lower Thames Navigation Commission Report " * is an excellent series of charts and text of the navigable channel opposite Leigh, though the shallower inshore waters are less specifically marked out. However, in that of Mackenzie's Survey, 1775, what is an entrance to the Leigh Swatch and one to that of Benfleet Creek are outlined quite apart, and with shallow bars but fairly deep channels within.

---

* Thames Conservancy's Report to the Board of Trade, March, 1886.

In Captain Bullock's Surveys, 1836-77, corrected to 1879 : " The Benfleet and Leigh Creeks discharged through a single channel, with a bar of 11 feet at low water, a little less than a mile westward of the old end of Southend Pier." In Captain Tizard's Survey, 1883, the bar was only 5 feet deep, Canvey Spit had been partially washed away (1881), and Holehaven deteriorated in tidal capacity. In Captains Pirrie and Jarrard's Survey, 1895, a reversion to the state of things of a century before is manifest. Leigh Swatch and the Ray (=Benfleet Creek) have again separate entrances. The former's entrance very shallow and not followed as a channel, the latter's " Low-way " being a breach cut through marsh-end sand, almost a mile west of the former.

From a fisheries point of view it would be useful could it be ascertained precisely what has been the predominating factor of this inshore accretion, which bodes ill for Leigh. Southend Pier was erected in 1832, and some regard this as one element of change of the Swatch ; others assert the cultivation of mussels has been the active agent (*supra*). But it should be observed that the shallowing of Holehaven, latterly combined with raised crossings to Leigh Marsh, doubtless also has con-siderably lessened the ebb scour.

Whatever may have been the impetus of one or other, the full significance of the problem lies in the fact that these Leigh shore alterations are part and parcel of modifications and inter-mittent phenomena occurring for centuries and still proceeding apace all along the estuary of the Thames. In some instances the change of type of fisheries have been due to them. One thing seems most certain—viz., that provided the present ratio of swatch and creek deterioration continues—remembering that of late it accelerates apace—the threatened extinction of Leigh as a fisheries (and even yachting) station is measurable and not far distant. Some preventative measures, therefore, ought speedily to be taken.

IV.—WHALES, FOOD-FISHES, CRUS-TACEA, SHELL-FISH, &c.

THE marine animals and plants referred to in this section are mainly those having material connection with fishery interests, whether directly or indirectly. It is but an enumeration, with remarks on such forms as have come under our observation, or we have authentic information regarding from others. A more complete account of the sea-objects within our Fisheries District is a desideratum; but at present this is out of reach, for many of the lower groups have as yet scarcely been touched on by the naturalists of Kent and Essex. No matter how apparently insignificant the living things, what they lack in size is made up in numbers. Moreover, the food of the early stages of the young flat-fish are some of these self-same minute pelagic organisms. Though the latter are more deserving of attention as concerns fishery, nevertheless we give precedence to seals and whales, as creatures with lungs (not gills), respiring air, though otherwise adapted to an aquatic life.

SEALS AND WHALES.

The Seals (=fam. *Phocidæ*) —(1) The COMMON SEAL (*Phoca vitulina*) may be regarded as the most likely species to be encountered along our coasts and estuaries. Ordinarily the fishermen do not capture them in their nets; more often they succumb to the gun of the sportsman. The old Leighmen say, so far as their recollection goes, that every other year an odd seal would make its appearance in the fall of year, and hang about for some time, unless misfortune befel it.

Such certainly has been the case for the last few years back. A favourite haunt has been the sandy bays and spits of Canvey Island. It has been observed that as the tide flows the seal follows the flood and fishes up and down the Leigh or Hadleigh Ray. At ebb it goes out with the tide, and reverts to its chief quarters outside Canvey. Its whereabouts is generally made known by its popping up its head, having a good look round and thus satisfying its curiosity of what is going on among the sailing craft. The lower end of the Ray at certain times is an attractive resort for shrimps and young fish, which *Phoca* has apparently appreciated.

In other localities within our Sea Fisheries District, one, sometimes two in company, frequents the estuaries : *e.g.* (the Stour, Essex), the Blackwater*, Roach, Medway, Stour (Kent), and even Dover and Folkestone harbours.

FIG. 1.

Common Seal (*Phoca vitulina*), showing its belly mode of progression when on land.

In none of these places, though, are they ever met with in such numbers as in the Wash, where, in 1897, some 125 were counted lying basking on the sands, besides numerous others in the water. The Fishery authorities there seem averse to their destruction, though the seals must play dire havoc among the fish and shrimps. It is quite possible that the stragglers to our estuaries may be derived from the above more permanent colony off Norfolk; while the chance ones at Dover and Folkestone may have come from the neighbourhood of Beachy Head, where, it is said, a small family have settled.

It is rather perplexing to distinguish between the Common and the (2) GREY SEAL (*Halichœrus gryphus*) when in the water, unless the latter happened to be an old animal, whose greater size would give the clue. Brief notices of specimens seen or shot, and suspected to be the Grey Seal, have generally turned out mere supposition ; but one, authoritatively identified, "was captured in fishing-nets off the Essex coast" about 1838.†

---

* Our Chairman (E. A. Fitch) has recorded repeated visits of *P. vitulina* thither ; one called by his informant a "tiger seal," Mr. Fitch hints may have been a Ringed Seal (*Phoca fœtida*) or a Hooded Seal (*Cystophora cristata*) ; but as the Common Seal exhibits great variety in colour, we are inclined to think it was this species.—" Essex Naturalist," Vols. II., III., 1888-89, also Dr. Laver, *op. cit.*

† Pagot. Ann. Mag. Nat. Hist., VII. (1841), p. 79.

The nearest breeding-station of the Grey Seal is the Farn Islands off the Northumberland coast;‡ but they occasionally stray to the Wash and Norfolk sands.‖

Lastly, a solitary example of the so-called (3) BLADDER-NOSE, Crested or Hooded Seal (*Cystophora cristata*), a true sub-arctic straggler, is recorded as having been secured in the Orwell, above Harwich, in 1847.*

The Whale Tribe (*Cetacea*).—There are two sorts, one with teeth, the other provided with baleen-plates, or whalebone, in the jaws. Specimens of both kinds betimes have been driven ashore or incautiously entering estuary, river or creek, have got stranded or been pursued and killed by fishermen or others. To Cetaceans the estuary and its rivers seem a fatal trap. The large whales, say between 20 to 60 feet in length, when following flood currents and their fishy food, suddenly find themselves on the ebb-tide among the sands and shoals, without a prospect of return to sea. The stranding of Sperm Whales on the North Kent coast at different times is quite remarkable, of which more anon.

Now and again a whale capture perchance leads to the fishermen's receiving recompense ; though, generally speaking, between time lost and other circumstances, the captors find it *not* altogether a profitable venture. For example, if the whale be of good size, a number of men and boats may be engaged tackling the monster, or taking it to a place of safety; then after much time, labour and trouble expended, even in the best of cases, the ultimate division of profit renders the share to each individual meagre. Again, frequently the Lord of the Manor steps in and asserts his privilege to the fishermen's detriment, or the Crown officers claim it as a Royal fish. If of moderate or small size, a temporary exhibition of the specimen may eventually recoup time, &c., bestowed; but the success of such

---

‡ Selby. Ann. Mag. Nat. Hist., VI. (1841).   ‖ Southwell. Zool. (1882-3).

* Seals when in numbers are decidedly mortal enemies of fish, instance the New-foundland Banks. In their annual four months' visits there it has been calculated they destroy three to four million hundredweight of cod. Their paucity in our Districts' waters render injury to the fisheries a trifling matter; but if the Thames and Medway are again to become Salmon rivers, as lately proposed, then a few Seals about might thin the stock, for they are particularly fond of the Salmonoid tribe.

a show depends on so many contingencies (season, weather, &c.) that nothing is certain. Frequently, then, a whale turns out not a valuable prize to the fishermen, but, on the contrary, a veritable loss in several ways.

Toothed Whales.—Of these, eight different species have been obtained within our Sea Fisheries District. Excepting the porpoise, there is great irregularity in the recurrence of visitations from the others. Those below numbered 1 and 2 (possibly 3 and 4 (?)) appear to reach our shores by the South Channel route, while the rest come rather with the flood-wave from the North Sea.

(1.) The WHITE-BEAKED BOTTLE-NOSE (*Lagenorhynchus albirostris*), whereof the adult is from 7 feet to 9 feet long, has had one example taken off South Kent by Folkestone fishermen, a second off Ramsgate; and of a school of seven or nine (?) which ascended the Colne, 11th September, 1889, five were despatched.

(2.) RISSO'S Grampus (*Grampus griseus*), which attains 9 to 10 or even 12 feet, has likewise been captured in the English Channel, seawards off Dungeness or Rye (?), besides in the River Crouch, 5th September, 1887 (Laver Zool., 1888).

(3.) The COMMON DOLPHIN (*Delphinus delphis*) it seems is not so commonly got on our eastern coast as its name implies. Yet it is numerous outside our territorial waters in the North Sea; whither it delights to follow vessels and gambol round them, or to pursue the shoals of herring and mackerel. Its size is 6 feet to 8 feet. One was secured at Herne Bay in 1868, which the late Frank Buckland purchased and made a cast of. Eels were found in its stomach.

(4.) The BOTTLE-NOSE DOLPHIN (*Tursiops tursio*) is often confounded with the preceding, which in outward aspect it somewhat resembles, though anatomically they differ. Besides being considerably larger when adult, and with a shorter snout, it has fewer, stouter teeth; whereas the Common Dolphin has double the number, these are quite diminutive in size; likewise a tawny tint along the sides of the body. The question arises, whether

the recorded examples of each have been correctly identified ?
It has been found in the Thames Estuary, below the Nore, at
Harwich (River Orwell), near Brightlingsea, and several times
up the Colne and elsewhere, besides a male, female and young
in the Blackwater in 1878 (Fitch), while a skull (semi-fossil)
was discovered at Herne Bay. As to food, whiting, cod,
haddock, conger eels, garfish, crabs, cuttlefish, and even whelk
remains, have been recognised among its dictary.

(5) The COMMON PORPOISE (*Phocæna communis*) may truly
be said to be seldom absent in one part or another of the Kent
and Essex waters. They are keen, wary fishers, and hunt about
in small "schools" regularly at the mouths of the Thames,
Medway, Roach, Blackwater and Colne, as also Harwich neighbourhood. Occasionally London receives a visit from them,
and they have been known to go beyond to as far as Mort-
lake, and even to Teddington Lock.* During the summers of
1886 to 1889, first one and then several porpoises daily
fished in the still water at the angle of Dover Pier, and
latterly the family, young and old, seemed to get accustomed to
the crowds of spectators watching their movements.† Porpoises seem to keep pretty well clear of the shrimp-trawlers'
gear; but in summer, 1898 a Leigh whitebaiter (H. Wilder)
caught a young one, 4 feet long, in his drag-net below
Southend. During the whitebait season they often rush close
inshore after the bait or its fishy enemies, and we have seen
them at high water rollicking about near the Crow Stone.
Shoaling fish, as sprat, herring and whiting, they pursue
vigorously. The porpoise's average size is from 5 to 7 feet.

(6) The KILLER WHALE (*Orca Gladiator*) reaches from 15 to
over 30 feet in length. A specimen measuring 31 feet was slain at
Greenwich in 1793, and others are recorded as taken in the
Blackwater. This rapacious, nay dangerous, animal, not
inaptly, is regarded as a terror of the ocean, being a constant
devourer of porpoises, seals and codfish, &c., which it swallows
whole. When in numbers they even successfully attack the

* "Echo," issue 27th Aug., 1892.   † Webb, "Handbook to Dover."

Greenland whale and other species, hanging on like so many bulldogs, or ferociously tearing off great pieces of the skin and blubber.* These attacks sometimes aided by Thresher Sharks.

(7). The HYPEROODON, or Beaked whale (*Hyperoodon rostratus*), has its headquarters in the Arctic regions, where they are gregarious, but usually they migrate south, in pairs, during autumn, and some of these North Sea travellers, once in a way, enter our estuaries.

Such were two seen near the Nore Sands, July, 1891. At ebb tide one got stranded, and was killed by the shrimpers and towed to Leigh. It proved to be a male, over 25 feet long, and after being exhibited for a couple of days was dissected.

Fig. 2.

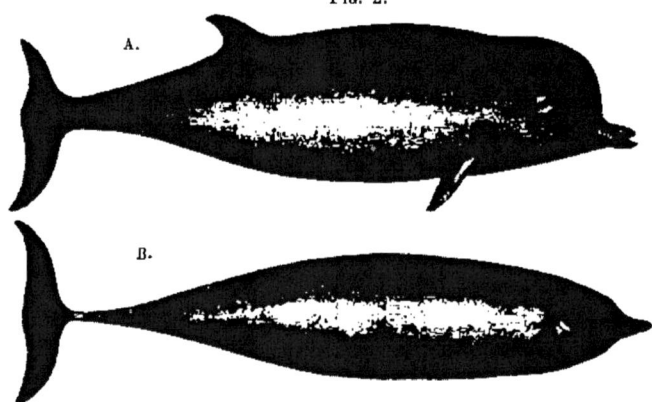

Nore Hyperoodon towed to Leigh, July, 1891, from sketches by Dr. Murie. ' A. Side aspect. B. Top view, showing obliquity of blowhole.

Its companion, also a male of equal size, went up stream, and was despatched near Barking Creek.†

After drifting hither and thither with the tide, decomposition set in, and it became a public nuisance; then the authorities paid £15 to get the carcass destroyed. The Leigh fishermen

* The foregoing series, Nos. 1-6, all belong to the true Dolphin group (Delphinidæ); but there is yet another not included among the *living* whales of our District, viz.:— the GLOBICEPS (*G. Melas*) a skull of which many years ago was dredged in the bed of the Thames. This, the Caaing Whale of the Orkneys, is driven ashore there in herds of hundreds, and such a school visited the Forth in 1867, and a single one was got on the Norfolk Coast in 1879, so that its occasional presence in the Thames Estuary in olden times may be deemed certain. †Notice in "Zoologist," 1891, by W. Crouch.

were more fortunate, receiving £10 for the oily blubber in addition to the exhibition fees. The boss on the head of this Nore animal contained much limpid oil (pure sperm), which unfortunately got mixed up with the dirtier blubber. Clarified Hyperoodon oil, on analysis, shews the closest similarity to sperm oil, being a trifle paler. However, at the date mentioned the market price of the former was £24, and of the latter £48 per tun.

The Hyperoodon* is recorded in our waters near Maldon (Blackwater) *circa* 1717; above London Bridge, 1783; off Whitstable, 1860, and Nore and Barking *supra.* Some years ago a Hyperoodon (?) run a tilt at Dover pier. The shock to the rammer was fatal, and the dead body was afterwards got off the North Foreland. (Webb, *op. cit.*)

The Hyperoodon's food is chiefly cuttle-fish, and such proved to be the contents in the Whitstable and in the Nore examples. The fleshy substance of both octopus and squids is often so digested as to be unrecognisable, but the horny beaks and "cuttle-bone" attest their favourite diet.

(8.) The CACHALOT, or Sperm Whale (*Physeter macrocephalus*). Although this usually immense whale (attaining when adult a size of from 30 towards 70 or 80 feet) is often regarded as a tropical, South Sea, and Antarctic form, yet it is widely distributed. It is found regularly roaming in the North Atlantic, though in that area much scarcer than the southern regions. It seems to follow the Gulf Stream, has frequently got stranded in Scotland and the Orkneys, and at wide intervals of time has come into the North Sea, and coursed southwards along the English East Coast. It is now over a century ago since, on two separate occasions, quite a number of enormous male sperm whales were, after a storm, cast ashore dead on the

---

* In possessing a back fin, and in shape generally, the Hyperoodon when young has considerable resemblance to some of the Beaked Dolphins; but the head of the male, with increasing age, assumes by degrees the remarkably swollen, blunted contour belonging to the Cachalot. The latter, however, is devoid of back fin, having a kind of low hump instead. Consequently, in these and other skeletal characters, Hyperoodon is regarded as an intermediate form. The extraordinary change in the shape of its head with age has been well illustrated by Capt. David Gray, a renowned Arctic whaler, whose observations thereon, with Prof. Flower's remarks on the genus, are published in P.Z.S., 1882.

Fig. 3.

Head of Cachalot. The prominent Boss contains the sperm oil.

Kentish and Essex coasts. One alive even got up the Thames to as far as the Lower Hope. The carcasses of the others turned out a valuable property, as the annexed quotation will show.

An old newspaper of May 17th, 1762, states that " the spermaceti and blubber of the four whales which were ashore at Burchington [*sic.*] and Broadstairs were sold last Wednesday for £374 18s., and that at Deal for £149, which was much more than was expected." Harting in " Zoologist," March, 1883.

Since then (1829) a male, 62 feet long and 16 feet high, was secured by the Whitstable fishermen. When frightened into shallow water, and tide receded, scythes at the end of poles had to be used to kill the monster. A London firm purchased the carcass from the fishermen for £80, and they sent down men and apparatus to flense and prepare the oil on the beach. However, as matters went, the Lord of the Manor came forward, followed by the Lord Warden of the Cinque Ports, finally the Crown authorities. Meantime, ere law proceedings terminated, the valuable material had been pretty well swept back into the sea.

Fig. 4.

Photo by   Geo. Cousins, Birchington.

Back view of the sperm whale lying on the groyne as stranded on the beach at Birchington, August, 1898.*

---

* Mr. Cousins, to whom thanks are due, has kindly shewn us another large photograph taken by him, wherein the head and mouth are amply shewn, but we have preferred the above as better displaying the position across the groyne, and behind the backhump, not fin, in this whale.

Still more recently, viz. : in August, 1898, Birchington came in for an unwelcome piece of flotsam in the dead body of what at first was supposed to be a Greenland whale ; but it turned out to be a sperm whale, $42\frac{1}{2}$ feet long. The coastguard took possession, but gladly got rid of it for a trifle to a local party, who sold it to a Ramsgate man for £5. An exhibition was attempted, but the weather being unusually warm the carcass soon became unbearable. After a ludicrous attempt to burn the body, Mr. Gerrard, a London taxidermist, relieved the District Council from an awkward position by cutting up the monster and reserving the bones for a skeleton. In this case the valuable blubber and spermaceti oil were lost, as also the chance of obtaining some of the still more precious ambergris— a marked contrast to the 1762 specimens.

As is well known, the main food of the cachalot is cuttle-fish, various species. One caught on the Cornwall coast had 300 mackerel in its stomach ; whilst South Sea whalers aver that other fish, even sharks, are indulged in.

Baleen Whales.—Three different species are acknowledged as occasionally straying into our district. All three belong to the group named Rorquals or Finners. These have a small back fin, besides throat furrows or corrugated belly-skin, thus differing from the smooth-bellied Greenland whale, which, moreover, has no back fin. The whalebone of the Rorquals it should be noted, is relatively short, their blubber thin and always fibrous, and less oily than in the Greenland animal; hence the very greatly diminished value of the former's carcass. The Rorquals are rather of a solitary, migratory habit, yet exceedingly active sea-roamers, and they swallow fishes by the hundreds, or strain through their bristle-fringed whalebone diminutive pelagic crustaceans (Copepods) and tiny jelly-fish in multitudes.

(1.) The LESSER RORQUAL, or Piked Whale (*Balænoptera rostrata*), has been got in several localities in our district. A specimen probably of this species, but full grown, is chronicled

c

as having floundered on to the Leigh Marsh, 1806 ? and two younger ones, 17 feet and 14 feet 8 inches, have respectively got up river to Deptford (1789 ? and October, 1842).*

If a Balœn whale is captured, say between 15 up to 30 feet, with a white patch on the front of the flipper, there is every chance of its turning out to be a Lesser Rorqual; if beyond this measurement, then as surely will it be one or other of the two subjoined species. The Piked whale is a dire enemy to the cod family, herring and dog-fish.

(2.) The COMMON RORQUAL, or Razor-back (*Balænoptera Physalus*), when full-grown, attains double the dimensions of the preceding, or more. Of Thames examples there have been several recorded. In June, 1658, a 60 feet long fellow was killed near Greenwich. Another, 46 feet in length, got ashore on the Foulness Sands, *circa* 1826 ?; some of its bones and the lower jaws afterwards graced the grounds of Middleton Hall, Prittlewell. In 1849, an example, 58 feet long, was secured near Grays. One, which must have been nigh 60 feet when alive, was captured off Margate, 1850, and its skeleton exhibited in that town for several years. In May, 1859, a male Razor-back, spied near the Lower Hope, perished by sword wounds inflicted by the Thames Haven coastguard. The huge creature was towed to Gravesend, there made a show of for a few days, then floated to the opposite shore, Grays Reach, where the late Frank Buckland and Dr. Murie dissected it.† It proved to be a full-grown male, 60 feet in length. The flesh and offal were used as manure, and the skeleton became a Rosherville Gardens attraction. The oil merchant who purchased the animal itself estimated the entire body at 45 tons weight, and the rough flensed skin and blubber at 4 tons. A Greenland Right Whale of equal length would weigh 70 tons, whereof 30 tons would be valuable oily blubber. In the above case, this Common Rorqual turned out a windfall

---

* The latest has been a female 17 ft. long, killed in the Blackwater 23rd Sept., 1900. See Fitch, Zool., Nov., 1900.

† Curiosities of Nat. Hist. 2nd Series, and Proc. Zool. Soc., 1865.

to all concerned. The Burnham dredgermen were not so fortunate in their capture, in the Crouch River, 12th February, 1891, of a female specimen 47 feet long.* The Customs authorities asserted their rights, and the whale was put up to public auction. An outsider purchased it for £17 10s., so that the 30 oyster-dredgers' salvage, after much hard work, amounted to a mere pittance for each. By judicious advertisement as a show, the outsider cleared his expenses, and, 'tis said, with a con·siderable margin of profit; but the fishermen sorely grumbled at their labour lost. Nor did matters end here, for the owner of the Royalty appeared on the scene and took law proceedings.† Within a couple of months after, another whale of the same species, and quite as large, was seen at the mouth of the Roach. According to Mr. Fitch, it got partially stranded, but managed to get off as the tide rose.

Still another fully adult example of this species of Rorqual made its appearance on the 27th November, 1899, between the Albert Docks and Barking Creek. Its chief interest lay in its proving to be a pregnant female.‡

The Common Rorqual is a famous fish-eater (pilchards, herring and cod tribe), as many as 600 and 800 having been found in one's stomach. In the Thames specimen (1859) examination shewed only fragments of medusæ and entomostraca.

---

* *See* Essex Nat. V. (1891) and VII. (1893).

† The skeleton was afterwards exhibited at Burnham and then Southend, and finally deposited in the Grimsby Museum (W. Crouch). Essex Nat. VII. 1893.

‡ Since then we have learned further particulars. It seems that after an exciting chase the whale was headed off by a steam-tug, and ran on to a bank on the Woolwich Arsenal shore. Afterwards the dead body was taken over the river and beached on the North Woolwich shore, close to the steam-ferry jetty. Here for a few days crowds of sight-seers, visited it, the interest increasing on a *post obit* parturition. Before long the London County Council ordered removal of the mother's carcass, and it was towed down to Price's Oil works, Abbeyville, and there boiled up. After the parent's death the gas generated had evidently caused expulsion of a pair of young whales, in a very advanced condition. One of these mysteriously disappeared, the other was purchased by Mr. White, landlord of the Pavilion Hotel, North Woolwich. This he exhibited in a tent in the grounds behind, facing the river, and by a very judicious use of creosote, obtained from the Beckton Gas-works, he managed to keep the juvenile whale on show for about three months. The Officer of Health visited daily, but could make no complaints on the score of its being a nuisance. Mr. White showed me the receipt for £40 which he presented to the Woolwich Town subscription to the Mansion House War Fund, and he reckoned his own profit on the transaction at as much or more. According to Mr. White, the young whale measured 10 feet 9 inches long. A County Council official reported the adult female as 66 feet long; but it may have been rather less, the tape, we understand, following the course of the body. (J.M.)

FIG. 5.

Rudolphi's Rorqual, taken in the Medway, August, 1888.*

(3.) RUDOLPHI'S RORQUAL (*Balænoptera borealis*) is intermediate in size between the above two species, the adults ranging
from 40 to 50 feet long. There are several Norwegian whaling-
factories round the North Cape for their capture, where they
abound. They yield less oil than does the Common Rorqual,
but the blubber value is made up by the whalebone being of a
better sort. Besides, their flesh (and *no others*) is extensively
prepared in tins at the factories, and afterwards sold as human
food. It has been remarked that this whale, unlike the last,
seldom consumes fish; but instead, its nourishment is derived
almost entirely from minute crustaceans, both Copepods and
Thysanopods.† Altogether, few of this Rorqual have been met
with on the British coasts. Of these, three specimens have
been taken in our Kent and Essex waters,‡ a reputed fourth
(Laver, *op. cit.*) being of a certainty the Razor-back, mentioned
supra as slain at the Lower Hope, May, 1859. A male, 33 feet
long, was taken in the River Crouch, November, 1883, and the
body exhibited at Southend. But question of its true ownership arose, resulting in a Chancery suit at the instance of the
Burnham Lord of the Manor, in whose favour judgment was
decided. Its skeleton is now in the museum, Sydney, N.S.W.
Another stranded in the Thames outside Tilbury Dock, October,
1887, and this also was a male, 35 feet 4 inches in length
(fig. 6). The third, a female, 32 feet long, was captured in the

---

* Drawing by W. Crouch, to whom we are obliged for loan of woodcut.

† Collett, Proc. Zool. Soc. 1886; but the Tilbury Whale was supposed to be pur-
suing sprats, shrimps and eels? (W. Crouch).

‡ Flower, P.Z.S. 1883, and W. Crouch, Essex Nat. If. (1858) and Rochester Nat. 1881.

Medway at Gillingham Reach, August, 1888 (fig. 5). The carcass was sold by the Deputy Receiver of Wrecks for £6 to the fisherman who first saw it, and who after exhibiting it a few days had it buried. Rudolphi's Rorqual is outwardly distinguished from the Razor-back by its jet-black colour above, clearer white below, higher back fin, and relatively smaller flippers and robust body.

FIG. 6.

Photo by   C. Arthur Pearson, Ltd.

Northern, or Rudolphi's, Rorqual, Tilbury, 19th October, 1887.
Specimen as mounted in the Nat. Hist. Museum, S. Kensington,
showing belly plaiting, front view.*

FOOD-FISHES AND OTHERS.

The Kent and Essex Sea Fisheries District is probably best known, and justly, for its shell-fish, small crustaceans and flat-fish generally. This, to a certain extent, might be anticipated, inasmuch as the great stretch of shallow water warrants the inference (Sect. II.). Moreover, beyond the said shallower shore fringe the wedge-shaped deep, mid-water strip (mentioned p. 14) at the Southern extremity of the North Sea, thinning towards Dover Strait, and a reverse wedge thence westwards along the English Channel, helps materially to alter the character of the fish and fisheries. Indeed, as a

---

* For the use of Figs. 4 and 6 we are indebted to the courtesy of the Proprietors and Editor of the "Royal Magazine," the illustrations having appeared there, January, 1899, in an article on Whales, by Mr. Charles Ray.

matter of fact, the most important among the marine food-fish families of market value, or some species of them, are at least moderately well represented within our district's fishing area. In short, the herring, mackerel, cod, salmon (*i.e.*, smelt), mullet, gurnard, eel and skate families (*plus* flat-fish) are all with us, and yield creditable commercial results. The aim of the present Report is primarily in connection with the Thames Estuary, indeed only a N. shore section of it; but to keep in touch with the wider area, we have run together a general sketch of the fish-fauna of our entire Fisheries District as most desirable to grasp a broad view of the subject.

The Flounder Family (*Pleuronectidæ*).—These flat-fish are well represented round the whole of our coast, more particularly by the flounder, dab, plaice and sole, all of which are redundant. Such forms as the halibut, turbot, brill, smear-dab, sand-sole and topknots are much feebler in numbers, or are but rare. While others—witch, long-rough-dab, thickback (or variegated sole), whiff (or sailfluke), megrim (or scald-fish) are rather conspicuous by their absence, or the merest chance incursionist.

Among the whole of the British Flounder Family the eggs are of the free floating (pelagic) kind. Their transparency is such that only close examination reveals their presence in the sea-water, and hence fishermen seldom observe them. Driven by the currents, tides and winds they may be carried and hatched afar from the original spot where spawned (*see* p. 12). Thus the resorts of very young fish does not always imply the spawning grounds are there, or close by, *e.g.*, plaice, dabs and sole.

The flat-fish are liable to variation in colour of both upper and lower surface, to deviation of so called right- to left- sided fish, and to partial arrest, in changed position of the eyes. These physiological questions we need not enter into; but what fishermen do notice is the contrast of colour assumed, according to whether the ground be sandy or muddy where the fish feed.

(1) The FLOUNDER (*Pleuronectes flesus*) has a wide distribution, but with essentially an estuarine, river and creek habitat. Thus Hamford water, the Colne, Blackwater, Crouch, Thames, Medway, Swale, and the Canterbury Stour are all less or more its resort. The brackish water and muddy reaches are its chief haunt, and, as is well known, they run far up the rivers quite into the fresh water. Even flounders at London have not been altogether strangers of late ; whilst previous to the river's becoming foul, they were regular part residents up stream as far as Teddington. Indeed, the Thames has always been celebrated for its flounders, and the Medway not a whit behind.

It has been further remarked that they seem to prefer the Essex side of the Estuary; the nature of the ground better suiting their habits than most of the N. Kent shore. They are in force at Holehaven and quite round the Hadleigh Ray all the year ; though the larger breeding ones thence towards Southend flats, Shoebury-sands guts, and the Maplin swins, gather there more during the autumn and winter. The flounder does not seem to have diminished in the slightest from years gone by, though in some years they are more plentiful than in others.

Among a basketful (30 to 40) caught by hook in the Swatchway in mid-December, the majority were big ones, both sexes. The lengths of those critically examined ranged from $9\frac{1}{2}$ to 12 inches; scarcely any of the others were below 8 inches, though 5, 6, to 8 are common sizes of adults in the same spots during mid-summer.

According to authorities, flounders *only* spawn in salt-water,[*] further from or nearer shore as the case may be. This may be applicable to the seaward portions of Essex (Wallet and Swins), but superadded there is evidence of spawning in the more brackish water of the Thames mouth. Some of the Leighmen

---

[*] Consult Cunningham "Marketable Marine Fishes," who gives a summary of evidence concerning this point ; also McIntosh "Marine Food Fishes"; and Herdman Rep. Lancashire S. F. Labor. for 1893, also Ascroft *ibid*, for 1899. But Parnell asserts they spawn in brackish water, and Patterson avers they spawn in January in the brackish Breydon Estuarine Broad, at the back of Yarmouth (Zool. 1897).

hold the opinion that they spawn quite within the Hadleigh
Ray itself, where without doubt little fish—1 to 3 inches or
over—literally swarm in the spring and early summer months.
Furthermore, we may instance that two Leigh fishermen, about
Christmas time, were surprised to find on several occasions at
low ebb tide ripe flounders in the mud within the Ray near
entrance to a side creek. The fish were full roed almost to
bursting, and bedded right in the mud so that they were caught
by hand, and " strings " of these flounders were thus brought
into Leigh. The inference to be drawn is that these flounders
would not afterwards proceed to sea to spawn, but do so either
in the Ray itself or in the channel close by. Unfortunately, we
have not yet got the free eggs in the neighbourhood of the spot
indicated as proof positive, though the larvæ, half-inch long, we
have frequently procured in the tow-net in places adjoining.

Whether the above find of ripe females be merely regarded
as an incidental catch or otherwise, the fact still holds (as
emphasized by such experienced flounder-fishers as G. Kirby
and W. Little) that as a rule flounders in spawning condition
(unlike dabs and soles) are seldom captured in the trawl or
fish-nets, nor do they seem when ripe to take the hook. If
spawning seaward in numbers, equivalent to the flounders' presence in the Thames and Medway, most surely would the
trawlers rout them up when they fish on likely grounds where
they might be supposed to spawn. But it is far otherwise, for
in such favourable spots as the Black-tail Spit their paucity in
the breeding condition is well known.

Even on the assumption that the Ray case is an unusual
one, so far otherwise as we can make out the matter stands
thus. Much depends on the mildness or severity of the winter.
When the season is mild, and no severe frosts (December to
April), from the Shoebury Sands to Sea Reach or the Lower
Hope, there are hosts of breeding and nearly ripe flounders
hovering about, either frequenting the 3 to 5 fathom channel
or feeding quite inshore. These shed their eggs, so to say,

within brackish water area, and the tidal flow carries the eggs into the creeks, where hatching proceeds apace. Thus it is that the sandy and muddy Ray, and other such like creeks, virtually become rearing places of the flounder, even supposing that the actual spawning ground is outside. We cannot say, then, that in our estuary, or hereabouts, we have detected a regular wholesale migration from the river far seawards, as has been assumed to take place in other districts; but alone a periodical shifting from the fresh to brackish water as mentioned.

The regular breeding season in the Thames is the first three or four months of the year, but evidently on quite exceptional occasions it is prolonged. For example, R. Johnson, a reliable observer, states that in the middle of August, 1899, he captured in his trawl a full ("hard") roed female near the Oaze.

The notion that in some cases young flounders are hatched out on the parent's back has still a few believers. One unusually well-informed fisherman insisted he would prove the fact, and indeed produced examples of the said peculiarity. Even when he was shewn under the microscope that the egg-like tumours contained parasitic worms and not embryo fish, he left only half convinced that he was wrong.

The food of these estuarine flounders are ragworms, lobworms, and minute annelids, also small shrimps, Mysidæ, Corophium, Idotea; in sparse cases young mussels, Tellina, weeds and other vegetable *débris*.

Of those flounders in the Ray, the average rate of first year's growth appears to be something near McIntosh's estimate of 4 to 5 inches; but the presence of smaller ones complicates the question; though Cunningham's suggestion that they do not breed at this age seems quite feasible.

What flounders are captured by the Leigh fishermen find local customers, for they are very rarely indeed sent to the London market. Though not much run on by the people, yet the winter flounders are firm in flesh and capital eating. The average size of those exposed for sale at Leigh is 7 to 9 inches, thus in general ripe or tolerably mature in condition.

(2.) The PLAICE (*P. platessa*) has an extensive range round our coast, and is as plentiful in the deeper extra-territorial waters as inshore and in the rivers' mouths. However, it is important to recognise the fact that the plaice of our Fishery District taken in the aggregate never attains the large dimensions of those trawled in the subarctic portion of the North Sea, or off the east of Scotland. In the latter area up to 28 inches long has been recorded (Fulton)*; still the medium size of those brought to market (say, Grimsby) is between 11 to 14 or 15 inches.

Cunningham,† in his researches, has shown that the plaice of the English Channel round the Straits of Dover, and in the shallow southernmost portion of the North Sea, are altogether a small sized race compared with those of the deeper northern parts of the North Sea. The Channel fish may become mature at 9 inches long, the upper North Sea ones at 13 in., or 4 inches difference in dimensions. It is well to keep this in mind in view of the fact that from Ramsgate, the most important fishing station in our district, the trawlers work on the grounds where the presumed stunted race of plaice are found. In other words, big plaice are essentially deep-water fish, and the smaller sized sort more often frequent the shallower grounds as pertain to the southern section of the North Sea, &c.

Now, referring to the Thames Estuary plaice, ordinarily it is exceptional to find one reach over a foot long.‡ Those of 7, 8 or even 9 to 10½ inches are fairly numerous at certain seasons, generally in the autumn, though they are also met with at other times of the year, but scantier in quantity. On the other hand, the smaller sized fish, from about 1 to 6 inches,

---

* Eight Ann. Rep. S.F.B. for 1889.   † Jour. Mar. Biol. Assoc. (N. Ser.) Vol. IV.

‡ But we may cite examples which have come under our own observation, viz. :—
11¾, 12¼ and 16 inches—this last weighing 2 lbs.

swarm in multitudes in the early spring till the beginning of autumn.

Among the Leighmen there is a flat-fish vernacularly known as the "Rogue-Plaice," and which they consider a different species from the ordinary plaice they catch. It runs from a foot to 14 or 15 inches long, sometimes looks thick and plump, at other times more emaciated; but, in whichever condition, is extremely watery, and, as expressed, "drains away to nothing." As a rule they are discarded as unfit for food. In far back years they are said to have been got in the Leigh Roads during early summer. Within more recent dates our fishery officer (George Kirby) has captured them on the Maplins towards the Swin, but only at odd intervals, and then occasionally "a tidy few."* Others have come across single examples in the neighbourhood of the Spile and "Off-the-Land" *i.e.*, more towards Sheppey. From descriptions given of the general appearance of these fish—their shape, spotting and knobby head, they would seem to be only spent female plaice, that have come into shallow water after spawning.

With respect to the sizes of those diminutive plaice alluded to above, the following gives the gist of observations carried on during the greater part of one year, of material taken in the shrimp trawl. On 1st January, one catch of 25 were from $1\frac{1}{4}$ up to 6 inches in their extreme lengths. On the 10th, the smallest were $1\frac{1}{2}$ to 4 inches in a sample of 19. Towards the end of the same month, in six picked specimens the shortest was $2\frac{1}{2}$, the longest 3·6 inches, these being the apparent extremes of a long series. In February some half-dozen were 2 to $2\frac{1}{2}$ inches, others over 6 to 9. In early March we found among 30 specimens one moiety 2 to 3, the other 4 to $6\frac{1}{2}$ inches. In the middle of April, in 26 specimens, about one-half were under 2 inches, the remainder not exceeding 4 inches. There were besides many others 5 and 6 inches long. In the beginning and

---

* Kirby has since stated that in former years he used to take 20 to 30 daily to Sheerness, caught in fishing at the Black-tail Spit and thereabouts. The fish "looked handsome," but purchasers soon found their appearances were deceptive, which put an end to their sale.

latter end of May some were $1\frac{1}{2}$ inches; but 3 to 4 inches was
the average size, intermingled with a moderate amount of a
larger sort. In June a few got of $1\frac{3}{4}$ inches, many others just
over 3 to 4 inches, and those from 5 inches and beyond quite
numerous. In August still a few were met with only $1\frac{1}{2}$ inches,
but the bulk of the catch in question were between 3 and 4 on
to over 7 inches long—the latter very abundant. In mid-
September the few smallest observed were $2\frac{1}{2}$ inches, but by
far the greatest quantity passed through hands were between 6
to 10 inches in length. In November, of some 70 specimens
chosen for measurement, the least sized were $4\frac{1}{2}$ and the biggest
9 to $10\frac{1}{2}$ inches long.

The fishermen are quite undecided regarding the plaice's
spawning grounds, for as they say the very smallest of the
brood are got less or more almost everywhere within their
fishing area. Howsoever, from what is known of the habits of
the plaice elsewhere, we are inclined to think the off-shore sands
and shelly banks (*e.g.*, the Sunk, Long Sand, and Knock
John) will be found to be their breeding haunts. On this
point, of course, investigation is needed.

All the data of authorities on fish and fisheries lead to these
conclusions :— (*a*) That the plaice frequents deep water for
spawning purposes; (*b*) that in the majority of instances this
is outside the three mile limit; (*c*) as hatching occurs, and at
earliest stages, the young (larval and post-larval) fish gradually
descend from the surface water and ultimately make their way
shorewards or up estuaries; (*d*) there they remain for a time,
forming communities or nurseries in company with small soles,
dabs, lemon-dabs, solenettes, and sometimes flounders; (*e*) as the
plaice grow larger they again migrate seawards, and maturing
sojourn with the congregations of older breeding fish in the
deep water.

The North Sea and Channel plaice are said to spawn January
to March, or even a month or six weeks later. Their period of
spawning in the Thames Estuary area can only be expressed

with uncertainty, inasmuch as they are rarely got in advanced condition ; the breeding fish doubtless taking seawards to the sandbanks, now seldom visited by the Leighmen. It is said, however, that during the early spring months plaice full of roe are occasionally captured in the kettle-nets on the Foulness shores. Such medium sized fish as have been examined by us at the end and beginning of the year have either had the ovary very imperfectly, or only moderately, developed. The puzzling subject of the presence of the small plaice in fewer or greater numbers almost throughout the year has given rise to considerable discussion.* Some would limit the spawning season to winter and spring months, others regard its being carried on to the autumn months, still others are inclined to put emphasis on temporary slow growth of some of the brood. So far as the Thames Estuary is concerned, we are hardly in position to offer a solution of the knotty point—therefore leave it *sub judice.*

With regard to the localities in the Thames Estuary, where the plaice are found in most abundance, and other matters, *see* under Fish-Trawling, Sect. VI. As to their food, we have examined quite a large number from $2\frac{1}{2}$ to 8 inches long and over. The younger fishes' stomachs contained, as far as recognisable, remains of minute crustaceans (=Isopods, Copepods, and Amphipods), Nereid, or rag-worms, and only a few Mollusca. The older plaice, however, besides crustaceans, and exceptionally even tiny fish *débris,* more distinctly shewed preference for lob-worms and shell-fish (cockles, Tellina, Mactra, &c.), with occasionally sand intermixed. Shell-fish are, indeed, the choice staple food of the adults.

Plaice are chiefly captured in the trawl, though they are also got by the Peter-net, banding, spruling, and at certain seasons parties of London amateur fishers use rod and line (Sect. VI., Spruling, &c,).

(3.) The SMEAR-DAB (*P. microcephalus*) is by no means a rare fish with us, though not nearly so plentiful as those

---

* Consult Masterman and Kyle, 15th and 16th Ann. Rep. F.B.S. ; also Cunningham Jour. Mar. Biol. Assoc., and Vol. Brit. Mar. Fishes, &c,

which precede, or the two which follow. It is not uncommon from the Chapman to the Knock Buoy, and the Maplins is rather a favourite place for them. They are caught frequently on the Leigh Middle-ground, and there generally from April to June. They are not confined to these localities, but are got along the Essex coast and mouths of the Colne and Blackwater. In June, 1894, Cunningham (*op. cit.*) found in the Wallet a very large number, the majority 3 to 5 inches long, in the company of soles and dabs of corresponding sizes. They are present at the entrance of the Medway, but how stands their distribution around Kent is doubtful. It has been recorded at Sandwich, 1792, as smooth sole; but is "a reputedly scarce fish at Dover" (Webb). Those obtained by the Leighmen are not large— namely, 4 to 6 or even 8 inches long. The medium size, 5 to 6 inches, are most frequent. We have been told of a specimen nigh a foot long, taken in deep water in the vicinity of Southend pier, but this must have been quite a chance example. The biggish ones are usually taken in the trawler's net, the smaller ones occasionally stray into the whitebaiter's stow-net.

In the Thames Estuary the smear-dab seems to prefer hard, sandy ground, and this appears to be the habit of the younger forms got in the Humber mouth (Holt), and at St. Andrews (McIntosh, *op. cit.*). But the latter mentions that "the adults haunt the somewhat rough grounds near the Bell Rock, for which their dexterity in passing along rocky surfaces and up perpendicular ledges peculiarly fits them." The Swedish name Rock-flounder may thus seem appropriate.

They are reputed to breed in the spring and summer, in deep water well off-shore, and Cunningham has shown a large percentage are mature when 7 to 9 inches long. We have no reliable data to offer concerning their spawning or migrations within our district. However, towards the end of April, spent fish are not uncommon. Geo. Gilson says "even those of 10 inches he then returns to the sea, as at that time they are in poor condition so as to be unfit for food."

Those examined by us seemed to have fed chiefly on marine worms and only occasionally on crustaceans. The paucity of numbers taken in the Estuary do not render them of such economic importance as at some stations. At Leigh smear-dab is the only name given them, elsewhere they are known as Mary-sole, lemon-dab, lemon-sole, &c.

Mention has been made in the introductory remarks to the Pleuronectidæ of changes in their early stages which the two cuts subjoined partially illustrates.

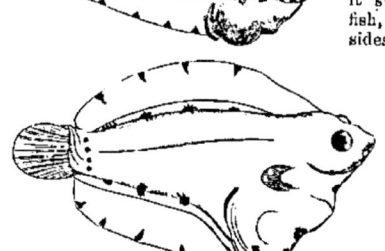

FIG. 7. Young (larval) stage of the Smear-dab, or Lemon-dab (*Pleuronectes microcephalus*), when it swims like an ordinary round fish, and with its eyes on opposite sides of the head.

FIG. 8. The young Lemon-dab at a later stage when it begins to lay flat. It shows the left eye shifting towards the right side and just appearing on the ridge of the head. Both figs. enlarged from nature (after McIntosh).*

(4.) The COMMON DAB (*Pleuronectes limanda*) is truly one of the commonest fishes in the whole of the Thames Estuary. It has a distribution nearly identical with the plaice. Occasionally, though, the dab is found to frequent the deeper water channels (swins and deeps) during the sprat season, being caught in the stowboat nets at all depths. These so-called "sprat-dabs" are generally well-fed, large and plump fellows. Although both dabs and plaice are at all times caught together, yet in the cold weather the plaice proportionally are quite the minority in number.

The winter dabs are usually the biggest; those of the spring time preponderating in the smaller sized sort. During summer they are still caught, but a great reduction in numbers.

* We are indebted to Professor McIntosh, F.R.S., for the use of these wood blocks, as well as Figs. 9, 10, 11, and 12, and beg to return the Sub-Committee's due thanks for the same.

As autumn wanes and the cold weather creeps on apace, they increase in ratio with corresponding improvement in condition and size ; indeed, their flesh then is excellent.

The Leighmen's markets for their trawl-caught fish, dabs inclusive, are Chatham, Sheerness and Leigh. The fish-hawkers there are the immediate purchasers, who afterwards distribute the fish to the population of these places and the surrounding neighbourhood. Unless those few dabs accidentally caught with the sprats in stowboating, none are sent to London. Those that the fishermen retain for home consumption, or for local sale, vary in size from 5 to 9 or 10 inches, more exceptionally they are got a foot long. A dab of 13 inches has been recorded as taken in the Crouch in 1891 (Fitch).

On two occasions we examined batches of dabs exposed for sale on a fishmonger's slab at Leigh towards the end of January, of which the following is an epitome : —

(*a*) Lot close on 50 in number. Six of these were chosen as representing, on hasty glance, the largest of the series. They proved all females. One was 9 inches and four $9\frac{1}{2}$ inches long, one 11 and another 12 inches in length. In the last the roe was quite ripe, in the others nearly ripe. All had young sprats or herrings in their stomachs, whereof two, those least digested, were $2\frac{1}{2}$ and $3\frac{1}{2}$ inches long. The remaining lot of forty dabs were not so critically examined ; however, the very shortest was $6\frac{1}{4}$, with intermediate sizes to 9 inches. Both sexes were present, and nearly every one appeared less or more in breeding condition.

(*b*) There were two dozen in this lot, of which a half were opened. Shortest, $6\frac{1}{2}$; longest, $7\frac{3}{4}$ inches. Seven males, remainder females, both partially or nearly ripe. The remaining half of series appeared chiefly females ; but all were in breeding condition, ranging from 7 to 9 inches.

The above fully confirms Dr. Wemyss Fulton's researches,[*] who even found mature females of $5\frac{1}{2}$, and $\frac{3}{4}$-mature males 4

---

[*] Eighth and 10th Ann. Report Fish. Board, Scotland, for 1889 and 1891.

inches long. It is important to bear such facts in mind when dealing with the knotty question of undersized fish.

The dabs' food is quite varied in character, depending somewhat on the time of year and much on the locality where fished; altogether, it is a gross feeder. In the early spring months in the Fairway channel and Hadleigh Ray mouth, small dabs feed on young shrimps, Mysidæ, Amphipods and such minor crustaceans, on worms, young mussels, &c. During midsummer, at the Girdler and Oaze, and towards the Nore, the dab preys upon larger crabs of various sorts (shore, swimming, spider and hermit crabs), adult shrimps, (rarely shell-fish ?), worms and zoophytes (so-called " whiteweed "=*Sertularia*, &c.).

In September, just above the Chapman Light, on one occasion we noted the stomach contents to be sand stars (=*Echinoderms)*, shrimps, crabs, molluscs (=*Tellina, Mytilus juv.*, &c.), and fish (=*Goby)*. In middle of November, on the Essex shore below Southend, we procured dabs whose food was mainly whitebait or young sprats, besides crab's ova in bunches, pieces of flat-fish, &c. Again, in December, in the upper Blyth Sand the food consists of lobworms, the flesh, and occasionally comminuted shells, of young mussels, Tellina and Terebella worm, &c.*

The spawning grounds of the dab have not of a certainty been located by the Leigh fishermen, nor have we ourselves satisfactorily cleared the enigma. The fish are well known to be full-roed during winter, and that spawning occurs in the spring time; nevertheless, some say examples with roe, though not ripe (immature fish ?), turn up all the year round. On the other hand certain old experienced fishermen assert that by the end of April, during May, even till June, all the dabs caught are in a spent condition, and then generally rejected by them.

During all the winter, however, ripe dabs are caught right up the Estuary, and therefore, as they believe, most probably spawn there. They add that the little dabs are generally *not*

* Compare Ramsay Smith, 10th Ann. Rep F.B.S. for 1891; and Herdman & Scott, 1st–3d. Reports Lancashire Sea-F. Labor. 1892–1894.

caught during the spring, but commence to be got about mid-summer, or thereabouts. This is not the case, though, with plaice.

Fisheries authorities are tolerably unanimous as to the dabs not making regular migrations to special grounds, deep or shallow, for spawning. Cunningham, however, qualifies this in its application to brackish estuaries—"where full-grown dabs are only abundant in summer and autumn, when they are not spawning." This may apply to some areas, but assuredly the opposite is the case up the Thames Estuary, as we have already mentioned.

As to the Leigh witness's statement (*supra*) of paucity of diminutive dabs in spring, our own observations are not quite in harmony. We are inclined to account for this by the young fish then taking to the shallow creeks where the tow-net secures them, whilst in the deeper waters the ordinary wide-meshed fishing net fails to capture them.

However this may be, it is unquestionable that young dabs of very small size are found scattered over a wide estuarine area most months of the year, and not alone confined to the early summer months.

We have examined quite a series of these brood catches in the autumn, midsummer and beginning of the year, where the specimens ranged from 1¼ to 3 inches and over. A similar prevalence of diminutive forms has been recorded elsewhere, and hence some authorities maintain this as proof of the inherent slow growth of this fish—supposing that it takes four or five years to attain sexual maturity.

Our view rather accords with Williamson's* reasoning of the spawning season being lengthened till autumn; though inasmuch as the Thames estuarine area is concerned, verification of such a thing being a fact is still wanting.

---

* Eleventh Ann. Rep. for 1892, F.B.S.; also Kyle, 16th Ann. Rep. for 1897; and Cunningham, Jour. Mar. Biol. Assoc., N. Ser., Vol. II.

(5.) The LONG FLOUNDER, or Witch (*Pleuronectes cynoglossus*), Webb states, has been several times noticed among ordinary soles sold at Dover. He gives no particulars regarding the specimens. It is indeed rare in the English Channel, has several times been met with at Yarmouth (Patterson), and otherwise frequents the North Sea. We have no knowledge of any Thames estuarine example, those seen by us at Leigh and Southend coming from Billingsgate (have the Dover specimens been thus imported ?).

(6.) The COMMON SOLE (*Solea vulgaris*) is everywhere distributed, and bears a high reputation in our Fisheries District— Dover, Kingsdown and Ramsgate soles bringing good prices in the London and midland counties markets. It may also be safely said that it is quite an abundant fish in the Thames mouth, from Hole-haven to the East Girdler. In other words, it exists in numbers over the whole area fished by the boats from Leigh-on-Sea. Nay more, from the beginning of June till the end of September soles of moderate size are continuously taken. By such are meant those from 6 to 12 inches long, or up to 15 inches; these last being scantier, though we have seen a couple brought in mid-October, one 16 inches, the other 19¼ inches long, 9 in. broad, and weighing 2lbs. 9oz. The more ordinary size, however, is about 9 to 10 inches, and those of 8 inches are quite numerous.

All the fishermen admit that the season 1897-98 was one of the most productive for soles, in the Thames, for a long series of years. It likewise was remarkable that through the winter months of 1896-97 soles only 2 inches long, or thereabouts were constantly caught; even during the succeeding winters they have been far from scarce. Indeed, it may be positively affirmed that nearly every year small soles are extremely abundant from the end of April to the first weeks in June; May being the most plentiful month. These fish run in size from 1½ to 6 inches. They are smallest in the early period, and very quickly grow larger as the season advances.

The places in which the sole is found in the greatest numbers in the Leigh fishing area are :—(1) The longer soles, *i.e.*, 6 to 12 inches onwards, are caught in the Oaze Channel and on the Warp. (2) The young brood, $1\frac{1}{2}$ to 6 inches, congregate in immense shoals at times heard of more eastwards, but particularly and regularly at Warden Point (Isle of Sheppey), and this so close to the clay cliffs on the shore as to be inside the fishing smacks' ordinary range of trawling. Their numbers diminish by degrees along the more stony Sheppey coast towards Sheerness. From the Grain Spit to the Yantlet Creek the nature of the ground is decidedly sandy, and there these diminutive soles are not found in any great multitudes. (3) Between the Yantlet buoy (near the datum posts) up to the middle Blyth buoy, however, the brood fish again muster in force, occasionally in packed family groups. It will be observed, therefore, that the young and immature shoals (Nos. 2 & 3) seem to have a preference for the Kent side in ascending; whilst the riper aged (No. 1), on the contrary, rather cling to the Essex side in their downward estuary progress. Thus it would seem that in the Thames area the migration of young and older flat-fish, to some extent, accords with what is said to be the rule on the north-eastern coasts. (*See* remarks, p. 12-13.)

Influence of currents, winds, temperature and food have been severally advanced as rational explanation of why and wherefore of these migrations and nurseries or gregarious association of juvenile soles, plaice, dabs, &c., inshore and towards estuaries. Possibly each and all these forces have a share, according to circumstances. From what has been said in Sect. II. of conditions extant in our estuary, the offshore spawned larval soles and plaice would naturally appear to be led towards the Sheppey cliff, with its marginal attraction of food, &c. Above the Yantlet again, sand diminishing and muddy clyte bottom superadded, ·provender for tiny fish undoubtedly abounds.

The following observations pretty well sustain the fishermen's statements of frequency of young soles nearly at all seasons. The numbers given do not represent the entire quantity in each haul of the trawl, but only samples of the general catch lifted at random in a baler along with other fish, &c., not here noted. The precise measurement of each fish was accurately determined, but here for brevity we only give the extremes of the sizes :—January 1st, 10th, 18th, Leigh Roads to just below the Nore—total, 47 soles, ranging from 2 to 3¼ inches; April 20th, between Spile and East Cant Buoy, 150 soles, from 2 to 3½ inches ; May 2nd, The Blyth, 164 soles, 2 to 3½ inches ; May 7th, Sea Reach and Leigh Roads, 275 soles, 2½ to 4 inches, and 4 soles from 5 to 6½ inches; May 10th, Girdler Buoy and Lightship, back to the Gilman, 7 soles, 3 to 3¼ inches, besides many larger ones 8 inches upwards ; June 16th, below Nore, New W. Oaze Buoy and neighbourhood, 20 soles, running from 2½ to 4 inches, besides quantities of moderate dimensions and others 9 and 10 inches long ; August 18th, area crossing the Red Sand, or from the Gilman to East Spile and East Cant, among a large series of soles of all sizes, roughly sampled after the shrimp-trawl had been emptied on deck, there were noticed a few 1 inch to 1½ inch extreme length, very many 2 to 5 inches, and a goodly proportion from 6 up to 14 inches long. In these hauls, besides prime shrimps, were abundant specimens of dabs and plaice (from 1½ up to 7 inches), a few solenettes, many sprats, whiting-pouts, gurnards, sand-eels, skates, blennies, pipe fish and others. September 10th, opposite Beacon, above Chapman Light, a fair assortment of soles, plaice, and dabs, the first-mentioned ranging from 2 to 10 inches, a few 11 inches and a foot long; those 2½ to over 3 inches were apparently preponderant; the mediums, 6 to 8 inches, numerous ; those above this sparse. Our notes, October to December, are not so definite, for the boisterous weather then often stands in the way of research. But we may state that puny-sized soles have been got in limited numbers each of these months, more particularly during the fast few mild winters.

The above catches with the shrimpers have chiefly been made in the daylight; but it is well known that the older soles are greatly night feeders, hence, those who go fish-trawling often take advantage of the darkness, remaining out over night on purpose. (*See* Fish Trawling, Sect. VI.)

The food of the sole in our waters is not so easily identified as in the case of plaice, dabs and flounders. This is, perhaps, due to their being dainty feeders, at least the young; the material swallowed, as a rule, is tender and quickly digested. Hence we have found often only a mass of straw-coloured or brownish gelatinous substance, which under the microscope showed no tissue structure, or occasionally was indefinitely cellular. In other examples sandy matter was added, or remnants of worms, minute crustaceans (shrimps and others), but only rarely shelly remnants. Evidently *Nereis* and *Sabella* ("Ross") and *Terebella* are the choice worms. Elsewhere, in biggish soles, observers have met with sand and brittle stars, sea anemones, razor- and other shell- fish, with sand-eels to boot.

Mr. Robert Johnson, senr., a trustworthy observer, is inclined to the opinion—one held by others of the Leigh fishermen—that soles breed within the Thames Estuary itself, and likewise in the Crouch river upwards towards Burnham. He further believes that the larger-sized fish, of which mention has been made above, are the parents of the aforesaid brood. According to him, the spawning ground of the sole in the Thames proper would therefore be in the neighbourhood of the Oaze Deep. He thinks that in the Crouch river spawning takes place from the river's mouth as far up as Burnham, and even beyond. He bases his reasoning on the circumstance that on many occasions he has found full-roed soles in the places stated, particularly during the months of May and June. Among his experiences, whereof some 20 years were spent fishing in the localities above-mentioned, he states that ordinary sole fishing would last a number of weeks at a stretch. At first the fish would be full-roed, but towards the end of the fishing, the majority of the soles caught were spent fish.* He adds, that whenever the cold weather sets in, but especially if accompanied with ice and snow, during the after part of the year, then the soles disappear and are not to be found by the shrimper and fish-trawlers in the estuaries of the Thames and Crouch.

These views of the soles' spawning-places would seem to receive support from what Andrews† and Yarrell affirm of their breeding in the Arun River, Sussex, and Eagle Clarke, in the Humber; besides, soles spawn freely in shallow areas.‡ On the other side it has been as firmly established that on some parts of the English coasts (Eddystone for example), North Sea, and west of Ireland spawning occurs outside the territorial waters. Our own idea inclines to regard the Thames soles' breeding-grounds as in the direction of the Long Sand. It is, however, quite possible that nearer spots for spawning betimes occur; for instance, ripe-roed soles have been got near the Nore in April, &c. At all events the subject is well worthy of further investigation in our own area.

The period of spawning is the spring and summer months; but we are left in doubt how to account for the very tiny ones at nearly all seasons. The subject of the rate of growth of the flat-fish—sole, plaice, dab and others—is still an unsettled one. Either the spawning period may in cases commence earlier, or at intervals extend longer than is reckoned. Again, variation in temperature, &c., it is known urges on or retards development. The age of brood has thus formed a fertile subject of discussion among experts. As we have not the data to decide how it stands in our waters, therefore the question must be left open. This may be said that, despite outcry of the shrimpers' wanton

---

* One Gravesend witness stated to the Commissioners, 1878, that soles spawned in the Lower Hope. Has the Blyth brood-crowds deceived him?

† Zool., 1853; likewise Yarrell, Brit. Fishes.

‡ McIntosh, Brit. Mar. Food-Fishes; also Holt, Jour. Mar. Biol. Assoc., N. Ser., Vol. III.

destruction of brood-fish, the Thames is still amply stocked with soles, plaice, &c., and full indications of more to come.

It may be affirmed that seldom or ever are those soles caught by the Leigh shrimpers sent to the London market. On the contrary, as a rule they are disposed of in the village, or to the fish hawkers who carry them to Southend and vicinity for sale. The fish trawlers again dispose of their ware chiefly at Sheerness and Chatham (*See* Sect. VI., Fish Trawling). Formerly at Leigh and Southend small soles, or "slips" and plaice, caught were only retained for use by the fishermen's families. But of recent years the great influx of visitors and increased price, scarcity and run on these fish have tended to smaller ones being exposed for sale. Eight to 9 inches is a common size, seldom or ever less for soles, though on extra occasions we have seen a few plaice of 7 inches in lots here at Leigh. Still to our knowledge the fishermen, as a rule, avoid bringing these in. The public, however, will have them fresh from the sea, and thus supply follows the demand.

Piebald soles are not uncommon : for instance, six turned up within a week in January, 1898.

(7.) The FRENCH SOLE, or sand Sole (*Solea lascaris*), and (8) the VARIEGATED SOLE (*S. variegata*), also known as Thickback are reported as appearing in the Dover market (Webb, *op. cit*). But we are left in doubt where and when caught; hence arises the surmise whether taken on the Varne or the Ridge shoals outside our territorial waters. However, there is an Essex specimen of the *S. lascaris* preserved at Brightlingsea (*Laver*).

(9.) The SOLENETTE, or Little Sole (*Solea lutea*), is not altogether so very rare a fish in the Thames Estuary as Dr. Laver's note of addendum* would seem to indicate; though otherwise we have no clear idea of its distribution, habits or spawning ground within the district. They are generally got in the trawl of such small size that they are at once rejected, and go over-

---

* *Op. cit.* p. 124.—A solitary specimen existing at the Marine Biological Station at Brightlingsea.

board as the young of the common sole. Indeed, as a rule, many of the fishermen know little or nothing of the fish as a separate species. Those observed have been captured beyond the Nore, so far supporting Cunningham's idea that it avoids brackish water. We may exemplify the sizes got, by citing one taken in the Oaze, May, 1898, 2½ inches long; another trawled by R. Johnson, jun., near the Girdler, summer, 1897, just under 4 inches; still others met with by us were only from 1½ to 2 inches.

The Solenette seldom exceeds 5 inches, and breeds at 3½ to 4 inches in length; the males being mature at 3 inches or less. Comparing their apparent numbers in the Thames district with those recorded as occurring on the Lancashire coast, the latter far and away outstrip. Prof. Herdman* gives data shewing that of a total of 1,531 soles and solenettes got in the experimental trawling of Mr. Dawson, Supt. L.S.F., May, July, August and September, 1892, the solenettes exceeded the soles as nearly 4 is to 1. Herdman therefore inclines to the opinion that in the area in question the solenette may compete and interfere with the juvenile soles. He even hints that the useless solenettes abundance materially swells the decried destruction of supposed brood soles.

A young common sole, measuring ⅝ of an inch, has been found in the stomach of a solenette (Herdm. Rep. 1895); but whether they regularly prey on each other is a moot point, for their ordinary food otherwise appears chiefly to be Copepods and other smaller crustaceans and molluscs. There are several clearly distinguishing characters between the solenette and the young common sole of similar size. But the most readily recognisable ones for fishermen are:—(*a*) Colour, sandy or reddish brown; (*b*) that the fin rays have a broad deep black one about every sixth or so apart.

(10.) The HALIBUT (*Hippoglossus vulgaris*).—This flat-fish is regarded, no doubt rightly, as a very rare visitor to the Thames

---

*Rep. Lancashire Sea Fish. Laboratory for 1892.

Estuary, at least within the bounds worked ordinarily by the Leigh-fisher. Our Sub-committee's representative has not seen one himself, young or old, vouched for as of Thames mouth extraction. Information as to solitary individuals having at times been secured is not wanting. Mr. R. Johnson relates his capture of one in 1856, or thereabouts; and he assures us several other members of his craft have on a few chance occasions come across a specimen. His own example was $2\frac{1}{2}$ or 3 feet long, and it was sold in Billingsgate for 15s. It was caught by hook and line, baited with plaice, which had been laid the night before. Mr. J. Tyrrel says that over thirty years ago he also caught a fine fellow on the south side of the North Knob, in some 12 fathoms of water; the spot was colloquially known among the fishermen as "Dengie Head." He reckons it was 5 feet long, and that it weighed nigh three-quarters of a hundredweight. He was not fortunate in its sale, 5s. being all he got for it at Billingsgate—" That morning being a dreadful bad market."

The halibut is decidedly a northern deep-water fish, still they are fairly numerous as far south as the Dogger Bank. Comparatively few reach the S.E. English coast, though recorded off Norfolk (Patterson). They grow to an enormous size, those above-mentioned being very far from full grown specimens. It appears among the " List of Fishes of Sandgate and its neighbourhood," by W. Boys, 1792. The Ramsgate fishing craft, we understand, occasionally land them, but these are from the North Sea grounds. We are not aware of any authenticated Kent specimens other than mentioned, though it is said to have been taken on the neighbouring Sussex coast.

(11.) The TURBOT (*Rhombus maximus*).—Some fifty years ago Turbot were comparatively plentiful in The Swin and along the Maplin Sands. Although many of these were small or of moderate size, it was not exceptional to get them nearly 2 feet long according to Mr. B. Baxter. Even yet, 'tis said, turbot are not altogether scarce, from the

Margate Sands seawards ; but the Leigh fishermen now
seldom go there, though they used to do so frequently
in the so-called " Long-lining days." Frank Buckland*
states that " magnificent turbots are also caught at the back of
the ' Falls,' near Margate ; there are sands near the Goodwin
which, however, the turbot do not frequent." The former
locality referred to is beyond the international limit, certainly
out of the way of our provisional Leigh fisheries boundary.
In the kettle-nets near Fisherman's Head, Foulness, small
turbot in times past and still are occasionally entrapped. Our
colleague, Dr. Laver, mentions (Introd. vol. cited) that at
the fish-pits adjoining the sea-wall, Foulness, where the catches
are temporarily stored, they tie a string round the tail root of
the turbot, &c., with a cork at the free end. The cork float
thus marks exactly where to dip for the fish when wanted.
When we visited the Fisherman's Head locality, perforated
floating store boxes were only then in use.

Turbot when secured by the Leigh fishers are brought up
in the shrimp-nets or beam-trawl, and then, as said, few and
far between.† The most usual time of year they are got is
towards the end of the summer or the beginning of the autumn.
Then, as a rule, they are obtained below the Nore, or as far as
the West Girdler or the Maplin Light. In the fall of 1870
a specimen $2\frac{1}{2}$ ft. long was brought up when dredging for
" Five Fingers " in the Bawley " Busy Bee," off Grain Spit, at
the mouth of the Medway. A week or 10 days later, the same
persons caught another in the shrimp-net on the Maplin Sands.
This plump one was about 2 ft. long, and fetched 10s. in Billingsgate market (J. Tyrrel).

Turbot are mentioned among the " Fishes of Sandgate "
neighbourhood (*l.c.*), and probably may be met with at other
places on the Kent shores. At all events, they are in plenty
on the Varne and Ridge sandbanks, whence the fisher-

---

* Nat. Hist. Brit. Fishes, 1880.
† A female, 25 inches long, weighing nearly 13 lbs., roe full in pinky stage, caught
in stow-net, near Knock Buoy, 21st Nov., 1900, by Ben. Emery.

men capture and take them into the Folkestone and Dover markets. At Ramsgate also the deep-sea trawlers land con-siderable sized ones in fair numbers. They are greedy fish-eaters, but don't disdain the crab and lobster tribe. In the North Sea they spawn from April to July, a few even in August, and beginning of September. Opportunities for comparing the period of those in our district have been wanting. It seems feasible that their breeding-grounds may be near the Galloper Sands or The Falls, likewise the Varne and Ridge shoals ?

(12.) The BRILL (*Rhombus lævis*) figures as an ordinary marketable product at our fisheries stations, Ramsgate, Dover and Folkestone—these being chiefly brought by the deep-sea trawlers. Its range in the North Sea, and more immediately in-shore round our counties' coasts, nearly corresponds with that of the turbot, neither being such a far northerly fish as the halibut. Speaking in a general way, it is more often the younger brill that ascend our estuaries, though in our wide, comparatively shallow seaward bays, larger fish are not infre-quent at a moderate distance from shore. It is mentioned as the " Pearl " (*Rhombus*), in the Sandgate list already cited.* Sale-able brill are somewhat scarce within the present bounds of the Leigh fishing quarters. Still one, said to be 18 or 20 inches long, was quite recently trawled between Sheppey and the Nore Sand. The small ones, as the men say, "are got anywhere." About 1885-6 (?) some 400 small live brill and soles were captured for and transported in tanks to the New York Aquarium by two of the Leigh fishermen (W. Little and G. Gilson).

Confining our remarks to a few among others of those coming under our immediate observation, we have had them in November from 11 to 13 inches long. But the biggest we came across measured 15 inches in length, fully half that broad, and weighed 1 lb. 10 oz. This was taken in a shrimper's trawl in

* Large catches of Brill have at various times been made in Whitstable Bay, during July, Aug. and Sept.; but the last few years they, like other kinds of fish that used to be plentiful, have become scarcer or absent. (Capt. Anderson.)

the channel-way between Leigh middle and River middle buoys
16th April, 1898. Thereafter, on 20th April, 2nd, 7th and 20th
May, several specimens were obtained; one between the Spile
and the East Cant buoy, four near the Blyth, and two in the
Leigh Ray—so they come well up to the brackish water. The
shortest of these was 3 and the longest 5·3 inches, or an average
of 4½ inches. These observations in the light of Cunningham,
McIntosh and others' researches, would seem to imply that the
younger fish were from 10 to 12 months old, whilst the single
older example (15th April) would be two years or over.

An examination of the above more juvenile examples
shewed they fed on shrimps, brown and pink; and in
one remnants of a small fish was found (Goby ?). In the older
ones fish predominated. The diet of the fully mature brill is
said to be 98 per cent. fish, chiefly sand-eels and sprats, while
shrimps and occasionally squids make the remainder (Holt).

In the female specimens which we have inspected in November,
the roe has either only been moderately developed or in a fairly
advanced condition. Judging in one case, from the latter's
appearance, it would be ripe in January or early February.
The spawning season of the North Sea forms has been stated
as from March to June. Our own only test example (16th
April) unfortunately had been eviscerated ere reaching us.

(13.) The SCALDFISH or Scaldback (*Arnoglossus laterna*)
has not hitherto been recorded from the Kent and Essex
waters. A single example, however, came to our notice last
spring. This was caught in the trawl by Geo. Gilson, in mid-
channel (4 to 5 fathoms) between the Leigh river middle and
·the Chapman, 21st April, 1900. It completely answered
descriptions and figures of this fish, even to its loss of scales.
Extreme length, 5 inches, which is an average size of adults,
the very largest not exceeding 7 to 8 inches. Its chief habitat
is the S.W. of England, Plymouth to Cornwall.

(14 and 15.) The TOPKNOTS (*Zeugopterus*) are flat-fish of no
commercial value, though of interest to the naturalist. Both

species—viz., Müller's topknot (*Z. punctatus*)—brought to us as a remarkable kind of brill—and the One-spotted topknot (*Z. unimaculatus*) we have found in the Thames Estuary. They are very rare, but here further comment is unnecessary, other than that Webb says (*l.c.*) they "frequent our rockpools" at Dover.

Previously we have referred to the translucent buoyant eggs of some fishes, but as these may neither be familiar to many fishermen, nor to all Members of our Committee, we venture to insert illustration of three different stages of development.

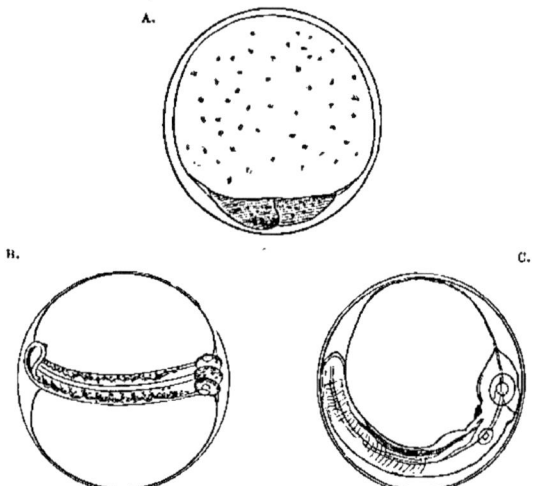

FIG. 9.   A. Egg of Whiting, shewing the commencing aggregation of the germinal substance at its lower part.   B. Egg of Flounder, containing the early long-shaped embryo ; colour points are already developed. C. Egg of Cod, with embryo at sixth day of hatching.   The natural sizes of these eggs are about that of a pin's head, and here, of course, are greatly magnified (after Prince and McIntosh).

The Cod Family (*Gadidæ*).—Compared with some places, our district's commercial returns in the cod family presents but a moderate show, yet at certain seasons a quantity gets landed at Harwich, Ramsgate and Folkestone.   Within our area migration seems related to prey, and in the case of the whiting sporadic visitations of countless hordes have been notable. The bulk of the Gadidæ are typically a northern group, our locality only getting the tail-end of their North Sea expansive distribution. Woe be sprats, young herring, or crab and lobster kind, when pursued by cod, whiting, or pout. Excluding a fresh-water form (Burbot), their eggs are surface-spawned, or of the floating type above shewn. Their breeding haunts are mostly outside our limits.

(1) The Cod (*Gadus morrhua*).—Codfish of great size are very rarely obtained by the Leigh boats in the localities now frequented.* The state of things was considerably different, say, half a century ago, when there was a regular Leigh cod and skate fishery, of which more particulars will be given further on, when treating of Long-line fishing, Section VI. Meantime, we here note that when it was in vogue medium—nay good-sized —cod were taken in quantity. These were obtained during the whole of the winter months, commencing in November, the fishing lasting till March. The regular fishing-grounds for both cod and skate then were comprised between the Oaze channel to the Naze, on occasions almost to Orfordness ; this both inshore and seawards towards the Long Sand and the Kentish knock. Roughly estimated, these market cod might be from 15 to 30 inches and over, though our information thereon is not precise. Doubtless some were sexually mature, for the critical period that the North Sea cod breed is (according to Holt) from 22 to 35 inches ; though ripe cod are found at 20 inches (Fulton).

Of late years many codlings of from 4 to 8 inches long have been regularly got by spratters, fish-trawlers and shrimpers in various parts of the estuary, more particularly in the Oaze, and even as far up the estuary as the Blyth and Holehaven, or up the Medway. These immature codfish are chiefly met with in the spring months. Unless of good size they are seldom

* As this is passing through press, we have seen a cod 3 ft. 3 in. which had been captured in the fish-trawl between Sheppey and the Nore Sand (28th April), by G. Gilson.

brought ashore, not being considered eatable, still less are they saleable. In December, 1898, several examples of hauls from Leigh Roads by John Harvey were brought for our inspection. Two specimens examined, females, were 16 and 11 inches long, and weighed 30 and 10 ounces respectively. In January, 1899, codlings were again numerous, and distributed well over the estuary mouth. Several caught below the Nore ranged from $3\frac{1}{2}$ to over $4\frac{1}{2}$ inches in extreme length, many considerably beyond. Later on, in March and April, even within the "Low-way," Hadleigh Ray mouth, small codlings were procured. The smallest of these fish was 4, the largest 7 inches. The shorter ones were in an interesting change of dress, just beginning to lose the side stripes, or markings, of the post-larval stage.

When or where the adult cod spawns that pay our district a visit we cannot say. Elsewhere, February to March are the chief months, though some ripe fish are got earlier and later. According to the cod-age calculations of various investigators, it would seem the above Thames codlings might be reckoned as from eight to ten, and others twelve months old, and over. Breeding does not commence before the second year. Codlings are abundant the whole entire stretch of our district—Ramsgate, Deal and Folkestone being well-known favourite resorts of sea-anglers for codling, silver whiting, &c. In all of the above Thames codlings, shrimps and remnants of fish were the chief food. In the larger-sized examples, besides the shrimps in spawn were shore crabs and Amphipods. These latter crustaceans gave a rich salmon tint to the stomach contents.[*]

(2) The HADDOCK (*Gadus æglefinus*) has never formed any part of the fishery followed by the Leighmen. What few got have been quite accidental captures, more often with hook-and-line. Mr. B. Baxter says that in former years when he followed stowboating for sprats, at odd times a few would come

---

[*] The so-called Lord Fish or Large-headed Cod (*G. macrocephalus*) of the Thames mouth is assuredly not a separate species, but only a malformed fish. This is of occasional occurrence in the Thames Estuary; but witness Patterson's figs. for examples noticed at Yarmouth. (Zoologist, 1898.)

up in the net. Some eight or nine years ago he himself caught a very fine haddock in Leigh Creek, quite close to the pier. They are brought into Harwich, the product of line fishing off-shore. Dr. Laver has occasionally taken numbers in the Crouch (*op. cit.*). Numerous haddocks were captured at Purfleet in March, 1879; and at the end of the same month a Mr. Hood reported that some years previously haddocks were known to have been found in Dagenham Breach ("Land and Water," 1879). Boys mentions haddock among "Fishes of Sandgate," 1792; one caught near Rochester Bridge, March, 1883; but of other Kent instances we have no information.

(3) The COMMON WHITING (*Gadus merlangus*), although amply represented in the North Sea, especially its more south-ern half, yet for size those of the S.W. of England surpass them. They abound from Dungeness to Harwich during the fall and winter season—around E. and S. Kent, affording famous sport to the pleasure-seeker, as well as gain to the boatmen and fisher-folks. At intervals they come as thick as hops. As an instance, in January, 1898, at the Dover pier the sea literally surged with them, and soon some 2,000 were landed, mostly by amateur fishers.*

There is no special fishing for whiting carried on from Leigh at any season. Fish from 6 to 8 or 9 inches long, occasionally larger ones, are caught by the shrimpers and stowboaters in their ordinary routine. Some seasons they are much more pre-valent than in others. In the spring-time and summer they are comparatively scarce, but more numerous other months. The noted place for whitings in our estuary—exceptionally that red-letter year for them, 1898—was the South channel of the Leighmen, the Knob channel of pilots. Here the fishermen were singularly successful; one fish-trawler (F. Rand), in Sep-tember, got 30 bushels in a single haul. These were good

---

* The "Daily News" of 7th November, 1900, mentions that—immense numbers of Silver Whiting are now to be met with off Deal. Two rods accounted for 440 Whiting, a rod and hand line took 380, and it is estimated 1,000 were caught from Deal Pier in one night.

E

market fish, many a foot long and upwards. He took them to Chatham, where they met ready sale.

The largest-sized whiting we have heard of is said to have been 16 inches, which was taken many years ago by a spratter, northwards of the Oaze. The more usual size got is from 6 to 8 or 9 inches. Yet fish 4 inches long are not uncommon, and when out with the trawlers we have measured a few only 3 inches in length. A dozen whitings bought from out a basket-ful on 16th November, taken up at random, ranged from $8\frac{1}{2}$ up to 12 inches long, the average of the lot being 10 inches. In years gone by, the whitings caught formed part of the Leigh fisher-families' ordinary diet, rather than a marketable product. Now-a-days they have commenced selling them to the fish-mongers and hawkers, as well as disposing of them at Chatham and Sheerness; at times, an item of income worthy of con-sideration. Such as we have seen exposed for sale have all exceeded 7 inches in length.

The following occurrence is thus narrated in Buckland's Appendix II. to his and Walpole's Sea Fisheries Report, 1879. " At the end of October, 1867, immense numbers of young whiting suddenly appeared in the Thames, and it was estimated that nearly 20,000 bushels of them were caught and used for manure; they measured from 2 to 5 inches long. A conviction was obtained against the defendants, at Dartford, under the Thames bye-laws. These fish were probably driven in by the great frost which occurred at that time." The Leigh fisher-men well remember the extraordinary glut of these fish, dubbed " Fenians " by them. They came about October, and they were still found nearly all the winter, disappearing in the spring. The fishermen are of opinion they were not true whiting, neither haddocks, nor codling, but " a different species by themselves " (*sic*). According to their description, they had blunter noses (" bull-dog fish ") than the whiting, and they never were found to have grown larger than the above dimensions of Buckland. They say that ever since 1867 there have always been some of them about all the year round. Indeed it is averred that numbers of these " Fenians " are still to be got in the Blyth and up and down Sea Reach. We repeatedly have had catches of these deceptive " Fenians " for study, guessing some might turn out to be diminutive Poor cod. But those brought us wanted beard (barbule), and invariably bore characters agreeing with the common whiting. If difference among them it was some sharper-nosed, others blunter.

As to the whitings' estuarine migrations, they are observed first to arrive in October and November, about the time that spratting commences (? following these fish), and then below the Oaze and South Channel. Afterwards they by degrees head up river; but it is only on the extraordinary occasions that they are plentiful beyond the Chapman. Presumably their spawning season is when they absent themselves from the river's month; but as to where they go exactly our evidence is deficient. In only a few, 7 inches upwards, have we found the roe indicating progress. One $13\frac{1}{2}$ inches long, at end of November, seemed likely to spawn in January. February to June are given as the Channel months of breeding; they commence a month later in the north. The smallest sexual maturity is given as 8 inches. We have found the whiting's stomach crammed with the following assortment:—Fish (viz., young whiting, sprat, sand-smelt, gobies, &c.); crustacea (such as shore and swimming crabs, hermit crabs, shrimps, Mysidæ, Idotea and Amphipods); occasionally worms and shell-fish; mixed up with these, seaweeds, and even decomposed bits of wood—these last possibly being swallowed in hot haste as they grab at other objects.

(4) The WHITING POUT, or BIB (*Gadus luscus*).—At Leigh some only know this fish by name as the Whiting Pollack; but it is not the *Gadus pollachius*, Linn. Dr. Laver says Essex fishermen call it " Wule," though we ourselves have not heard this vernacular expression.* The Pout is common round our coast. In the neighbourhood of Ramsgate, Deal, Dover and Folkestone they form a sure take of amateur fishers during the

* It is their only name on the Blackwater (Fitch).

season. At the latter port, when skinned, trimmed down, tail twisted round and poked into the eyes, the converted pouters are passed off as genuine silver whiting (Buckland). It is got pretty much everywhere in the Thames Estuary, probably most frequently about the South or Knob Channel, thence to the Margate Sands, &c. Above the Nore it is scarcer, though occasionally it turns up within Sea Reach. It appears to be most numerous in summer, but we have notes of its occurrence in January, May, September, October, November and December, so that it may be regarded as less or more with us all the year round.*

The light paternoster and Kentish-rig chopstick are the approved tackle for its capture on the Kent shores, but in the Thames it is only by chance brought up in the shrimp and fish-trawl. In the latter quarter those caught are not always brought ashore, for they are not prized, yet they eat excellently. The old whiting pouts seem rather to frequent rocky ground; our estuarine examples are seldom full-grown. Specimens usually run from 2 to 3 up to 7 inches, the average being $4\frac{1}{2}$ to 5 inches. The largest we know of measured 10 inches, obtained in mid-December. Our information with regard to their migration, spawning-ground and rate of growth is indefinite. We are more certain as to the nature of their food, having examined many and at different seasons of the year. Shrimps were preponderant, occasionally Mysidæ, then rag-worms, the fleshy parts of crab's claws and legs, and now and again small fish of various species; betimes in May an odd, small octopus.

(5) The POOR COD (*Gadus minutus*).—This diminutive member of the Cod family, so far as we know, has not hitherto been recorded from our district. Yet inasmuch as the Thames Estuary is concerned, it is not altogether at times a rare fish. Its distribution is pretty much the same as the whiting and the pout; indeed, it is usually got with them in the trawl-net It

---

* Extremely abundant in the Blackwater May and June, 1898. Mr. F. O. Rush and three friends hooked 864 in one night tide on 9th June, 1900 (Fitch).

never grows beyond $8\frac{1}{2}$ inches, but those we have examined have been under that, or from $5\frac{1}{3}$ to 7 inches long, some even less. It seems to be most nearly allied to the pout (some think it a variety), but it has quite as close a resemblance to the whiting, from which, however, the presence of a barbel at once distinguishes it. Most fishermen see no distinction between them and whiting; any big enough to pass muster being disposed of as such. Those that I have shewn the difference to, and interrogated as to its being their mythical " Fenian," have not been disposed to take that view.* Such as we have opened have proved shrimp-eaters.

(9) POLLACK, or Whiting Pollack (*Gadus pollachius*).—Webb says this is hooked from the pier at Dover. In the summer it is regularly caught at Deal (a 16 lb. fish recorded in 1889), and towards Ramsgate. Said also to be brought into Harwich (Dale). We have hinted how some Leigh fishermen call the Pout a Whiting Pollack, but others believe they have caught the true pollack.† We have not been fortunate in coming across any Thames Estuary examples.

(10-12) On the authority of Webb (Handb.) we name (10) the COALFISH or Green Pollack (*Gadus virens*)as having been obtained at Dover. (11) The HAKE (*Merluccius vulgaris*) is another of the uncommon gadoids that seldom pays us a visit. Dr. Laver (*op. cit.*) vouches for one captured on the Essex coast, and quotes Dale and Lindsey for their presence at Harwich. Webb likewise announces it as landed at Dover. (12) Again, such is the rare LESSER FORK-BEARD (*Raniceps raninus*), whereof one $4\frac{1}{2}$ inches long is said to have been taken by Mr. S. W. Waud in the Crouch river, May, 1858 (Day), and several times brought ashore by fishermen on the South Kent coast (Webb).

(13) The LING (*Molva vulgaris*).—We are inclined to believe that this member of the Codfish family has not hitherto been recorded from the Kent and Essex district. It has appeared,

---

* One individual recognised it as the "Grass Whiting."
† An old fisherman assures us the true Whiting-Pollack frequented the Crouch above Burnham a few years ago, but we have had no corroboration of this.

however'as an occasional visitor in the Sussex waters (Merrifield).
G. Gilson has seen several Thames examples, 9 to 12 inches,
during winter and spring.   One was obtained in the trawl below
the Southend pier on 1st April, 1897.   It measured a foot long,
and contained in its stomach a rockling half as big as itself
(*i.e*, 6 inches).   Besides being a scarce fish in our area, this
ling was interesting in its exhibiting a stage of development,
just prior to its assuming the more sombre fully adult dress.
But we must refer to Professor McIntosh's descriptions of the
remarkable changes which this fish undergoes from its post-
larval condition onwards ; Fig. 10 being from his volume, by
favour.

Fig. 10.

Young Ling when it has assumed the barred stage ; about 6 inches
long.   (After McIntosh.)

(14–15) The Rocklings (*genus Motella*) serve a useful
purpose as food for other more valuable fish.   In a very young
stage they are known as the mackerel-midges by our Channel
fishermen.   At times they shoal in myriads at the surface of the
sea, pursued unrelentlessly by the mackerel, &c.*   As they grow
older they assume the appearance of the Blenny tribe, scatter,
and take shorewards thereafter, oftimes leading a more
solitary life, and then go by the name of Rocklings.   Mr.
Fitch remarks (Essex Nat. II.) "These dull orange fishes are
locally known as ' Newcome ' or ' Lucome' in the Blackwater."
(14) The Three-Bearded Rockling or Whistle-fish (*M.
tricirrata*) and (15) the Five-Bearded Rockling (*M. mustela*)
are tolerably, though irregularly, distributed in the Thames,
Blackwater and Colne estuaries; whilst the former has
been taken in 30 fathoms off Folkestone, and there named

---

* Off Dover a shoal pursued by mackerel had dogfishes hanging on latters' skirts,
and porpoises in turn hunting them (Webb).

" Goss " or " Gossat " (Buckland). We have seen an odd one or
two of both sexes taken in the shrimper's net above the
Chapman Light, near W. Shoebury Buoy, again between
the Nore and the Jenkins, as also near the Oaze and
Spile. In the winter months, especially December and
January, they seem to congregate rather numerously in the
Hadleigh Ray, but apparently take more seawards as spring
advances. The smallest we have obtained in August was $2\frac{3}{4}$
inches, and the largest in November and December 6 and $8\frac{1}{2}$
inches long. They, however, grow to twice that length. At the
end of December we have found a female with full but not ripe
ovary, but others less advanced. As to food, shrimps and
Amphipods, small shore and pea crabs has been their diet.
Though their flesh is fair eating, they are never used as food.

The Herring Family (*Clupeidæ*).—Some of these (sprat and
herring) frequent our outer coast in immense shoals during the
latter part and beginning of the year from Dungeness to Dovercourt. But the herring and sprat are also, in more scattered
groups of different ages, more or less always within our estuaries
up to the brackish water. The shads, however, push right up
into the fresh water of the rivers annually for spawning purposes. The above three furnish considerable revenue to our
fishermen, whereas pilchard and anchovy do not; they being
scanty in numbers and irregular in their visits, which are chiefly
round South Kent. The clupeoids, unlike the cod and flatfish
families already described, present striking diversity in their
modes of spawning. For example, the herring has eggs which
are adhesive and sink in the water (=demersal), becoming
fastened in clumps or in flat patches to stones, seaweed, or
hydroids, fig. 11 (*i.e.* " whiteweed " of Leighmen). The sprat,
pilchard and anchovy, on the contrary, have surface-floating
spawn (= pelagic). The shads again bear an intermediate
character, for their eggs, while quite separate, and not attached
to foreign bodies, still have a tendency to gravitate, and lie
towards the bottom.

(1) The COMMON HERRING (*Clupea harengus*) may be regarded with us as of two kinds, or, as some would infer, demonstrating two races—one the sea-herring, the other estuarine-herring, so called autumn and spring herrings. There appears to be no hard and fast line distinguishing these other than size, the areas they occupy and their times of spawning.

(*a*) The *Sea-herring*, which frequents mainly the deep central depression of the southern portion of the North Sea, seems to come more landwards, and be found in spawning condition from October to December, according to circumstances. At least they are pursued and captured in drift-nets by the fishermen of Margate, Broadstairs, Ramsgate, Deal, Kingsdown, Dover, Folkestone and Dungeness. The Essex men seldom use drift-nets, hence sea-herring fishing at the present time is purely a Kentish industry.

So far we have not yet learned the exact whereabouts of the spawning-ground of these sea-herrings, though the area between the Galloper and Kentish Knock, and the shallow water near the Falls have been suggested. Howsoever this may be, it appears that some of the spent fish from these North Sea shoals evidently make their way up the estuary. One old spratter states that in the neighbourhood of the West Spile Buoy and the flats thereabouts they used to catch in their stow-nets, towards the end of November and December, from 500 to 600 herring on a tide. These usually were full sized and clearly, or in the majority of cases, shotten fish. There also has been other occasions when these sea-herring have ascended the Medway and Thames to the limits of the fresh water. G. Kirby recalls such a case occurring some 20 years ago, when in February a great shoal came up the Medway and were caught in numbers. As stated by him these were quite like Norway herrings in appearance and size, ranging from 10 inches to a foot long. However, they turned out of little value, "eating quite dry, and woolly"—evidently spent fish. Ab. Robinson and others further tell us that in their fathers' time (about 1820 ?) extraordinary shoals of sea-herrings visited various parts of the

Essex coast. One lot in immense numbers crowded up the estuary to Sea Reach, as far even as the Lower Hope, or beyond that So great was their mass right opposite Leigh in the Fairway Channel, that one boat with a brand new set of nets got these at once so full as utterly to destroy them. Other smaller craft put off, and it was said literally baled them in, so heaped up had the fish got. Almost simultaneously a branch shoal penetrated the Crouch to above Cricksea, and at Burnham quay they were easily lifted out in bucketfuls.

While small lots here and there annually congregate together at the Thames mouth apart from the larger shoals outside, others more solitary, in one and twos, get scattered all over the estuary, and appear often to keep company for a time with the smaller river-herring and yearling fish. Occasionally the shrimpers may bring up these, but more often they find their way to the whitebaiters' stow-net.

A few examples, among others within our notice, may be cited, to give an idea of the differences of condition, &c. On the last day of December, 1896, one, a male, $14\frac{1}{4}$ inches in extreme length, was brought for examination along with three of the female river-herring—$7\frac{1}{2}$, $6\frac{1}{2}$ and 6 inches in length. The milt of the former was well-nigh spent, whilst the ovaries of the latter were only in an early stage of development. They had all been feeding on young sprats and whitebait. On 14th December, 1899, a thin elongate-bodied female, $10\frac{3}{4}$ inches long, clearly a North Sea herring in shape and appearance, was procured. There were only a few eggs left in the ovary, otherwise this last was watery and flaccid, with other proofs of being a fully-spent fish. With this was a $6\frac{3}{4}$ inch herring of the estuarine or river type. On 5th March, 1900, two long gaunt specimens, a male and female, respectively $10\frac{1}{2}$ and 10 inches long, both shotten, were taken in the whitebaiters' stow-net along with a number of "yawlings," sprats, and whitebait. Such another pair of sea-herring were taken by the same party on 19th March. Another characteristic example on the 20th March was 11 inches long. By April and May these

spent sea-herrings are seldom met with. Improved in condition
after temporary sojourn around the coast, presumably they
rejoin seawards the retiring shoals of their brethren in the
North Sea. The conclusion to be drawn from the preceding
seems to be that these sea-herrings begin spawning in early
November, the maximum by the end of that month and till
mid-December. Then comes a falling off, and late ones may
continue to the end of January, after which only spent fish
are met with. The size of these fish which approach our
shores apparently ranges from about 9 to close on 15 inches.

(*b.*) The *Estuarine or River Herring* of the Leigh fishermen
are usually recognised at a glance, partly from being of smaller
dimensions than the sea-herring, but more particularly by their
general shape. Contrasted with the North Sea fish they are
shorter and relatively deeper bodied. As the fishermen express
it they are of a snugger build with a small head and altogether
plumper shape. Inasmuch as our observations trend, there
seems to be no difference in the numbers of the fin rays from
those of the sea-herring, nor could we detect any trenchant distinction in the position of the dorsal to the anal fin, or to the
length of body, &c. Such combination of characters in herring
are insisted on by Heincke, a German naturalist,* to denote
racial differences. Our comparisons thereon have certainly
been more limited than Heincke's or of Matthews'† examinations
of the summer and winter herring of Scotland; but the results,
nevertheless, incline us to the latter's opinion of the difficulty
of assigning variations sufficient to positively base race
character on.

Yet, on the other hand, race or breed has an elastic source
in physiological functions (*e.g.*, nutrition and reproduction)

---

* Dr. Heincke's researches "Die Varietaten des Herings" are altogether of an
elaborate nature. His earlier memoirs in 2 parts with illustrations were published in
1877 and 1882 respectively, in the Bericht der Commis.-Untersuch, deutsch meere (Rep.
German Sea Fisheries Commission, in Kiel), which we have duly consulted. Since
then he has issued another work "Naturgeschichte des Herings" (Nat. Hist. of
Herrings), which unfortunately we have not seen. But an excellent Review of this
by Mr. Kyle, has appeared in the 17th Ann. Rep. S.F.B. for 1898.

† "Variety among the Herrings of the Scottish Coasts." Append. 5th Ann. Rep.
S.F.B. for 1886.

rather than in anatomical details. Hence, for all practical purposes, the sea- and estuary- herring of our district may be regarded in the light of two different races, notwithstanding that we cannot define distinctive bodily points of variation.

As to Yarrell's separation of the Thames February spawning herring into a species—his Leach's herring (*Clupea Leachii*)—this cannot be maintained; but Cunningham's suggestion of there being a spring spawning brackish-water herring seems quite justified. It is, however, not alone confined to the Thames, as we shall proceed to show.

Regarding its distribution we may refer to a herring fishery which formerly existed in the Medway. Witnesses before the Sea Fisheries Commissioners, held at Rochester 14th November, 1878, stated that up to near 1860 some 20 to 30 boats, with two men and an apprentice in each, used to seine for "river-herrings" every October, November and December.* A last†‡ was then not unusual to be obtained; but they dwindled away, so that later on not a tenth of the numbers were caught.

Latterly this Medway river-herring fishing has practically been restricted to irregular catches of only a few. About the same period there was a regular herring-fishing on the Essex coast, namely, the Pont herring fishery. This we understand was carried on by the Wyvenhoe, Brightlingsea, and particularly the Tollesbury and Mersea fishermen generally. From the descriptions given us of these short, plump herrings, they doubtless were of the same estuarine breed as the Medway fish. Short drift-nets were used for their capture, and the men used to blow horns to warn off the spratters from their drift-nets (Baxter). The herring frequented the Pont or estuarine bight of sea at the mouths of the Colne and Blackwater; the fish, it is said, running up the latter to as far as Osea Island. This fishery, we understand, still continues, but the number of boats engaged are fewer (French).

---

* At Rochester, called by the fishers " White herring."

† In the North Sea fisheries a "Last" of herrings is nominally 10,000, but practically 13,200. What numbers were in the Rochester men's last we cannot say. Theirs only seems a broad expression.

We have only incidentally heard of the possibility of such a herring fishery in the Harwich neighbourhood; but our information thereon is too meagre and contradictory to be relied on—hence further inquiry is therefore necessary. Estuarine herring, however, seem to frequent the Yarmouth shore, for Patterson (*loc. cit.*) mentions a 6-inch example full of roe, and another of similar size, April, 1890, containing 143 opossum shrimps. According to Holdsworth (Deep Sea Fishing, 1874) there was in the Wash "a small variety of the common herring, which appears in December and spawns in February and March." He further adds, that it agrees with Yarrell's reputed species of those of the Thames mouth (*supra*). Taking these data into consideration, it may be inferred that the estuarine or spring-spawning herring is not restricted to the latter river, but is spread in fewer or greater numbers along the seaboard of East Anglia—from Kent to Norfolk and Lincolnshire.

Pursuit of herring seems never to have formed a distinct branch of the Leigh fisheries. Nevertheless for several months of the year in the Thames estuary and the creeks along the Essex coast, herrings of various ages and stages of growth muster in considerable force. Among those got in the stow-net a certain percentage of the adult larger sized ones—from 6 inches upwards or thereabouts—are recognised by the Leigh. men as true herrings. But others of smaller size—2 to 5 inches and over—captured in company with them, and locally known as " yawlings,"—most of the fishermen will not admit are young herrings.

They, indeed, insist these are a separate species of fish [*sic*], though belonging to the herring tribe. Many of the men declare in support of their assertion that they frequently get these fish full of ripe roe, though some fishers of older standing avow this does not tally with their experience. We have examined specimens, but unfortunately those hitherto received have proved rather unsatisfactory evidence in confirmation of the above view. Take for example among other cases examined by us one batch of 13 received 20th May,

1898, and said to be " Yawlings " in spawn. Two were males. One of them 6·7 inches had a small milt not ripe, in the other 5·7 inches the milt showed non-development. The sizes of the 11 females, were : three of 6·3 inches, others respectively, 6·2, 6·0, 5·10, 5·9, 5·7, two of 5·6, one 5·2, and another five inches,

Fig. 11.

Eggs of the Herring attached to a Hydroid (*Antennularia antennina*), reduced half nat. size after Prof. Ewart, 3rd. Ann. Rep. S.F.B. for 1885. The above hydroid with others go by the name of " Whiteweed " among the Leighmen, who inaccurately consider them plants, and not animal forms, from their being rooted to stones and shells, &c. But see remarks on hydroids further on.

all extreme lengths. In each of them the ovarian organs either were in an imperfect, very early stage, or in others not apparently developed. None of the entire batch could be said to have had the slightest semblance of sexual ripeness.

Probably most Leigh fishermen would have allowed that the largest of the set were really herring, even although they clung to recognising the shortest as their typical " Yawlings." *
Still where would come the line of separation in such a graduated series ? As a climax it may be added, avoiding detail, that examination into specific characters left no doubt of their all being immature herrings.

As to where those herrings spawn that frequent the estuary, ignorance is to be confessed. The Leigh shrimp trawlers, so far as we know, have not hitherto brought up or observed any samples of spawn that could be construed as that of herring. To wit, within their area of fishing which in the lower estuary chiefly compasses the Oaze, Redsand, Gilman and the Girdler. As mere conjecture on our part, the vicinity of the Shingles, Barrow Sands, Sunk and Long Sand would seem the most likely grounds. This inasmuch as the diminutive brood (part whitebait) which literally swarm westwards towards mid-summer cannot be derived from a great distance.

Regarding the period of their spawning : In December we have noted some specimens between 6 and 7 inches long, with the ovary in the early vascular stage, while others were less advanced. In February similar sized specimens were much in the same condition, though examples male and female of 8 and $8\frac{1}{2}$ inches (extreme length) had full milt and roe, both nigh ripe. In March and April the completely adult forms seem scarce or absent in the whitebaiters' stow-net (Southend neighbourhood, as well as at Queenborough), so probably during these months there is a migration towards their spawning grounds, not visited by our fishers. At all events, during April and May the quite young translucent scaleless fish, and those with partial

---

*A few of the fishermen, especially the lads we have conversed with, are rather confused in their notions how to distinguish a " yawling " of small size. An invariable reply is " I knows it," or some will say "he's got a big head." But the clearest expressions characterizing yawlings we heard from the brothers Bundock. Their method of judging is based :—1. On general length as compared with depth of body. Sprats being deepest and plumpest, the yawlings are so to say leanest looking. 2. Head relatively largest in yawlings. 3. Eye largest in yawlings, and the lower jaw below the eye protuberant. 4. The sprats are brightest throughout (more sheen), the " yawlings" tending to a darker coloured back. 5. The prickly belly when old enough.

silvery sheen, appear abundantly among the baiter's catch (*see* " Whitebait "). In the latter month stow-netting ceases, and the drag-net comes into use. Then and in June and July fishing is carried on from the shore, and fewer big fish got. In a few of the so-called " yawlings," nearly 6 inches long, at the end of May we have found the roe commencing to expand, or in what may be termed the " pinky " or vascular stage, but without trace of eggs,—similar, in fact, to the conditions met with in December. Whether this indicated a later spawning we are not prepared to say, though other circumstances point to the likelihood of their being among the later autumn spawners.

Concerning migration, our limited data barely allows a sound conclusion to be drawn. It would appear, though, as if they were to a certain extent local in habitat. Except when the ripe adults shoal and go seawards—in the spring breeding season— those of the yawling stage apparently are resident hither and thither in various parts of the estuarine area nearly all the year round.

Their food within the estuary depends somewhat on age and season. Among the younger fish the stomach often appears empty, or the contents, of a gelatinous consistence, are not definitely recognisable. In some, though, by the aid of the microscope, we have detected remnants of minute crustaceans— Ostracods, Copepods, Amphipods and Mysidae, as well as Crab-Zoëa (early swimming stage). and embryos of tiny soft-bodied Mollusks that creep among the *Zostera* weed. In many older fish, likewise, gelatinous residue is all that can be seen, for the yawling and adult herring's rapid digestion of tender material soon reduces most of their food to a pulp. This has given rise to the fishermen's notion that the herring " lives on suction." Certainly the North Sea tidal wave brings up stream myriads of the diminutive crustacea mentioned above.

But the so-called " yawlings," from a few inches up to the adult herrings, by no means confine their diet to these, for we have found stuck in their throats and in the stomach their own brood (herring larvæ), and that of sprats or other small fish composing the whitebaiter's catch. Occasionally also nereid worms, and at certain times Mysidae and Amphipods.

Their rate of growth we discuss further on, under " Whitebait." So far as Leigh fishermen are concerned, herrings bring them profit chiefly in the form of whitebait. Within our waters, as elsewhere, herrings, like all the defenceless Clupeidæ, have hosts of enemies ever on the watch. The cod family generally, the garfish, mackerel, skate, and dogfish tribe, &c., besides porpoises, are perfect harriers of shoals. Nor do the gulls and cormorants, &c., wait long for share of the plunder, whenever their quick eyes detect them near the surface.

(2) The Sprat (*Clupea Sprattus*).—Kent and Essex alike have long been noted for the numbers and quality of their sprats. These frequent the whole extent of the coast. Particularly are they found at the estuarine mouths and up the rivers and reaches to the furthest limits of the brackish water. The immense shoals of adults are annual, but somewhat capricious winter visitants. The juvenile sprats associated with the herring-yawlings may be met with at one part or another of the estuary and creeks at least nine or ten months of the year.

The sizes of sprats that have come under our observation have ranged from $1\frac{1}{2}$ inches up to a maximum of 6 inches in extreme length. The former are the post-larval stage, or their whitebait condition. The latter, which are probably not less than three year old adult fish, are very rare. We have not met with half a dozen of such all told, though we have had a sharp eye to the big ones in boat loads of fish we have scanned both at Leigh and Brightlingsea. Those of 5, $5\frac{1}{4}$, and $5\frac{1}{2}$ inches, however are not altogether uncommon. From $4\frac{1}{2}$ to 5 inches, though, may be considered the ordinary size of the prime adult sprats, while $3\frac{1}{2}$ to 4 inches are those of ordinary dimensions. Possibly 4 to $4\frac{1}{2}$ inches may roughly be reckoned as the average size of the adult market fish sent from our neighbourhood. The south-east Kent sprats, however, have a good reputation for bigness and plumpness. These are caught by large meshed drift-nets, and not stow-nets, so doubtless the lesser sized fish escape entanglement.

According to the records of the Scotch Fishery Officers, among herrings males and females are almost identical in numbers, viz., in the proportion of 100 of the former to 99 of the latter. In the case of the sprat in our English waters the females out-number the males—at least, of some 200 adult specimens examined 75 were males and 125 females. Whether this inequality in sex would hold good were a longer series inspected, remains to be seen. Taking the data for what it is worth, it seems to lend countenance to Fulton's suggestion* of a preponderance of females in those fish having floating (*pelagic*) eggs, *e.g.*, sprat, in contradistinction to its close ally the herring, whose eggs are sunken (*demersal*) or fixed to various substances.

Sprats with us are very irregular in their abundance and scarcity, barely two seasons following resembling each other. This periodicity of plenty and the reverse appears always to have been the case. Certain red-letter years have occurred with a perfect glut of them all round the coast; or again, at one part of our district they would be more plentiful than at another. Some spratters of long standing maintain that they formerly were more numerous, others are of a contrary opinion.

In Buckland and Walpole's Commission, 1878, a witness at Southend stated that taking five-yearly averages there had been no difference in the sprat fishing for 40 years. At Gravesend they said sprats had fallen off 75 per cent.; at Leigh they were decreasing. Rochester and Queenborough men had the same tale, though the latter admitted it was rather that they now fished for them off the North Foreland and Prince's Channel; one boat in 1877 having caught £50 worth of sprats in a week west of the Tongue Light. Meantime superfine sprats were got at Dover, and four years previously very plentiful at Ramsgate

---

* 10th Ann. Rep. F.B.S. for 1891.

in Pegwell Bay. In such evidence, unfortunately, memory and
bias may have served rather than reliable statistics; for the
river and estuarine fishermen were then at loggerheads, un-
wisely opposing one another's methods of fishing, which time
has changed and much modified their views thereon.

The subject of the migration of sprats has not hitherto
received so much attention as that of the herring, yet both are
distinctly of nomadic habit. From our informants we glean
that the adult sprats visiting South Anglia come almost simultaneously with herring shoals from the North Sea about October.
Usually they appear to strike shore either a little north of or
somewhere opposite Southwold and Aldeburgh in Suffolk.
Thence, with erratic wandering, they trend southwards along
the Essex and Kent coasts in November and December; branch
shoals heading up the several estuaries. In short, they seem
to follow the course of the strong tidal current from the north
which sweeps into the great bight of the Thames estuary.

Sections of the huge shoals would seem to progress towards
the Straits and English Channel, for Deal, Dover and Folkestone
drifters not infrequently receive full share in their nets. So
far as their approach to the Thames is concerned, it is vouched
for by those who pursue the winter avocations of spratting, that
they never know where to look for the advance shoals. Some
seasons they are first met with in one Channel, then another
year in quite a different one. Moreover, on occasions, strangely
enough, the first indications of them have been near the
Chapman Light, viz., quite in the most western portion of
the estuary.

Betimes the golden opportunity of big and paying catches
has first been made in the neighbourhood of the Wallet; at
another season around the Princes, the Queen's Channel, and
the Girdler would seem to be their earliest gregarious centre,
or even more shorewards towards Kent, in the South, the Gore
and the Copperas Channels. The more observant fishers, however, incline to think the balance is in favour of the common
route being through the Swins and Deeps towards the Oaze.

There is a notion that if they come thus in preference to the southerly passages "there are bound to be a good lot of fish."

How far they may ascend the brackish water of the Medway and Thames, their daily whereabouts, or how long they may remain in the neighbourhood, are always questionable events. It is noticeable though that with S. and S.E. winds the sprats keep to the south side of the Estuary; but should N. or N.W. breezes arise the fish cross to the north shore. Sharp cold weather though does not seem to have great sway in retarding first arrival of the shoals. But on gloomy days and fog, or during low tides, they seldom swim on the surface; thus their presence in lower currents may be undetected. Earlier or later in February there is a tendency to a retrograde or seaward movement. The breeding sprats are noticed to congregate somewhere about the outer Kentish flats, and ultimately retire to their spawning grounds outside.

As to the period of spawning, our observations point to this as commencing about February or beginning of March, and it continues for several months. Among series examined at different dates as to the condition of the sexual organs, the undermentioned is an abstract.

About mid-December the large females (say from $5\frac{1}{2}$ to 6 inches long) had the ovary in what may be termed the "pinky" (=vascular) stage, and in which minute eggs were discernible by the hand-lens. That is in a moderately advanced stage, but by no means ripe. Males of equal length had the milt firm, but not ready for extrusion. On 31st December a series of females, from 4 to 4·9 inches in extreme length, had the ovaries only slightly developed, the shortest of the fish still less so. On 2nd and 5th January, series ranging from $3\frac{3}{4}$ to $5\frac{1}{2}$ inches long showed different stages of advancement. The smaller ones possessed quite undeveloped roe; the larger ones only were assuming the "pinky" condition in which minute eggs of varied sizes lay disseminated in the vascular ovarian substance. A 6-inch male had the milt full though not ripe. Other sets examined on the 12th and 19th

January were in a very similar state to the preceding. It was clearly evident though, that all those sprats of 4 inches and under were in a backward phase, or late spawners, as compared with the 4½ to 5 inch ones. On 11th February in a total of 100 specimens half of these were examined to ascertain their sexual condition and food. Their sizes were from 3½ to 5½ inches, whereof 31 were females and 19 males. In the former sex the ovaries were either moderately or fairly well developed, some among the bigger fish exhibiting well formed eggs. Among the males the milt corresponded in stages of ripeness. None were absolutely in fit spawning condition, though some very close to it. The other 50, of from 2½ to 3½ inches length, were all individually measured, but not critically examined as to their sexual phase.

In company with the above were a lot of younger sprats of 2 inches, or what may be deemed the whitebait stage. The whole boat load was taken by a spratter, but what between the rather numerous sprinkling of under-sized fish, the day of catch at week's end, and adverse weather, the London market was not attempted, so the Salvation farm had them (7 to 9 tons) for manure. On 15th February two males and a female (= 4¼ to 5¼ inches) showed ample milt and roe in an advanced stage, still not thoroughly ripe. On 27th February a catch, 3½ to 5½ inches long, exhibited similar condition, the smallest least developed. On 5th March among 13 males and 11 females (=3¾ to 5 inches) most of the large fish were almost ripe, the smaller ones, however, less advanced. Our memoranda, on 6th March, record ripe and a solitary supposititious spent sprat ?

Meanwhile spratting had practically ceased, but occasionally the whitebaiters would get a few in their stow-net along with herrings and "yawlings." Instance two females on 20th March, one 4¾ inches, the eggs within a trice of ripeness, the other 4 inches, ova fairly advanced ; others along with them were under a couple of inches in size, or whitebait proper.

From all these data we infer :—(a) That the sprats principal spawning season is the spring months ; (b) that the older fish first become mature; (c) that breeding condition is not attained until they are well nigh four inches in extreme length ; (d) that a large proportion of the younger fish are temporarily resident, and distributed hither and thither in the estuary and creeks from autumn till spring, the majority of yearlings then join and migrate with the adult shoals ; (e) that while no racial distinction exists, yet practically the fishermen's notion of sea *versus* river sprats deserves consideration.*

The location and area of the sprats' spawning ground, viz., those frequenting our district, is not known to the fishermen— no more than that of the herrings. It is presumed to be seaward by the eastern movement of the breeding fish. These just leave us at the critical juncture of sexual maturity, accompanied by the immature sprats, which have been temporarily sojourning in the shallow brackish waters. There is a strong probability of the spawning area being at only a very moderate distance from land, possibly near or within territorial limits. Judging by the sets of the tidal currents and likely action on buoyant eggs, spawning may occur outside any portion of the North Sea facing Essex.

The opinion of fish-experts differs considerably. Professor McIntosh and Masterman† believe that, from the place of capture of eggs in the Firth of Forth, the sprat spawns well up the reaches of the estuaries. Cunningham‡ reasons from his observations in the Plymouth neighbourhood that the sprats go some distance off shore in order to spawn, and Holt's §

* Mobius and Heincke evidently hold such opinion, inasmuch as in their account of fishes of the Baltic, they state that there are two local races of sprats, spring and autumn spawners, similar indeed to the herring races (Commis. Untersuch deutsch meere, 1883). According to this view on our coast the larger fish caught at Dover might represent sea sprats (autumn spawners), the smaller Thames sort to be equivalent to brackish water form (spring spawners). But there is no decided testimony to this effect. Hence, for the present we can but regard our S.E. Anglian sprats as exhibiting no prominent racial distinction. From the mode of fishing at Dover, the sprats there caught, plausibly are a selection of the oldest, best conditioned, premature breeders, the bulk of those frequenting the Thames ripening slower—here taking their inshore autumn visit in precedence. But, if such is the case, it tends to render ambiguous the significance of herring races.

† Brit. Mar. Food-Fish, 1897 ; and 11th and 16th Ann. Reps. S.F.B. for 1892 and 1896.

‡ Marketable Mar. Fish, 1896.

§ Jour. Mar. Biol. Assoc., April, 1898, Holt & Scott, Tabs. p. 156 onwards.

record of eggs and larvæ collected thereabouts, verifies the
idea of their transportation from the outer to the inner
waters of the Sound. Our inquiry into the subject at the
Thames mouth is in favour of Cunningham's view.

Prior to and when the full-roed sprats are leaving the
estuary in the spring there is no appearance of eggs or spent
fish (one noted above) remaining in the river, nor evidence
of breeders about afterwards, until their return the following
winter. Furthermore, it is subsequent to the adults' departure
that the larval forms begin to swarm from the West Swin and
Barrow Deep, and advance up stream. Ostensibly a similar set
of phenomena occurs in the North. Witness Masterman's
analysis of the work of the "Garland" in the Firth of Forth
under the auspices of the Scotch Fishery Board (*l. c.*). His data
and admission of the eggs drift from E. to W., and their
further spread, according to directions of wind and tide, does
not, however, substantiate the sprats' spawning ground to be
in the brackish water of the inner Firth or estuary, as he and
McIntosh believe.

The rate of growth of the sprat we shall have something to
say about under Whitebait (*postea*).

As to their food, this in a great many instances is often past
recognition, partly from its original delicate nature, and from
its quick digestion. Frequently gelatinous glairy substance
(as in the herring's stomach) alone remains. In December we
have found Mysidæ and Copepods. In January Amphipods,
Copepods, and remnants of crustacean larvæ; in one large
female was an annelid, but this worm was not determined; still
another contained a small fragment of rotten wood. In
February, in a batch of large and otherwise good sized sprats,
every one seemed to have been feeding on whitebait, and so far
as could be made out from the partly digested material these
were clupeoids. We expected to find in some of the series examined minute shrimps, but if these were present they escaped
our observation. In the March specimens the food was doubtful,

though the sprats themselves were in admirable condition, fat and oily.

Their economical aspect is best attested, oddly enough, in the "Essex Dialect and Folk-lore," by "Weavers Beef," of Colchester.* As nutritious food this goes without saying. But what doubtless detracts from their more frequent domestic use in the better class households, is the strong pungent and penetrating, oily odour given off in cooking—a counteracting agent for which we are not aware of. Their free use at times as manure is often censured by those interested in fishery matters ; but remedies are easier suggested than carried out. This is to be regretted ; but practical emendation still awaits those who clamour when there is a glut of fish, and rather glibly talk of waste unmindful of the needy or deserving fishermen ceasing their occupation. Such would be the essential outcome of the contingency, were the drastic measures carried out which some critics have urged. All the while the matter deserves our committee's serious consideration.

Take, for example, Professor Stirling's hints† as to extracts being made on other products utilized, or Mr. Fryer‡ and others suggestions as to preparation of sprats as sardines, which are steps in the right direction. Nevertheless, the alpha and omega of the question is a monetary one. Connecting the sprat therewith, some years back at Deal, factories for canning them were established, and much profit expected, seeing boat-loads of sprats were almost going a-begging. In 1892, a poor spratting year, values were kept up by the factories' needs. In 1893 the factories offered low prices, though at Brightlingsea and Leigh sprats could only be sold as manure. In 1897, with sprats plentiful, the tinning establishments dropped their prices. In the 1898 Reports,§ only one factory said to be working, and difficulties arising between

---

* Essex Naturalist, Vol. VIII.
† 4th Ann. Rep. S.F.B. for 1885.   ‡ 5th Ann. Rep. S.F.B. for 1886.
§ See Annual Reports of Inspectors English Sea Fisheries, years mentioned.

the fishermen and the manager. Thus the inexorable law of supply and demand sets at nought theoretical utility. (*See* Sect. XI., Fish Product Manufacture.)

Among the sprats' greatest foes, besides man, are the same ravenous fish families, the sea birds and the porpoises, mentioned as devastators of herrings. In batches of sprats, never in herrings, generally one will be found with an "eye-sucker," viz., a double-tailed worm-like parasite, streaming away from the orbit. This is phosphorescent, hence such sprats are known vernacularly as "lantern sprats." The parasite in question (*Lerneonema*) does not seem much to affect the health of the fish, which are usually in as plump a condition as their companions.

WHITEBAIT.

Appendix to Herring and Sprats.—By the popular term whitebait is to be understood, not one particular kind of fish, but a mixed series of small fish, &c., which are sent collectively to the market under this commonly known appellation. It is true that naturalists from the beginning of last century to about the eighties, were not of one mind as to their identity. Pennant declared them young bleak, Donovan and Fleming young shad, Yarrell a separate species of supposed adult fish, his *Clupea alba** ; Gunther more judiciously recognized in them the young of herring, substantiated by Day with addition of sprats, which last view has received ample confirmation from extensive examinations of Thames and Forth whitebait by Ewart and Matthews.† Nearly all these authorities confined themselves to ascertaining what was the bright and silvery fish that predominated in the so-called whitebait, ignoring the other material.

---

* A view supported by Cuvier and Couch; Valenciennes went further in constituting them a new genus, his *Rogenia*.

† 4th Ann. Rep. S.F.B. for 1895, and other articles in 2nd Ann. Rep. for 1893.

Buckland, who usually seized the practical side of a thing, overhauled direct the nets and baskets of the whitebaiters. His list runs—1, herrings ; 2, sprats ; 3, gobies ; 4, weevers ; 5, sand-eels ; 6, smelts ; 7, pipe-fish ; 8, sticklebacks ; 9, buntings or brown shrimps ; 10, red shrimps ; 11, gorebills or garpike.* This is correct as far as it goes, but requires expansion, for to our knowledge the following forms also occur : 12, sand smelts ; 13, shad ; 14, eels ; 15, eel-pouts ; 16, White Goby (*Aphia*) ; 17, plaice ; 18, dabs ; 19, flounders ; 20, soles ; 21, bass ; 22, mullet ; 23, lump fish ; 24, Sea-horse (*Hippocampus*) ; 25, lamprey ; 26, crabs (= shore and pea-crabs) ; 27, Isopods (*Idotea*) ; 28, Opossum shrimps (*Mysidæ*) ; 29, octopus ; 30, star-fish (five-fingers) ; 31, jelly fish (the fishermen's " flat " and " round-gall," see Whitebaiting, sect. VI.) ; even another might be added in an occasional dash of seaweed.

Such is the heterogeneous assemblage despatched to Billingsgate vouched for from our oft-repeated scrutiny of net, box and basket, added to which frequent gustatory experience of what is served up in the dainty dishes at hotels and restaurants. Of course, the relative numbers of each sort are most unequal and uncertain. Some are present quite by accident, others in profusion or the opposite, according to season, weather, and tides where fished for, and the net in use.

In fact, whitebaiting requires experience, discretion, and careful picking to be successful in choice results. But if an odd creature by hazard now and again gets into or is sent off in a box, as several animals mentioned exemplify, it is to be impressed on the reader that the men often are placed under most disadvantageous circumstances. To work in partial darkness, or in rainy, roughish weather, and to get the catch despatched in hot haste, in time for market train—for it must go fresh from the sea quickly or spoil—the culling necessary has to be bustled through somehow. If sorting and picking could be performed leisurely and systematically, then there

* Append. Commissioners Rep. Lond. 1879.

would be a different tale to tell. Still, we are dealing with
the facts as they present themselves irrespective of bias and of
what are considered true whitebait, of which more hereafter.
We here offer some critical remarks on the above lists grouped
differently.

(A.) Invertebrates generally.

Jelly fish, exemplified further on, are a source of great
trouble to the fishermen. The "flat-galls" (Medusæ) perchance in early summer effectually clog the stow-net; the "nut-
galls" (Ctenophora) seldom absent during the greater part of
the year, betimes defy hand picking. Therefore the latter are
frequent among fresh whitebait, but their jelly-masses disappear in cooking. Star fish (five-fingers) do get into the nets,
but are quickly routed out. Even the very small ones pass so
sparsely into the boxes that we have never noted one there *en
route* to market.

Among several Crustaceans (see Figs. *postea*) such as the
opossum-shrimps (Mysidæ), and slender-bodied Idotea (Isopod)
the Wriggler of Leigh-lads, from their diminutive size and
rarity, they play a very inferior part. So do the little pea-
crabs. The shore-crabs that unwittingly slip into the boxes of
a surety may be guessed as dwarfs. Still, we have detected
both crab kinds in whitebait served up. On the other hand,
the ubiquitous shrimps are rather to the fore, for few boxes in
summer are without some representatives. Their colour when
alive so assimilates to the surrounding mass of fish, that a
spring of their body or wag of their antennæ first calls attention to their presence. They freely pass on to the cook, get to
table and are eaten with crispine relish, though the juicy, saline
flavour given to the shrimpers' boiled ones, is preferable. Once,
when enjoying a plate of whitebait, we espied a cooked Octopus
not much bigger than a nut, and once again saw such another
alive in a box of bait. It seems these mollusks empty their ink-
bag among the "bait," to the latter's saleable deterioration in
appearance, so the baiters keep a sharp look out for them.

(B.) *Vertebrates.—Fish.*

(a) *No set Fisheries in District.*—Taking the Stickleback first: this, as everyone will allow, is not much of an eatable commodity. Only seldom have we observed a specimen. The fishermen feel their prickles before sight warns. During the season many Lump-fish get caught, but, unless exceptionally small, do not find their way into the boxes; though we have once caught sight of a very small one. A solitary example of a diminutive *Hippocampus* was taken out alive, and kept by A. Bundock for some days in a dish of seawater as a curiosity, afterwards being given to us. The Gobies (whitethroats or polywigs of Leighmen) are in marked contrast, for one or other sort may be numerous or again few present. At special times they are a marked feature in the boxes, and, though strenuously attempted to be picked out, circumstances often prevent, when they are freely sent to market. Indeed, it can be asserted that a fat One or Two-spotted goby, especially if in spawn, is capital eating, and preferable to certain dry stages of the young herring (yawlings). Here, therefore, in the gobies we have an instance of plentiful little fishes which ordinarily are rejected as food, when dressed up as whitebait becoming useful and indeed expensive diet. Moreover, we may incidentally remark that we have reason for suspecting that the transparent white goby (*Aphia pellucida*), so abundant in the river Thames, was the original of the Thames whitebait of the beginning of the 17th century.

That diminutive, even fairly large, Weevers get caught among the " bait " is certain, for the men dread their sting, so whenever seen they get short shift. Extremely few indeed must ever reach the market. Only once or twice at most have we detected examples of the Lesser Weever (*Trachinus vipera*) in a very large number of boxes of whitebait overhauled by us prior to their transit. Buckland's statement that " The ' Rooshians ' that come into the river about May are the young of the weever fish; they have little colouring and are very jelly-like " is evidently founded on error. What he refers to, is in reality the fully adult or nearly mature and very transparent White Goby (*Aphia*). Put before a Greenwich or Gravesend fisherman, as we have done, he at once pronounces them " Rooshians," as do the Leighmen. Their abundance during the Crimean War gave rise to the cognomen still retained.

Pipe-fishes from late spring to autumn are of frequent occurrence among the catches. Usually they are in great part weeded out; notwithstanding, from their narrow needle-shape, a few escape observation, and those $2\frac{1}{2}$ to $3\frac{1}{2}$ inches long are found among cooked whitebait. Eel-Pouts (or Viviparous Blenny) $3\frac{1}{2}$ and $5\frac{1}{2}$ inches long have come under our observation in the "bait" boxes; though this fish is wonderfully abundant in the Hadleigh Ray during winter. It is said that at Queenborough sometimes a large number are caught and got rid of.

As to the Lesser Sand-Eels, they, like the gorebills, create immense havoc among the shore whitebait, &c., during the summer months. Those from 3 to 4 inches long and over simply crowd the drag-net from June to July. In a most unusual instance at the end of July we reckoned by guess in one box of whitebait there would be nearly a quarter (25 per cent.) of these sand-eels—this after culling. Other boxes in June and July might contain $\frac{1}{6}$, $\frac{1}{8}$, or $\frac{1}{16}$ sand-eels. These fish pass muster with the cook, and as prepared with boiling dripping eat deliciously.

While the Sand-smelt along the shores of the English Channel is fished for and does duty there for the true smelt, yet within the limits of our District no special fishery for them exists, though in summer its presence in the several estuaries—Medway particularly and towards Dungeness—is most frequent. The young sand-smelts ordinarily are the reverse of rare among whitebait despatched to market. We have got them of $2\frac{1}{2}$ inches long in February, again in June turned 3 inches, and over 4 inches in July. Their shiny striped

sides match well with the glittering ",bait." They also are excellent food product, which the cuisiniere converts into almost
as tasty morsels as the sand-eels.

(b) *Fisheries Extant.*—Both the Sea-Lamprey and the Lampern are caught in the whitebait nets.   The first quite
exceptionally and then more often of good size.   Altogether
not many of them are taken by the "baiters" downstream, and
only the very smallest ever get into the box, for their movement attracts attention.   One specimen, 9 inches long, we took
out of a box in April.   The men regard the lamperns as good
omen of whitebait being about.   The Common Eel as a rule does
not much trouble the "baiter," for whether small or a little larger
they usually manage to wriggle through the meshes of the nets,
as more often does the lampern.   They are particularly reten-
tive of life.   An odd silver eel, even 6 inches long and over, we
have seen in the boxes during the spring-time, but with no regularity.   Much larger river eels besides congers at intervals are
captured in the stow-net.   The former the fishermen prize for
home consumption, the latter they are not so fond of.

Small-sized Bass are rather a numerous fish close to the
precincts of favourite spots for whitebaiting near Southend
Pier.   It is said they are not infrequently seen in a haul, and
some possibly may escape the men's eye and get sent off; though,
usually, being an active hardy fish, they get pitched overboard,
and dash off none the worse for capture.   Not many, surely,
can get to market, since we can recall only one example, 3
inches long, picked up by us out of a box.   Some of the " baiters "
assure us that, now and again in the Shoebury neighbourhood,
they have found young Mullet in their drag-net.   We doubted
their identification, for previously young bass had been brought to
us by shrimpers believed by them to be mullet.   However, from
the " baiter's " description of the fish, their shoaling and habit
of leaping over the net, &c., we must accept the statement of
their being mullet—which after all is not unlikely.   We ourselves have never seen specimens of those thus caught, nor
found any whatsoever in the boxes forwarded to market.

About midsummer the Gar-Pikes or Guard-fish (Gorebills of Leighmen) regularly pay a visit to where the drag-netters are at work, and in companies voraciously hunt up the whitebait, among which they are caught. On the Shoebury sands they appear in plenty during summer. Big ones are eaten, moderate sized not allowed to escape, and only the little ones get into the " bait " boxes. The very smallest are needle-shaped like the pipe-fish, hence apt to pass hasty observation. Gorebills are dire enemies to fry and fish of all kinds, so the " baiters " may render service in their diminishment; though, oddly enough, ours is the only Sea Fisheries Committee that have a bye-law (No. 4) in their favour.

Flat fish.—Respecting the asserted ruinous spoilations of the valuable flat-fishes by the whitebaiters, we have judiciously used our own eyes, and made searching inquiry into the subject so far as concerns the Leighmen's practice. At different times we have been witness to the capture of both the young stages of the Plaice and of the Dab. Looking to their catch by the shrimpers, those obtained by the whitebaiters are trivial in comparison. From what we have noticed and learned from others the whitebaiters always assiduously pick them out, and return them to the water with all speed. Practically they seldom are got in the stow-net, and when so are usually large enough at once to be perceived, and the great majority rejected while alive. In the use of the drag-net the short interval of pulling round the net ashore truly does little harm even to the youngest, for they smartly scuttle off immediately they get pitched back into their watery element.

The presence of flat-fish among ordinary mercantile whitebait assuredly is quite a rarity. Their appearance does not simulate " bait," while detracting from its market quality. Though on the watch for examples of flat-fish, we have only been successful in poking out but few plaice and dabs in the boxes for Billingsgate, and those at wide intervals. Only on very sparse occasions have we found 1½-inch examples among the cooked whitebait.

As to both the Flounders and Soles, they are habitually ground feeders, and never enter the stow-net. The flounder constantly steals away beneath the ground-rope of the drag-net, which is lightly leaded, and usually, at the centre, does not touch ground until within a very short distance of shore-margin. The larval forms of flat-fish we have examined left us in doubt whether flounders were among them, though we have noted, but rarely, presence of bigger ones.

Regarding the Soles, larger or smaller, these we have not seen in any hauls when we were present, nor have discovered them but very seldom indeed among the " bait " in the boxes, and never had them presented at table in the restaurant. Still we have learned that annually, but altogether under exceptional circumstances, a haul will be made on the broad, flat, shallow sands of Shoebury, or on Lapwell Bank, Queenborough, when good and lesser sized soles have been taken in moderate numbers. This is to be explained by the fact that the long level sand permits the ground-rope and bunt of net to trail, and prevents the soles shuffling under. On the other hand, alongside the steeper slopes of sea-walls or in deepish spots it leaves a space beneath as mentioned in flounder. With a catch as above the bigger soles are retained, the lesser ones, which survive with impunity their capture and handling, get off scot-free.

Admitting a certain amount of flat-fish perish at the white-baiters' hands, these altogether appear relatively so limited that they can only infinitesimally, or in a very minor degree, interfere with our fisheries.

The habits of the Smelt and of the Shad are a barrier to any wholesale sacrifice of the young below Leigh by the white-baiters. Darkness or night-time best answers for smelting, whereas daylight is preferred for whitebaiting. This distinction greatly reduces chance of smelts capture by " baiters."

The adult breeding Smelt travels up the estuary in the winter season, and makes chiefly towards the brackish, or on with flowing tide to the fresh water, there to spawn. This accomplished, it descends in the spring months. At the upward migratory period (as in its allies of the salmon tribe) there is a danger of capture. Undoubtedly large ripish and moderately-sized ones, 5 to 7 or 8 inches long, drive into the stow-net in scattered manner at intervals. But then, there is this anomaly, that smelt fishing by the Thames Conservancy's Bye Law, No. 21, is sanctioned, and indeed exclusively carried on, when the smelts are full of ripening, and ripe spawn and milt. The maturer their condition, so is delicacy in proportion, and one has only to examine the fish legally sent to market and exposed for sale in the shops about Christmas, and after, to get unanswerable proof of this. If the "baiters" down stream then get a paltry share, while smelters are hard at work swooping in netfuls, it clearly shows the former's minor captures are a very unimportant factor in the problem of smelt decimation at the breeding season. Moreover, the younger stages that are taken in the drag-net are, after all, very moderate in numbers, for with misgivings thereon we closely examined into this aspect of the question. We have found them from $1\frac{1}{2}$ to $3\frac{1}{2}$ inches long, in the net and boxes, and enjoyed young smelts dished up with the whitebait.

The Shad is not nearly so valuable a food-fish as the smelt. Its river ascent is spring, its descent autumn, and as a rule it spawns well up in the fresh water. The shad's migrations usually concur with the use of the drag-net ; there we mostly look for them, seldom in stow-net. Large shads turn up quite irregularly below Leigh, but not in quantity. Very few of the young have been observed by us among the whitebait. We have no evidence or reason to think that estuarine whitebaiting impairs the up-river shad fishery.

Sprats and Herrings (="Yawlings")—Coming to these we get at the root of the matter. Their admixture in various proportions and sizes assuredly constitute the merchants' whitebait of the present markets. Other marine forms are manifest, but play such an unimportant rôle as has justified naturalists in confining inquiries to the sprat and herring view.

As a prelude to the clupeoids referred to below in Ser. I.-VI., we had previously made a critical examination of between 900 and 1,000 others, between 9th February and 16th March. On the first date 61 specimens ranged from 26 millims. (1 inch) to 50 millims. (2 inches) ; there being only three of the latter. On the second date 65 specimens, the extremes were from 25 millims. (1 inch) to 67 millims. (under 2¾ inches), with the addition of a herring 4¾ inches, and a sprat 3 inches long. These were not picked, but fair samples of catch. The sizes in the other lots at intervening dates agreed with the above.

We now take the inventory of the entire contents of a box of whitebait, caught on 17th March, 1899, near the Knock Buoy. It was open, moderate weather. The fish were not culled, but simply placed in the receptacle as taken from the whitebaiter's stow-net. We dispense with minutiæ of data, merely giving results in the table (p. 99).

After general examination of the material and a study of the developmental conditions extant the following method was employed. Division was made into six typical series *infra* by placing these aside for constant reference—a plateful of each. In these type-sets every individual fish was rigidly measured in millimetres, a rough conversion into inches being superadded. Then, lot by lot of the others were taken out haphazard from the boxful, separated into dishes according to size and condition by the eye, comparing them with the types whenever doubt arose, and their numbers counted. The 1st and 2nd series differ from the others, inasmuch as while they represent a single series so far as general size is concerned, they are each a double series, or contain a sub-series with regard to their stage of development.

In what follows in tabular form, it should be borne in mind that the enormous numbers of fish in this box does not necessarily hold good throughout the season. It is the exception, not the rule, and represents only what occurs when the larval stages are pre-eminent. Moreover, as described further

G

on under "apparatus for transport, &c.," Sect. IX., there are two sizes of boxes. No. 1, which usually contains about four gallons of "bait," the other, more capacious, No. 2, equals six gallons; only used by a very few whitebaiters.

It was a register of one of the latter—6 gallons—that was attempted. Hence an ordinary box would be ⅓rd less. Besides, at other times of the year, when the mass of "spratty-stuff" and "yawlings" averages 3 to 4 inches long, with stoutness in proportion, then the total would be probably no more than half that here given, or even less. When whitebait are redundant the boxes are filled to the brim. During midwinter or in stormy weather, "bait" being scarce, they are not so crammed. Indeed then ¾-full is not unusual, or even a ½-boxfull has to do duty; its value enhanced. To hazard a guess of ordinary numbers in the boxes throughout the year this might be put down as from 8,000 to 10,000 each.

Fig. 12.

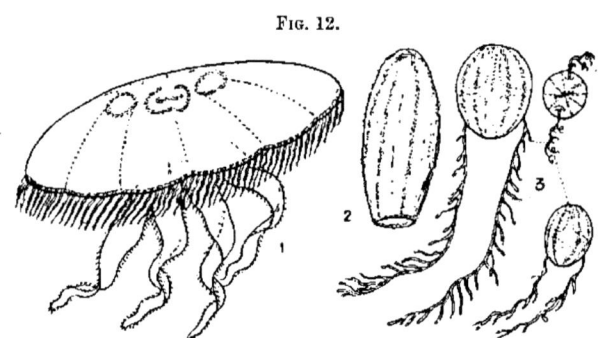

FLAT-GALL AND NUT-GALLS OF WHITEBAITERS
(described further on).

CONTENTS BIG BOX WHITEBAIT,

During Spring when Larval Conditions Superabundant.

SERIES I.—Fish ranging from 32 to 42 millimetres (1¼ to close on 1¾ inches), calculated approximately to be from 6 to 8 weeks old.

(a) Clupeoids of pale yellowish or buffish tint with a thin, elongated (eel like) body, translucent or diaphanous generally, excepting a single, narrow stripe of silvery sheen along the gut (inside or peritoneal). No silvering whatsoever outside the body. These numbered ... . 883 }

(b) Having a similar translucent body and gut stripe; with the addition outside the body of faint silvering on the gill covers, and a thread of same along the lateral line. ·None on back. Numbers ... ... 578 } 1,461

The larval stage I.a, and possibly a few of the smallest of I.b, appear to correspond to what the Thames fishermen know as " heads and eyes."

SERIES II.—Fish from 41 to 51 millims. (under 1¾ to 2 inches), conjecturally 8, 9, or 10 weeks of age.

(a) Clupeoids in part translucent, still elongate, a trifle deeper bodied than Series I., all with a most delicate thin silvery film on the surface of the skin ... . 1,152 }

(b) A further set a little more full bodied, and distinguished by possessing silvering of an iridescent kind ... ... 4,822 } 5,974

SERIES III.—Fish of from 49 to 61 millims. (2 inches to close on 2½ inches), supposed to run from 2½ to 3½ or 4 months. Well shaped fish, relatively deeper bodied than in Series I.,II., and the majority just beginning to assume a sprat-like appearance, others probably young herrings. Still further iridescent than in Series II.b, but not yet scaled 5,795

SERIES IV.—Fish from 63 to 72 millims. (about 2½ to over 2¾ inches), assumed to be from 4 to 5 months advanced. Most of a somewhat sprat-like contour, deeper bodied than Series III., and neatly formed, with a remarkably bright metallic sheen or lustre, and among only the largest a commencement of scaling 2,779

SERIES V.—Fish running from 75 to 85 millims. (3 to over 3½ inches), say, from 6 to 7 months old. Quite evident their being composed of sprats and young herrings in the yawling stage, and all fully scaled. The relative proportions were 20 of sprats and 24 yawlings. Total ... 233

SERIES VI.—Fish from 86 to 136 millims. (over 3½ to nearly 5½ inches). These may be reckoned to have ranged from 7 to 10 or 11 months, some doubtless a year old. Among them were nine adult sprats, and some of these with the roe fairly developed. The young herrings, numbering 43 in the so-called yawling stage, exhibited no signs of roe development. Rather less than half of them were above 4 inches long 52

Total amount of clupeoids (=herring-sprats) 16,294

In addition to the above (fisherman's whitebait) were 48 specimens of extraneous material, pipefish, &c. (including 17 white gobies, but excluding the numerous small nut-galls, &c.).

In this particular catch the relative proportions of outside forms to whitebait proper stood as 3 to the 1,000, or only a third of 1 per cent. But analysis of Ser. I.—VI. denotes more. From them something can be learned of the conjectural dates of spawning, probable ages of the fish, and their more marked developmental changes.

Kuppfer, Meyer, and Ehrenbaum have respectively devoted attention to the incubation and development of the herring and sprat, both in confinement and in their free natural conditions.[*] Speaking generally, they show these fish grow about $\frac{3}{4}$ of an inch monthly, less or more, according to temperature, food, and other circumstances. The sprat's egg hatches out within a week, the herring's egg from a week to a month; heat accelerating, cold retarding the process. The newly-hatched larva of the herring is just under a $\frac{1}{4}$ inch, that of the sprat about $\frac{1}{8}$ inch. At the end of the first month they have attained nigh $\frac{3}{4}$ inch in length.

Reasoning from all these premises we derive the evidence given approximately in Ser. I.—VI. As we find a 1-inch example on 9th February, it follows spawning must have commenced in January, and the hatching, &c., in this and the other fish relatively keeping pace, to have gone on continuously to the later dates. Further avoiding details, we have found a regular succession of brood up to the 23rd August and 2nd September, when a sprinkling of larval forms 28 to 73 millims. have been secured. So that there can be little doubt of there being a spring and late autumn spawning of herrings within the Thames estuary, as Cunningham surmised.[†] As to the sprat's period of spawning it seems more continuous, *i.e.*, with early and later spawners—the older fish at the beginning and younger fish following later in the season. Altogether, probably extending for five or six months; the ripening fish of Ser. VI. indicating presence of late spawners. It is the intermingling or

---

[*] In papers embodying their researches for 1874-76, 1892, and 1896 in Commiss. Untersuch, Deutsch meere.

[†] Jour. Mar. Biol. Assoc. II. (1891-92), p. 241 and p. 330.

overlapping of the sprat's longish single with the herring's double (spring and also late autumn) spawning periods that enables the fishermen truly to say, "we can get whitebait all the year round."

In connection therewith the main points of Ewart and Matthews' examination of Thames whitebait may be cited.* They show that, in their numerous samples obtained, the sprat's maximum numbers (over 93 per cent.) were in February and March, declining in April and May. In June, the minimum (13 per cent. by a sudden drop), with a slight revival in July and August. The herrings were the reverse, the minimum (5–7 per cent.) in February and March, rising steadily in April and May, with a leap to maximum (87 per cent.) in June, and steady decline in July and August—but still high, viz., over 50 per cent. But the fact stands out that sprats are in preponderance, and in the whitebait stage come in advance. In part support of the above, the fishermen well know their best "spratty-stuff" is obtained in the fore part of the season, the relatively inferior "yawling material" about midsummer or later on.

Our own observations in some measure accord with those of the Edinburgh fish experts, though in several items we do not see eye to eye. For example, their per centages, though weighty for 1885-86, were taken when the "baiters" freely fished up river (Gravesend reaches, &c.), which now is strictly forbidden. Again, something is due to whether catch is on north or south shores, whether within the Queenborough reaches, creeks, or whether from Burnham waters; for it is not infrequently conveyed by trap from there to Southend, and thence despatched by rail to Billingsgate. Again, they hazard the guess of about 1 per cent. as extraneous material. No doubt, as in our case of 17th March given above, it was under 1 per cent., but manifestly far above this when sand eels, &c., are about. Even to strike a low average it would be higher than they reckon.

* Fourth Ann. Rep. Scot. Fish. Board for 1885. Append. F. No. 5.

But the net result of the whole data and argument is that brood fish other than sprats and herrings are a mere bagatelle of the " baiter's " destruction. Then arises the knotty question : should whitebaiting be entirely abolished, or how far its restriction ?—Mark with the idea that the fishermen and the fisheries interests are to be benefited in the future ? This is attempted to be tentatively replied to later on under sub-heading Whitebait Fishery.

(3 and 4.) The SHADS.—These are the TWAITE SHAD (*Clupea jinta*), and the ALLICE SHAD (*C. alosa*). The Allice Shad of a certainty inhabits the Thames (*see* Yarrell) ; but we have not seen it among those taken in the lower reaches. In continental rivers it spawns far higher up stream than does the Twaite, which seems more estuarine in habit. It appears in Boys' " Fishes of Sandwich " (*op. cit.*).

Dr. Laver records the Twaite Shad as occasionally common in the Colne, many in August, 1886, and one the same year, on November 29th, at East Bridge, Colchester. Doubtless they enter all the estuaries of our Sea Fisheries district. At one time the Upper Thames was noted for its shad fisheries ; shad then being much in vogue as a cheap article of diet. In this respect there is a great change in the taste of the public ; nor is shadding now so hedged in by rule as the Bye Law of 1697 enunciated.* They are still as abundant as ever though they don't figure conspicuously in prices current at Billingsgate.

The longest we have seen at Leigh measured 12, 13½, 14¾, and 15½ inches in extreme length, with depth of over 3 inches. These were all females. The smallest have been between 2 to 3 inches. As the breeding females are most often caught we

---

* " That all persons using the Art, Mistery, or Craft of a *Fisherman*, that use to
" take *Shadds*, in *Shadding-time*, shall observe and keep their true Orders, of Shooting
" a Drove-length off from One Another : And that none of the said *Shadders* shall go
" forth to Fish, within the Bounds and Limits aforesaid, until he or they, shall have
" received Leave and License, in such manner as is herein after particularly mentioned
" and provided for, upon forfeiture of Twenty Shillings for every such Offence."

suspect this sex preponderates. We have not had opportunity of ascertaining the rate of growth nor development generally.

In December we have found the roe only in an early stage, in March half advanced, in May nearly ripe. This is consistent with their spawning up river May to July. But it is a question whether some fish may procreate in the brackish water below the Lower Hope, and eggs and larvæ be carried still lower down by ebb tides. One "baiter," Joe Deal, relates how at the end of July near the Yantlet in one haul of drag-net there was quite a lot of transparent brood, like needles ("heads and eyes"), which in appearance he took for young shad.* Unfortunately none were brought to us for identification.

The older shads, presumably the Twaite Shad, frequent the Queenborough Swale, where we know of a 10-inch specimen having been obtained in October. At various times of the year odd ones are brought up in the trawl in the neighbourhood of the Leigh roads, the Blyth, &c. Among these are got fish 6 to 8 inches long. Shad have been landed by hook and line while spruling at the mouth of the Hadleigh Ray. Good sized ones are also secured by the flounder-net fishermen on the Maplins, and up to near Southend Pier. Some Leighmen set small value on them, and even throw them away. Yet split up, sprinkled with salt and pepper and fried in butter they are very good eating, their numerous delicate rib-bones being the only drawback. In those examined by us their stomachs were crammed with whitebait, as many as 20 to 25 being counted in one fish. The food of juveniles we failed to investigate.

(5) The PILCHARD (*Clupea pilchardus*), known in its young stage in French waters as the sardine, is on the British coasts found numerously, chiefly around Cornwall and Devon. It now seldom passes up the English Channel beyond the Bill of Portland. Over a hundred years ago it is reported to have been annually taken in large quantities off Yarmouth and east coast

---

* Consult Metzger and Hoek, Tijdsch. Nederland. Dierk. Vereen, Leiden, 1888, and Ehrenbaum, Deutsch. Fisch. Verein, 1892, freely criticised by Cunningham, Jour. Mar. Biol. Assoc., May, 1892.

of England. Still a few stragglers are brought in with the
herrings at Yarmouth (Patterson, Zool., 1897). Yarrell obtained
one in the Thames in 1838, and according to Dale occasionally
they were brought to Harwich by the herring fishers. Our
Dungeness, along with the Rye, fishermen captured a biggish
lot in that neighbourhood in September, 1868. Boys recognised its presence among the fishes of Sandwich fully a century
ago. The decrease of pilchards on the east coast is interesting,
as clearly showing this has not been produced by over fishing
or capture of the young.

(6) The ANCHOVY (*Engraulis encrasicholus*), like the preceding, is a southern form, and only occasionally rounds Kent
or is taken on our eastern borders. Yarrell merely gives it as
a report of inhabiting the Dagenham Breach (?) and mentions
his having received one caught in the Thames (May, 1838).
Curiously enough, at the same date one pilchard was obtained
by him in the Thames. We, perhaps, are not justified in
attributing an error, or doubting such an authority on fish, but
at all events the coincidence is remarkable. Whatever may
have been the case as respects Dagenham Lake in years gone
by, we may at least refer to J. Hilliar, an experienced angler
on that piece of water, who (in Essex Nat. VI.) says that in
1892 he did not find them there. Day's habitat "Coasts of
Essex" is somewhat vague, though doubtless correct. Frank
Buckland has recorded in *Field*, July, 1864, an anchovy $4\frac{1}{2}$
inches long caught in the whitebait nets at Purfleet in June,
1864. Some years ago Carrington received a few anchovies
which had been obtained by the Southend whitebaiters. On
21st November, 1900, H. Wilder, of Leigh, got a specimen in
his stow-net near the Knock Buoy. On examination we found
it to be a female, roe non-developed, and it had been feeding on
minute crustaceans. It measured $4\frac{1}{2}$ inches in extreme length.
In South Kent the anchovy appears sporadically, large numbers
having been captured in the drift-nets at Dover in November,
1889.

We have no evidence of the anchovy breeding within
our District, but on the Dutch coast there is an important
summer fishery,* and there they spawn freely. According to
Cunningham's data, the anchovy heads up channel in spring,
whence it wends its way to the Scheldc and Zuyder Zee;
there they spend summer, spawn, and return down the English
Channel during autumn and winter. In passing to and fro the
Straits of Dover, at times they come close to the Kent shore,
and on such occasions are caught by the spratters and other
fishermen. Wherefore comes it the anchovy prefers the coast
of Holland to our estuarine flats and creeks, which are a
counterpart ? Cunningham † believes it to be a matter of
warmer temperature. The two preceding southern fish therefore illustrate how that physical conditions play an important
part in their distribution and migration.

The **Weever Family** (Trachinidæ), whereof the two forms,
viz., The GREATER WEEVER (*Trachinus draco*) and (2) the
LESSER WEEVER (*T. vipera*), are notoriously dreaded by whitebaiters and shrimpers for their stinging propensities. Most
fishermen only know them as of one sort, be they big or small.
Both species are widely scattered around Kent and Essex.
They mainly keep to sandy ground, irrespective of depth of
water, and are greedy feeders on whitebait and shrimps,
hence are numerous at the mouth of the Thames. They are,
however, not restricted to the many sands below the Nore, for
they regularly haunt the neighbourhood of the West River
middle buoy, and shores opposite (particularly Essex side), to
whitebaiters' peril. If by chance a weever is seen in a haul
or in culling, it is instantly crunched under boot, and thrown
away. As a rule, they are captured in the nets ; but Mr.
Fitch has noted an instance of a 10-inch *T. draco* taken with
logworm bait while spruling in the Blackwater, Oct., 1889
(Essex Nat. III.). Kent coast anglers occasionally land them

---

* Beaujon, Hist. of Dutch Sea Fisheries, Lond., 1884.
" Immigration of the Anchovy," Jour. Mar. Biol. Assoc., III., N. Ser. (1893-06).

to their chagrin. We have obtained the Greater species between 8 and 9 inches long, though they grow bigger; and the Lesser, the more dangerous, from $1\frac{1}{2}$ to 5 inches. The latter is a constant source of anxiety to the whitebaiters, by remaining more inshore throughout the year; the former more often falls to the shrimper's lot; but is scarcer during the winter months.

Some fish authorities have maintained that the spine prick in itself is harmless unless where slimy substance gets into the wound and sets up irritation. Later investigations have clearly established the presence of true poison glands.[*] The neck spines and gill-cover spines both have them. They are situated towards the base and alongside the grooved spines. When the fish strikes by a simultaneous muscular pressure on the glands the virus enters the wound. Instantly an excruciating stinging pain is felt. This, with swelling and numbness, often lasts for hours or days, or is followed by more serious consequences. Few "baiters" or shrimpers escape a prick, and many retain stiff finger joints.[†]

At Leigh and throughout Essex, with a few exceptions, weevers are not used as food, though their flesh is good. At Dover the Greater Weever at times may be seen hawked about for sale as food in barrow loads. (Webb, Handb.)

Salmon Family (*Salmonidae*).— (1) The SALMON (*Salmo salar*) question has cropped up within recent times in connection with the Thames, the Medway, and the (Canterbury)

---

[*] *See* Parker, Proc. Zool. Soc., 1888; Allman, Ann. and Mag. Nat. Hist. VI., (1841).

[†] Treatment.—The shrimpers dip the finger into their almost boiling brine—the remedy being as painful as the disease. They, as well as "baiters," may casually suck the wound, oftener tie a cord tightly round the wrist or finger, or rub the parts with grease or with turpentine. An old much-vaunted remedy among fishermen is the application of the liver of the fish itself. This from its oily nature acts as an emollient, and from the men's experience is said to have a good effect. But the conditions are often such that the extracting of it is attended with risk, or the body is crunched and overboard in a trice. Sometimes a wet handkerchief is wrapped round the hand as a temporary expedient.

Practically each vessel or rowboat should always have on board a bottle of olive oil with a little opium in it. This mixture quickly applied externally acts most soothingly. Freely anoint the finger or hand with it, or use it with gentle friction. Then dip a woollen stocking in water as hot as can be borne and wrap around hand and wrist. At intervals renew this, and continue assiduously after returning home, or use poultices of poppy-heads, or linseed with a sprinkling of laudanum. When on board, if hot water is not convenient to be got, then sea water will do, without its renewal, the great thing being to retain the moist heat engendered.—(J.M.)

Stour. Suffice to say that from 1861-62 onwards the "Thames Angling Preservation Society," and from 1866 the "Association for Preservation of Salmon in the Medway," and the (Canterbury) "Stour Fishery Protection Association," have each assiduously endeavoured to stock the rivers above-mentioned with salmon and various species of trout.

The late Frank Buckland, who took an active interest in the matter, was so sanguine of success accompanying their efforts that at one meeting he said : "So sure as I am standing here, at no distant day salmon will come up the Thames as abundantly as ever they did " in the good old times. Over 30 years have passed since then, with unceasing efforts on the part of the above societies towards the maintaining young salmonoids in their hatcheries and preserves ; but the results we fear have not come up to expectancy. Notwithstanding, in midsummer, 1899, again a movement has arisen culminating in the installation of the "Thames Salmon Association." Whether their experiments will be more successful remains for time to prove.

It may be remarked that at the starting of this last association there was not complete unanimity. Some considered the river still unfit for salmon ; others viewed the subject with a tone of askance, hinting that ulteriorly the public rights of fishing might be interfered with. Indeed, already in 1868, discussion arose between the Canterbury Town Council and the Stour Fishery Association on this very point. Hence the words accidentally dropped by Buckland (1866), "then will arise the question as to whom the right of fishery belongs," were more prophetic than he then anticipated.

Whatsoever the outcome of the above, it may pretty surely be affirmed that no Thames Estuarine Salmon Fishery has existed during the 19th century.* There is reliable evidence extant that long prior to the river's pollution and introduction of locks and weirs—namely, about 1750—there had begun to

---

* In Sect. III. we have already drawn attention to the salmon and general fishery in the Hadleigh Ray from the 13th century onwards.

be a diminution of Thames salmon,* the numbers dwindling by
degrees until we hear of the last salmon caught up river,
June, 1833.

There follows an interval of some thirty years duration,†
when in 1864 a salmon was got in the trawl by the Southend
fishermen. Again, in July, 1866, the Southenders were fortunate in a 2 lb. fish—an authenticated salmon—and others were
said to have been captured about the same time. On 2nd
August of the same year came a salmon to be taken in a net
in the Long Reach, below Purfleet. This so-called Gravesend
salmon was 26 inches long, and weighed 7½ lb. Another was
seen about Sunbury Weir in June, 1867. Two specimens were
seined near Folkestone in 1868. A salmon was captured in the
Crouch above Burnham (Battles Bridge), 10th December, 1870.

In 1875 the Southend fishers were lucky in a capture,
and the same season was another got opposite Leigh. Still a
finer fish was secured in their drag-net by two Leigh whitebaiters while plying their craft at the marshend below Canvey
Spit, May, 1880. The men at first were rather alarmed at the
splutter and dashing about of the creature in their net,
so totally different to anything in their ordinary catch.
Pleasure followed their discovery of its being a salmon 27½ lb.
weight, and for which they received 1s. 9d. per lb. from the late
Rector, Canon King. In 1882 a capture is recorded at the
mouth of the Blackwater, and Dr. Laver, referring to it, adds
some are caught there annually. Just within the Lowway, at
entrance to Hadleigh Ray, in June, 1891, a fine conditioned
salmon, nigh three feet long and weighing 33 lb., met its fate in
"baiter's" drag-net. Mr. Cadman purchased it at 1s. per lb.,
had it stuffed, and made a presentation of it to the village. It
now graces the walls of the Board School, serving as a practical

---

* Consult Venables' series of articles in *Land and Water*, 1867; and Marston in
Nineteenth Century Magazine, April, 1899; besides Senior in *Field*, January, 1898.

† Regarding this 30 years blank period of Thames salmon, Mr. Senior ("Red
Spinner") is of opinion that annually some must have been caught by the Estuary
fishermen, though unrecorded. On this head all we can say is that the very oldest of
the Leighmen cannot remember of any being taken during the interval in question.
—(J.M.)

lesson to the fisher lads of historic times when royalty deigned to interest itself in the stake-net and "Kidell" (salmon) fisheries in the creek running up from the spot in question. To round off, salmon in the (Harwich) Stour, and their presence in the nets of the Dungeness (and Rye) fishermen so lately as 1898 serve to show the fish sporadically visits our Sea Fisheries District from one extreme to the other.*

Whether some of the above salmon have been examples reared in the upper waters of the Thames must remain a matter of pure conjecture, for there is no record of smolts or kelts having been found descending; though the fact that the occurrence of Thames salmon has followed, not preceded, the formation of hatcheries † suggests the possibility of their being true Thames reared salmon. Still, at the present rate of produce, salmon fishing as a commercial product in the estuary, or angled for in the upper waters, is yet, we fear, far distant.

(2) The SEA TROUT, or Salmon Trout (*S. trutta*).—This appears to be more numerous than the salmon around our District, and possibly some presumed captures of the latter should be credited to the former fish. Buckland,‡ in examining a supposed salmon got near Colchester (*infra*), was led to think that our local small, sluggish rivers might be more fitted for the bull-trout. Mr. Fryer,§ finding their numbers considerable in the Orwell and (Harwich) Stour, questioned if these East Anglian fish were bred in the neighbourhood or wanderers from rivers further north. Then arises the point whether the several Societies' efforts in the Thames, the

---

* The above references are not intended as a complete register of salmon captures within our area, but only incidentally illustrating the question at issue.

† It may be interesting to note the numbers reared by the Thames Angling Preservation Society during the first few years of their start—

1861-2	...	2,300 Salmon ;	1,500 Salmon Trout ;			30,000 Trout.	
1862-3	...	7,000 ,,	—— ,,		,,	40,000 ,,	
1863-4	...	5,500 ,,	750	,,	,,	29,700 ,,	
1864-5	...	19,500 ,,	800	,,	,,	17,000 ,,	
1865-6	...	14,500 ,,	900	,,	,,	20,700 ,,	

Thus between 1861 and 1866 some 48,000 salmon fry were set free in the Thames. To this might be added others set free from hatchery in River Lea, 1905, &c.

‡ *Land and Water*, March, 1867.

§ Twenty-ninth Ann. Rep., Inspect. (Engl. and Wales) Salmon and Fresh Water Fisheries for 1889. *See* also Thirtieth Ann. Rep. of Inspectors for 1891.

Medway, and the (Canterbury) Stour, may not have had an unlooked-for side influence. On this head it is to be regretted that explicit data are not forthcoming. Howsoever stands the case, a few examples of their presence in our estuaries and streams may best plead their cause. The rivers that meet at Harwich have been cited. Likewise the Colne, where at East Bridge, Colchester, March, 1867, a 4½ lb. fish was captured. Dr. Bree announced it as a salmon, but it proved to be a bull-trout. A specimen weighing 1½ lb. ascended the Blackwater and was netted in the Chelmer, close to Beeleigh, near Maldon, 23rd February, 1889 (Fitch, Essex Nat. III.), A salmon-trout of 3 lb. was taken in the Roach, 25th February, 1890, there considered unique by the old fishermen. At times these migratory trout get entangled in the V-shaped kettle-nets off Foulness (Thames side). Among Southend and Leigh fishers an odd one is not infrequent, though seldom recorded. The last we know of (good-sized) being in a whitebaiter's stow-net, March, 1899. Their ascent up the river has often been certified; among others, a pair between Hungerford and Waterloo Bridges, full of whitebait, 12th February, 1880. These measured 9¾ and 13½ inches, and weighed 5¾ and 14½ ounces.

The Medway, well known of old for its salmonoids, still annually yields a few, *e.g.*, one, 2½ lb., October, 1866; another caught near Rochester Bridge, 11th March, 1883. In Pegwell Bay a fatal barrier is the stake-nets. As for the once prolific (Canterbury) Stour, not yet deserted, mention need only be made to a prime fish 3 ft. 11 in. long and 21 lb. weight, secured March, 1868; paucity of weight being accounted for by its being a kelt in descent after spawning. The so-called Fordwich trout have long had good reputation for size and condition, and find markets at Ramsgate and Margate. Lastly, the Dover, Folkestone and Dungeness fishermen, at intervals, find sea-trout among their catch; whilst on the sandy shore stretch between Dymchurch and Romney Marshes they get meshed in the numerous kettle-nets.

(3) The SMELT (*Osmerus eperlanus*).—The true, or Cucumber Smelt or Sparling, is the most important of the marketable salmonoids within our District. Speaking in general terms, it is limited to our eastern border. From Dover westwards it is supplanted by the Sand-smelt or Atherine, a fish of quite a different family, of which more anon. While the Stour (Kent) has borne a good reputation as a smelt river, it nevertheless has been far surpassed by the Medway and the Thames. It likewise inhabits the other rivers, *e.g.*, Blackwater, Colne and Stour (Essex), in less plenitude.

The opinion of some of the fishermen is that the smelt does not leave the Thames estuarine waters, but for an interval "beds in the muddy holes." This is doubtful! We can say, though, of a certainty that we have got smelts, few or many, during every month from the end of October to the end of May, *i.e.*, seven to eight months. The intervening months, June to mid-October, we have made no entry of fair-sized ones being taken. Still, we have detected diminutive smelts among catches of whitebait at the turn of midsummer.

In the Medway fishery the smelt season commences in July and continues till the end of March. When in the eastern seaward portion of the estuary they appear to be irregularly distributed, and only on chance occasions taken in the trawl on stowboat-net. As to their further movements, the adult fish seem to migrate from the lower to the upper portion of the estuary during the late autumn and early winter months. So far as we can learn, they do not frequent much the neighbourhood of the Maplin sands, apparently preferring muddier ground, but the sand-smelt is found on the Maplins. We first hear of the ascent of good-sized true smelts in the neighbourhood of the Knock Buoy, and from it towards Southend Pier. Some of the smelts evidently strike the opposite Kent shores, and run up the Medway. Others direct their course up the Thames on both south and north margins; but whichever side they skirt they everywhere penetrate the brackish creeks and guts, where they spawn, and also find plenteous supply of food in minor crustaceans, diminutive fish brood, &c.

Thus in their peregrinations they enter the Yantlet Creek, St. Mary's and Egypt Bay, Cliff and Higham Creeks, indenting the Kent shore; whilst Hadleigh Ray, Holehaven, Shellhaven, and the creeks and guts about Mucking Flats, represent places where the smelts visit the Essex side. Meantime, a body of these mature fish go right up the Thames into the fresh water areas. Some years they go higher than others. A regular smelt fishery at London, with its 20 to 30 boats a-fishing (Yarrell), is a thing of the past. Still every other season we hear of their capture, even beyond the city—for example in 1868 at Kew Bridge and Teddington, in 1898 at Richmond, and in 1900 beyond Blackwall.*

Reverting to the estuary, the most noted strip of ground where they seem to congregate about spawning time is along the Blyth Sands, from Lower Hope Point down to the Grain Spit. Here there is a regular winter and spring fishery, which is nearly all carried on by Southend boats (*see* Sect. VI. Fisheries No. 4). The spawning places must be close by, for females with ripe ova and males in full milt are caught abundantly in the area in question. On the Essex side, immediately opposite, they are much scarcer. Nevertheless we have found them tolerably numerous during the winter in the Ray Creek inside Canvey Island Spit. Here, for the winter at least, they appear continuously resident, and of various ages, from less than half to the fully adult fish.

Reviewing a series of sometimes daily observations, made between November and May, and in which the smelts were measured in their extreme length, and the sex and nature of food ascertained, the following may serve as an abstract. Their sizes (those with pronounced smelt characters) ranged

---

* The *Field* (22nd April, 1899), in noticing members of the Lond. C. C. having partaken of a dish of smelts caught at Westminster, gently hints a share of credit is due to the Old Board, the Council's predecessors (the belied Metrop. B. of Works), who inaugurated the steps towards subsequent cleansing of the river.

from $2\frac{1}{4}$ up to 8 inches.* Both sexes present; the females predominated. The smaller, say $3\frac{1}{2}$ or 4 inches long, had the ovary or milt generally in an undeveloped stage. From $4\frac{1}{2}$ to 5 inches the sexual organs were a stage further advanced. The sizes beyond this were irregular in condition; that is, some fish, though small, had the roe fairly well developed; while others, a little bigger in size, were not so forward. But throughout December and January most of those 7 and 8 inches long had eggs of a size almost fit for extrusion. The bulk of the largest smelts were met with in December, evidently the precursory spawners.

Unfortunately we have not been successful hitherto in securing spent fish as they descend the stream, nor know with exactitude their subsequent movements. Opportunities for comparing growth-rate of the young were sparing. During the autumn several specimens, turned an inch to $1\frac{3}{4}$ inch long, were got out of the "bait" boxes, the shortest tolerably well agreed with Ehrenbaum's descriptions of river Elbe specimens.† At first glance ours, though in some respects resembling the elongated sprat and herring fry, yet differed in their more yellowish tint and absence of silvering. With hand lens their pigment markings, &c., easily distinguished them. The largest sized ones, in shape and appearance of eyes, head, fins and tail-forking, clearly denoted their salmon extraction. When $2\frac{1}{2}$ inches long there was no mistaking them for smelts.

Amongst the food of those examined were larval fish of various kinds, clupeoids and young gobies, &c., several kinds of crustaceans—shrimps, Corophium, Gammarus, Mysis, Idotea, Copepods and Amphipods, of sorts, with more rarely annelid remains.

Smelts continue in abundance, and we have not heard of symptoms of their diminishment. Economically the Southend

---

* It is said they reach 10 inches and over, though such have not come under our observation.

† Biol. Anstalt auf Helgoland, 1893 (1896).

fishermen derive a considerable income therefrom, though the Leighmen never seem to have taken to smelting as a special fishery.

Two other salmonoid forms claim mention, neither of marketable value. (4) The HOUTING (*Coregonus oxyrhynchus*), whereof we can only quote two observers of this fish in Kent and Essex waters. Dr. Day states he obtained a specimen from the Medway, February, 1881, and Dr. Laver (*op. cit.*) saw several which had been captured in the smelt-nets in the Colne in 1886. (5) The ARGENTINE or Pearl Sides (*Argentina sphyræna*) is under 2¼ inches when full grown. Some place it among the Salmonidae, others in a separate family. Its occurrence in Boys' meagre list ("Fishes of Sandwich") is our only authority for its Kent habitat.

Mackerel and Blackfish Families (*Scombridæ and Stromateidæ*).—These are truly pelagic or high-sea fishes, in contradistinction to the shore-frequenting or estuarine groups.

(1.) The MACKEREL (*Scomber scombrus*) seems to pass and repass the Thames estuary without making any protracted stay there. As a matter of fact there is no fishery for them. Our information as to its presence even is very meagre.

Several of the Leigh and the Southend fishers assure us that they never have caught a mackerel in the lower waters, which accords with our own trawling experiences. Some of the aged Leighmen, however, hazily recall scattered instances. For example, B. Baxter distinctly recollects getting a few while stowboating for sprats in the neighbourhood of The Deeps during the winter season. Even then they were considered rarities, and seldom more than one or two at a time were taken. Still, at the end of October and about mid-November, 1900, some mackerel seem to have made a passing visit up the Estuary. Wesley Bundock caught a fine specimen in the stow-net just above the Knock Buoy, 20th November, and the day after, Ben Emery got several in his stow-net off the Shoebury Sands.

Notwithstanding the above, the mackerel holds high importance commercially among our District's fisheries on the south and east Kent coast, but in Essex it is nowhere. The west end of the English Channel is a kind of headquarters for them. Whence passing eastwards in spring they strike somewhat landwards about Dungeness, and rounding the South Foreland keep northwards towards the Suffolk and Norfolk coasts. Spawning during summer, thereabouts in the North Sea, they appear to return channelwards during autumn and winter. It is during their migration hither and thither that drift-net, seine and kettle-net fisheries off Kent take place. As, however, these important fisheries are aside from those of our Estuary, we propose to leave them out of the present report, for they more properly belong to the Ramsgate, Folkestone and other stations data.*

(2.) As to the TUNNY (*Orcynus thynnus*), a gigantic mackerel in its way, its fisheries are afar off, namely, in the Mediterranean, though it frequents the Spanish, French and Cornish coasts. Single fish irregularly pay our shores a flying visit, coming, it is presumed, like the mackerel, by way of the south. Most specimens obtained within our Sea Fisheries District have come to grief at the Thames mouth. The following may be cited: In 1801 three were taken off Margate. In 1880 part of the skull of a large one (identified by Buckland) was got in the trawl of a Margate smack at the N. Foreland. About 1857 one was stranded on Foulness ; still another came ashore there in October, 1897. This one was 9 feet long, and as much in circumference, and its weight estimated at 5 to 6 cwt. Its reddish, firm, oily flesh tasted like eel when fried, and skate when boiled, though stringy (Fitch).

---

* The most complete history of Mackerel Fishery is that of the N. American Atlantic Coast, U.S. Fish. Commiss. for 1881. Of late the subject of the mackerel's movements in the vicinity of the S.W. of England and Ireland has received attention at the Plymouth Mar. Biol. station. Garstang regards the mackerel of the Channel and North Sea as a race of fish distinct from the S. and S.W. Irish stock, and that the American mackerel is quite distinct from either. He, Cunningham and Allen agree as to a to and fro movement of the mackerel from the neighbouring deep-sea to the shallower waters, and that our British fish are not migrants from southern climes or far Atlantic, as was formerly supposed to be the case.

The *Stromateidæ* is a closely allied family, whereof one form even rarer than the Tunny was captured at the mouth of the Colne, 20th December, 1881. Our colleague Dr. Laver (*op. cit.* and Zool. 1882, p. 75) called attention to this fish, showing it to be the rare Black-fish (*Centrolophus pompilus*).*

The Scad and Dory Families (= *Carangidæ and Cyttidæ*).

(1.) HORSE MACKEREL or SCAD (*Caranx trachurus*) Webb says is common about Dover, but the fishermen there more often throw them overboard as worthless. It is mentioned in Boys' List of Fishes of Sandwich, 1792. Though they are at times numerous, westerly in the Channel they appear but rarely in the market. Still in some parts of Cornwall they are split and salted for food and possess a mackerel flavour. Hitherto the Scad does not seem to have been included among the Thames estuary fauna. That they visit it is tolerably certain, for we have obtained young specimens on several occasions (November and December) during the winter of 1898. These were obtained in the trawl almost right opposite Leigh at the mouth of the Hadleigh Ray. The smallest was 1·6 inch long. One 4 inches long came up in G. Gilson's trawl when shrimping off the Shoebury Sands, 18th December, 1900. We have not met with adult forms, so remain in doubt whether the above were bred in the neighbourhood.

(2.) The BOAR FISH (*Capros aper*) has appeared vicariously all round our Fisheries District only within the last 20 years or

Fig. 13.

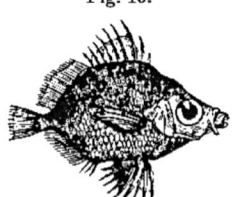

BOAR FISH (*Capros aper*).
(Young; reduced.)

so. In June, 1879, two were got in the shrimp-trawl off Harwich. The same month about a dozen or more were taken by the Leigh shrimpers off Sheppey, below Sheerness; and the Southend fishermen were also fortunate in getting a few. The men called them "Red Dorees,"† though none remembered seeing them before in the

* Gunther, Ann. and Mag. Nat. Hist. IX. (1882), p. 204 and p. 338; *see* also Harting Zool., 1882 p. 152.   † Carrington, Zoologist, Aug., 1879.

estuary. About the same time others were secured near Rye. At Dover since then single ones occasionally turn up. The kettle-nets in the neighbourhood of Dungeness, it is said, have entrapped them on several occasions. This small fish, seldom above 6 inches long, is rather noted for its gaudy, rich orange-red hues than value as food product, though averred to be of delicious flavour.

(3.) The PILOT FISH (*Naucrates ductor*), a wanderer from foreign climes in following an inward-bound ship, is quite a chance visitant to our coast. One was taken in the mackerel nets of a Folkestone fisherman (Mr. Baker) in October, 1868. Another seen in Ramsgate Harbour, September, 1868 ?; a fisherman stunned and caught it with a boathook. It is said they have been hooked at Dover.

Fam. Cyttidæ.—The JOHN DORY (*Zeus faber*). Authorities on British fish state that this fish is rare on the east coast of England, yet small and moderate sized ones are not altogether so in the Thames estuary. Here it certainly is not very common that the adults are taken in abundance, but nevertheless every year a good few are caught both in the stow-net and in the shrimp-trawl. It appears to be pretty well distributed below the Nore, but rarely is caught above this. By way of examples we may note—one 8 inches long got in stow-net in the South Channel, 1868 (Baxter); a similar capture when spratting in the "Deeps," winter, 1872 ? (R. Johnson)—to the best of his recollection, say 15 inches long, and he well remembers it providing a good meal to all his family; over a dozen have passed through J. Pryer's hands of late, 10 inches to over 18 inches in extreme length. Indeed, for the last couple of years few boats have failed to bring in an odd one at intervals, small or big.

The extremes of sizes of those we have more particularly examined have been $4\frac{1}{2}$ inches to 17 inches. The former in beginning of May, the latter end of November. The big one had a bodily depth of 7 inches minus fins, and weighed $2\frac{3}{4}$ lb.

It was a female, with ovary fairly well developed, and had been feeding on young fish. Its condition suggests a winter or spring rather than summer or autumn spawning. Good sized Dory are taken round Kent, but there are no special fisheries for them. The shrimpers, Blackwater and Colne mouth, chiefly get the small sized sort (Laver, *l.c.*). Josh Pitt caught two fair-sized John Dorees in the Blackwater, 18th September, 1896. He called them "Jackdaws" (Fitch).

Red and Grey Mullet Families (*Mullidæ and Mugilidæ*).—With a similarity in common name these two families nevertheless are very distinct in fin position, shape of head, dentition, scales, &c. The Red Mullets have long barbels, the Grey Mullets have none. The former comes near the Perch tribe, the latter is allied to the Sand Smelts.

(1.) The Surmullet or Striped Red Mullet (*Mullus surmulletus*), so far as we know, has only been recorded in Boys' List (*op. cit.*) within the limits of our District; though, from its reputed occurrence on the Sussex coast and erratic appearance off Yarmouth, the probability is that we have occasional visitors though unnoticed. One specimen, however, we can certify to as having been captured in the Thames estuary, end of July, 1897. It was taken in the trawl. It measured 5 inches with a body depth of $1\frac{1}{4}$ inches. Quite recently Geo. Gilson told us he has caught red mullet at rare intervals in the Estuary, and of a size somewhat larger than that above described. This species has its summer headquarters on the Cornish and Devon coasts, lessening in numbers eastwards up Channel, and retiring to deep water during the winter. Breeding occurs July to September. Whether the so-called plain Red Mullet (*M. barbatus*) and the above are varieties of one species, or are distinctly separate, ichthyologists are not agreed on.

Fam. Mugilidæ.—Of the Grey Mullet group there are (1) The Thick-lipped (or Lesser) Grey Mullet (*Mugil chelo*) and (2) the Thin-lipped or Grey Mullet (*M. capito*) more or less residents with us. At Harwich, during June to September,

some half-dozen small craft regularly use seines for fishing both
for mullet and bass. They are periodically netted at Dover
and neighbourhood, and thence regularly forwarded to the
London market. The fact is the grey mullet is ordinarily a
restless, impulsive fish. At times they rove in a scattered few,
at other times they are gregarious and very lively. They
frequent nearly all the Kent fishing harbours and piers seeking
the garbage, and then small and moderate-sized ones are taken
by rod and hand-line ; at Margate jetty, in 1880, an Italian even
speared them while devouring mussels on the piles. But the
big mullet seem to prefer grubbing among the muddy, weedy
creeks and shallows of the estuaries, where they feed on the
tiny crustacea and mollusks found on the *Zostera marina*, &c.
Thus the whitebaiters secure a few occasionally in their drag-
nets, while only by chance an odd one is taken in the trawl.

The Stour (Kent), Medway, Thames and Blackwater are all
noted haunts. Near Havengore and thereabouts in the old
times a nice lot would now and again be got (Tyrrel). In the
Blackwater they often run from 10 to 11 lb. weight—one of the
latter was caught in the peter-net August, 1900—a 10 lb. fish
taken 9th July, 1898, measured 2½ ft. long (Fitch).* A similar
large fish was met with by whitebaiters in the Queenborough
Swale in the autumn of 1899, but it leaped the net and was off
in a trice. Small ones occasionally are hooked at Southend
pier, but some anglers there are apt to mistake young bass for
mullet. Although not a rare fish, yet few have been brought
to us; extremes 5 to 10 inches. But around North Kent
annually many of the big ones find their way into the amateur's
basket. With regard to the grey mullet, rod-and-line fishers
admit it is most capricious in taking baited hook, and such is
the general experience of Kent and Essex sea-anglers.

The Sea-Perch Family (*Serranidæ*).†— The BASS or SEA-PERCH

---

* In the Essex Nat. II. (1888), p. 20, Mr. Fitch states that mullet are diminishing in
numbers in the Blackwater. This he attributes to decrease of the *Zostera* weed within
the last 30 years, and to the eel-trawlers disturbing their feeding haunts.

† Laver (*op. cit.*), evidently following Gunther and Day, places the bass under the
Fam. Percidæ. We prefer Boulenger's grouping of it (2nd. ed. B.M. Cat. of Fish I. 1895)
under Sea-Perch, *Fam. Serranidæ*, though retaining the old generic and specific
names, and not that of *Morone labrax*. *See* also Smitt's Scandinavian Fishes I. (1887).

(*Labrax lupus*) is irregularly distributed in few or greater numbers over most of the Kent and Essex seaboard, though rather sparingly at Dover.* In Kent generally it goes by the name of salmon-dace or sea-dace, and at Herne Bay by white salmon; the Leigh fishermen know it only as the bass. It is a fish rather affording sport to sea-anglers during the summer months than regularly followed by fishermen for sale in market. The anglers take bass by rod and by line (fly-fishing or spinning) either from the pier-heads and jetties, or off shore in small boat (whiffing and drift-line fishing); while the fishermen procure the bass with the seine and peter-net, or accidentally in the trawl. Herne Bay, Margate and Deal on the Kent coast, and Harwich on the Essex coast, are noted for bass fishing. Besides the pier-heads and open harbours, the favourite localities where bass congregate are in the creeks, the swins, and the swatchways of the estuary mouths.

For instance, Mr. Fitch records three large fish (16½ lb., 16 lb., and 12½ lb.) caught by Joe Handley in the peter-net in the Blackwater during summer 1887. Previously, about 1860, a bass of 19 lb. weight was captured by Wm. Handley in the Upper Blacklow Creek, near Bradwell. Our fishery officer (G. Kirby) for many years every autumn made good seine hauls of bass among the swins of the Maplins; particularly the Black-tail swin. On one occasion he remembers capturing 50 great fellows in the aforesaid locality. At another time some 30 were taken in his peter-net in exceedingly shallow water, at the head of a gut, not far from the preceding spot. Dr. Laver mentions having seen some nearly 20 lb. in weight, and Buckland states one of 22 lb. was taken in a net close to Herne Bay Pier. Besides, fish of smaller size run further up the estuary, and are regularly caught at Southend Pier-head by amateur fishers during the autumn.

---

* As there is no rule without an exception,·so in this case our eye alights on a paragraph that between 800 and 1,000 bass were captured by Dover fishermen, 17th November, 1900. Some weighed 9 lb. to 10 lb., and such sold at 1s. per lb. The catch is unprecedented. Evidently the fish were returning south.

Hitherto we have not received any accurate or authentic information as to the migration and movements nor of the spawning grounds of the bass frequenting our waters. There is, though, every probability that they come round from the English Channel in the spring and spawn in our estuarine waters during summer; but these adult fish apparently recede to the deeper water as winter arrives. What, however, is less known to ichthyologists, is that the young bass remain in the shallow brackish creeks during the whole of the winter months.

Our attention was called to this subject by an old fisherman, who is allowed to trawl in the Leigh Ray mouth, bringing us in the fall of the year what he deemed a few young grey mullet. These proved to be specimens of the bass. Our further observations were continued during the winter till spring. On some occasions they were got in vast numbers, and at other times seldom a day passed without few or many being got in the net. We measured over 200 between the 1st November, 1898, and the 28th March, 1899, besides roughly examining a great many more, and the remarkable fact was that the sizes remained pretty much on a level during the whole of the five months, namely from $2\frac{1}{2}$ to 4 inches in length. Now and again a few larger ones, 5 to 6 inches, would turn up, but the great majority were of the first-mentioned lengths. Even in the beginning of January and on to March, fish were still got 2·2 to 2·6 inches long. From this it may be inferred that the bass are slow of growth during their first winter. Moreover, there is some reason for thinking that such fish as grew faster, and therefore bigger and bolder, betook themselves to the Sea Reach for sustenance, the smaller remaining and feeding on the mussel bed within the Creek.

The adult bass, as is well known, lives chiefly on fish and crustaceans, and most actively pursues these. Among the above small bass, in the Ray, in some it was difficult to be sure of the nature of their food. In others, though, there could be distinguished gobies or young of the eel-pout, crustaceans such as diminutive shrimps, Mysis and Amphipods, while some evidently preyed on logworm.

Sand-Smelt and Sand-Eel Families (*Atherinidæ and Ammodytidæ*).—We place these two families together for convenience sake, whereas structurally they diverge considerably.

The SAND-SMELT (*Atherina presbyter*), as we have already hinted, is not to be confounded with the true smelt. The former is readily known by absence of cucumber scent, short bluntish head, large eyes, and specially bigger rayed hindmost back fin, besides silvery side band. The true smelt is a salmonoid, with quite small post-dorsal fleshy or adipose fin, &c. Dr. Day* says (evidently citing Montagu†) : "In Kent the atherine appears to be unknown" ; though, oddly enough, further on he quotes Yarrell that, "It is found off Dungeness." As a matter of fact, the sand-smelt is tolerably well represented in our two counties. Doubtless its headquarters is along the English Channel, Sussex, Hants, westwards, where special fisheries for it obtain. The Colne smelt fishermen capture them in their ordinary smelt-nets (Laver); they are got on both shores of the Thames estuary, also in the Medway mouth, and in certain spots from Dover to Dungeness.

Those which have come under our observation in the Thames have mostly run from 4 to 5 inches long; several shorter have been taken either in the stow or drag-net. But one of the whitebaiters at work in the Queenborough grounds in 1899 tells us that during the summer season they regularly procured a few daily, and towards the end of October they seemed to get more numerous, from 20 to 30 a day in the drag-net, many of these 6 to 7 inches long. He further said they seemed to be present in the Swale "one end to the other." In early times, when the Leigh middle-ground was shallower than it is at present, report says sand-smelts were frequent there ; now they are caught chiefly from Southend eastwards.

---

* Fishes of Gt. Brit. and Ireland, I.   † *see* Parnell, Fishes, Firth of Forth (1839).

Our knowledge of their food and spawning in the Thames area is defective. In the west of England their spawning season is June to August, and their eggs are of the adhesive kind, that is demersal.* Sand-smelts are of little economic value in our neighbourhood (excepting small ones as whitebait), consequently some fishers use them only for home use, others reject them. On the Channel coast stations they meet a ready sale.

Fam. Ammodytidæ.† Our District is credited with two species—(1) The GREATER SAND-EEL (*Ammodytes lanceolatus*) and (2) The LESSER SAND-EEL (*A. tobianus*). As to No. 1, the larger sort, which grows to a foot long, Dr. Laver mentions it as inhabiting the Essex coast; but we have not been fortunate in obtaining any, probably by its keeping to deep water. We have been informed, though, by an old fisherman that at one time both the kinds of sand-eels were numerous off the Leigh middle ground. Doubtless the larger form may also be found in places on the Kent coast, but our knowledge thereof is limited.

Regarding No. 2, preferred by Yarrell to be called the sand-launce, this in the summer is very abundant, and in large assemblages, wherever there are sandy bays, or in those parts of the estuaries where brood fish congregate, both in Kent and Essex—though it seldom ascends to the limits of brackish water. They head in to the shores in spring, continue thereabouts during summer, but, as winter or cold weather approaches, retire or bore into the sand—at least, they are then seldom got. They grow 7 inches long, but $5\frac{1}{2}$ inches to 6 inches is the longest we have come across; indeed, the average length of most has been $3\frac{1}{2}$ inches to 4 inches. Occasionally we have noted a few about half that, but have not been favoured with a sight of the eggs —diminutive larval and post-larval forms — so graphically described by authors ‡ In the Thames estuary they are found

---

* Holt, Reprod. Teleost, Fish in S.W. Distr., Jour. Mar. Biol. Assoc., April, 1898.

† Here we follow a recommendation of Boulenger; the Sand-eels usually coming under *Fam. Ophidiidæ.*

‡ McIntosh and Masterman, Brit. Mar. Food-Fishes.

in plenty between the Grain Spit and the Blyth, mayhap in
diminished numbers on the Chapman side. The great bulk of
our examination have been obtained by the whitebaiters from
the Crowstone downwards on the Essex shore. Indeed, when of
smallish size they are not readily culled, and hence, at certain
seasons, go to market in profusion with the whitebait, as already
stated. In Kent they are eagerly sought for as bait, to be used
by the rod fishers from the piers. The Essex people do not seem
so partial to them for baiting purposes. The whitebaiters well
know what a dainty dish they make, though the trawlers chuck
them overboard whatever their size.

The Garfish Family (*Scombresocidæ*).—(1.) The GARFISH or
GARPIKE (*Belone vulgaris*) goes by quite a variety of names
in different localities; but in the greater part of our District,
and particularly the Thames estuarine area, "Gorobill" or
"Gobble" is the familiar cognomen. They seem to come
round the coast in their breeding time in the summer months,
and to retire during the fall and winter. They ascend our
estuary about the middle of the whitebait season, that is May
to July, though generally most numerous in June. On the
Essex side they are moderately numerous, but are said to be
exceedingly abundant off Whitstable and Herne Bay. They
appear to keep near the shore, and consequently are taken in
the drag-net, seldom or ever in the trawl or stow-net. The adults
are taken either singly or in small family parties. Instance two
caught at a haul by a whitebaiter a little way below the Crowstone 2nd June, 1899 — one, a male, 22, its mate, a female, $18\frac{1}{2}$
inches long, both in breeding condition, and feeding on the
whitebait quite close in shore. They spawn in nooks amongst
the *Zostera* beds, to which latter and other objects their eggs are
affixed. Buckland[*] tells of a wooden fishing weir near Herne Bay
where the owner used to catch an enormous quantity of gorebills.
He further says, "Upon this weir I have obtained some very
good specimens of the eggs and young of the gorebill; the eggs

---

[*] Rep. Sea Fisheries, 1879, Append. II.

are covered with *spiculœ*, like spider's web, which enable them
to adhere to sticks and weeds."

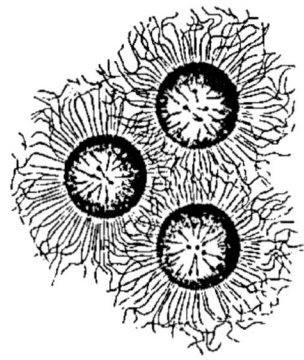

Fig. 14.—Eggs of Garfish
(greatly enlarged) showing the
fine filaments binding them together, and by which they likewise adhere to foreign bodies.
(After McIntosh and Masterman).

Now and again young gorebills, resembling needles over a
couple of inches long, get sent off in the whitebait boxes. Their
tenuity prevents them being readily detected amongst the mass
of glittering fish. The larger garfish caught at Leigh are only
used by the fishermen's families; at Brighton they " are likewise
disregarded " (Webb) ; but on the other hand they are often
brought for sale by the fish-hawkers to Maldon and vicinity
in quantities.

There is a limited special fishery for the garpike in the
neighbourhood around the mouth of the Blackwater. The
interests involved in the said fishery were not large, nevertheless
they gave rise to a lively discussion at the July meeting, 1890.
Hence separation of Nos. 3 and 4 in our Committee's Bye-Laws.
The most curious thing is that the more valuable smelt gets
less protection in size of net mesh than does the rapacious and
destructive garfish.

(2.) The Flying Fish (*Exocœtus volitans ?*). We have here
to add to our District's fish-fauna a rare traveller from the
Atlantic. This unique example got up the Medway as far as
Rochester at the end of September, 1898. A person noticing a
fish leap from the water and skim along the surface, struck out

with his walking stick and secured it. It proved to be a flying-fish measuring 15 inches in length.

Gurnard and Bullhead Families (*Cottidæ*) and allies. —As a matter of convenience we propose to include three families under this heading.

Fam. Cottidæ.—Of the GURNARDS (*Trigla*) nearly all the British species frequent our coasts and estuaries. Some of them are neither so big, so numerous, nor such marketable fish as on the S.W. English Channel or partly E. coast. The following five sorts are recorded as common at Dover (Webb) :—(1) The STREAKED or STRIATED GURNARD (*T. lineata*); (2) the GREY or BLOCH'S GURNARD (*T. gurnardus*); (3) the PIPER (*T. lyra*); (4) the TUB-FISH or SAPPHARINE GURNARD (*T. hirundo*); (5) the ELLECK, RED or CUCKOO GURNARD (*T. cuculus*).

Under Striated Gurnard, presumably the Streaked Gurnard, is mentioned in Boys' Sandwich Fishes, and a small one has come under our observation in the Thames estuary.

The Grey Gurnard, most readily distinguished by its short breast fins, Dr. Laver has only once caught in numbers, during September, off Mersea island. Dale got it in Harwich harbour. It is not unusual " off the land," Sheppey coast (Gilson), more frequent in the Leigh middle-ground, though rarely as high up stream as the Chapman; and small ones are got near Southend (Tyrrel). The *fish*-trawlers, shrimpers and whelk baiters each take a moderate number. Sometimes they are obtained full-roed, though our information thereon is restricted. They and Red Gurnard come to market at Ramsgate and Folkestone, but both are chiefly eaten at Leigh for home consumption only, few falling into the fishmongers' hands. The fish are small, 7 to 10 inches at most, and only the largest in spawning condition. Our knowledge of its Thames migrations is limited, yet this fish possesses considerable interest, and deserves further attention.[*]

---

[*] For instance, concerning said Grey Gurnard and other fish, there has been much thorny argument. Consult Dr. Fulton—"Review of Trawling Experiments of Garland, 1886-1895," in 14th Ann. Rep. S.F.B. for 1895; also 17th Ann. Rep. for 1898—

Besides Dover and S. Kent the Piper is recorded near Harwich, but is rare in the Thames estuary.

The Sappharine Gurnard, better known to fishermen as the Latchet or Tubfish, is, however, much more frequent in the latter locality. During the summer, June to August, we have not infrequently observed them—sometimes a good number at a time—in hauls of the shrimp-trawl. These ranged from 7 to $9\frac{1}{2}$ inches long, were of both sexes, roe and milt undeveloped, and were feeding on shrimps and small fishes. The North Sea trawlers know it as the Latchet. Boys mentions it as Tubfish in Sandwich list, which is its common name in the S. W. of England. Dover is another station, and Laver has procured it in the Blackwater.

The Red Gurnard is regarded as probably the most constant habitant of the Thames mouth during winter, though it also turns up in the summer months, when the Grey species predominates. It comes into the stow-net of the whitebaiters, from 3 to 4 inches to nigh a foot long, but is also got by the shrimpers and fish trawlers. It frequents the hard ground in the Channel-way, and is got from the Low-way to the Knock buoy, which is a favourite haunt. It is obtained in spawn in the fore part of the year, though irregularly. Opposite West Mersea, Blackwater, Dr. Laver has often caught this fish, where it is taken by hook as well as captured in the trawl. Like the Grey Gurnard at Leigh, Sheerness and Chatham, it does not figure much as a mercantile product; indeed, taken in the aggregate, the several Gurnards are but moderate in numbers.

BULLHEADS—the fishermen's common name for which, indiscriminately applied to every sort, is "Bullrout." "Father-lasher"

" Migratory Movements and Rate of Growth of Grey Gurnard." *Versus* Prof. McIntosh, F.R.S., vol. on " The Resources of the Sea," Lond. 1889. As side issue pamphlets, "Trawling and Trawling Investigations," Banff, 1899, and " Reply to same, &c.," Aberdeen, 1899. Without entering into the merits and demerits of the case—like the hard-worded argument and facts of the (brain) "hippocampus question" between Owen and Huxley—it is our earnest wish both may live to sound the praises of his opponent. Although a "rough and tumble" proceeding, wherein the action taken by the Scotch Fishery Board in closure of great areas, trawlers *versus* line, fishers' interests at stake is questioned yet a great principle underlies, directly affecting our Kent and Essex fisheries, as well as others. Hence, however disagreeable to all concerned, it is far better the subject should be so thrashed out and sound conclusions established, either way, than that fishermen and fisheries, and the public, should suffer through false notions, local jealousies, or sordid interests.—(J.M.)

is another colloquial, and sometimes " Lucky Proach." With us
they are practically of little account unless occasionally as
bait.   They perfectly swarm in our estuaries, where their
pinkish egg-clumps, adherent to various ground objects, are
torn up by trawl or dredge.   (1.) The SHORT-SPINED COTTUS
(*C. scorpius**); (2) LONG-SPINED COTTUS (*C. bubalis*); and
(3) The FOUR-HORNED COTTUS (*C. quadricornis*) are representative forms.   The latter is scarce, and met with
chiefly in the Deeps and southern outer channels, not now so
much frequented by the spratters.

The Short and the Long-spined species, at all seasons, con-
tantly come up in the nets.   We have trawled in May in the
neighbourhood of the Girdler and Gilman, and again in September near the Chapman, and there, as elsewhere, their numbers
small and bigger, were something extraordinary.   In one haul of
fish-trawl three trunk-fulls were gathered and shunted overboard (Gilson).   In brief, where there are shrimps, minute
crustaceans and brood-fish, there follow the voracious Sea
scorpions.†   On the South Coast they are said to haunt the
lobster pots and steal the bait placed in them (Webb).   The
Skates and Rays in turn as greedily seize them, hence during the
long-lining from Leigh, a regular bullrout hunt in the swatchway was a preparatory step (special Fisheries *postea*).   Their
usual size is from 4 to 7 inches, but at intervals examples
8 and 9 inches long turn up, both in the Thames and Blackwater.‡   During spring and early summer post-larval stages
obtain of much smaller dimensions than the above.   The fishermen say they get them in roe most of the year.   We have
obtained lumps of ova and ripe fish in early spring, and even
a Father-lasher (*C. scorpius*) with nearly ripe eggs towards the

---

* There is a variety of this named the Greenland Bullhead, which is distinguished
by its gaudy colouring : white spots edged with rich carmine and brown.   Carrington
called attention to its presence near Southend (Zool., 1890), and identified by Dr. Day
(fig. in Brist. Fish.)   We have seen other specimens from the estuary since then, and
Dr. Laver has caught them in the Colne area.   With us they are ordinarily 6 or 7 inches
long, but in Greenland they run up to several feet in dimensions ; there and in
Scandinavia being a regular article of diet.
† Fitch records a Bullrout in the Crouch containing a whiting as long as itself ;
others with crabs, shrimps and prawns.   Essex Nat. V. (1891).
‡ Fitch, Essex Nat. I. and II. (1887-1888).

end of June, so spawning season evidently extends fully half
the year. Though with sweety taste and fairly good to eat, yet
they are rejected as food by the Thames fishers, save a very few
poor elderly people; but we are told that at Queenborough,
Wivenhoe and Tollesbury they are frequently used among the
fishermen's families—paucity of flesh being said to be their
chief drawback.

Fam. Cataphracti.—A near relative of the foregoing, and
one of our very common small fishes, is the ARMED BULLHEAD
or POGGE (*Agonus cataphractus*). By the Thames fishermen it
is known as Hardhead, sometimes as Miller's Thumb,* and
receives from them immediate despatch overboard as rubbish.
It has quite an old world form, with great broad head, tapering
body, clad entirely in a coat of mail in spiny rows. The
Pogge seems to prefer hard sandy ground, and feeds on minute
crustaceans. Females with eggs are got in January and
for several months afterwards. On 16th June, when with
shrimper, hauls were made near the West Oaze Buoy, when
these fish were brought up in amazing numbers—some 50 of
them were measured, and there was a regular gradation of size
from $2\frac{1}{4}$ to $4\frac{1}{2}$ in. Such forms Tosh† computes are over a year
old. Howsoever be it, these and younger stages are freely
devoured by other fishes. The Spaniards is another spot where
at times the Armed Bullhead congregate in hordes. Elsewhere
older fish are got scattered in fews, and they become scarce
above Southend. Mr. Fitch has obtained specimens in the
Blackwater 5 to $5\frac{1}{2}$ in. long. There and in the Crouch it is
abundant and only familiarly known by the name "Miller's
Thumb." A few 6 in. and over at intervals come up in the
trawl-net Thames mouth.

Fam. Pediculati.—The ANGLER (*Lophius piscatorius*) is locally
known as the "Pocket Fish," but elsewhere goes by such fanciful
names as Sea Devil, Fishing-frog, Kettlemaw, &c. It is a common

---

* The Pogge is not to be confounded with the true Miller's Thumb (*Cottus gobio*),
which inhabits our fresh-water streams.

† Twelfth Ann. Rep. S. Fish. Board, (for 1893).

I

fish in the North Sea, and the Ramsgate and other deep-sea trawlers sometimes get them up to 6 ft. long. Those obtained strictly within the Thames area are sometimes smaller fish, merely stragglers in their way. Take for example one of 32 in. caught in the Colne 1866 ?; another off the Maplins 1863, 4 ft. 4 in. long, and a third trawled between the Nore and Jenkins, November, 1898, whose dimensions were $10\frac{1}{2}$ in. long, the body half that, and not much less in breadth. This latter fish contained a whiting only a couple inches shorter than itself. Among others a large one captured close to Holehaven (Thames) in 1867 ?; a considerable sized example taken in stow-net near Whitstable, January, 1869, ? which W. P. Coleman sent to Buckland for casting. Fitch tells us of a 30-inch specimen got in the Blackwater, 8th June, 1890. At Dover and Folkestone the fishermen often bring them in. They are ugly fish destroyers, and their eggs float as a great sheet of spawn.

Regarded in the light of a food-fish the flesh of the Angler is not unpalatable, but like the Cat-fish, the great head is so repulsive as to raise prejudice.* Hence at Grimsby the fleshy sides only are cut out and exposed for sale. When taken in our District it graces the fishmonger's slab as gazing-stock, or the fishermen make a show of them.

The Blenny Family (*Blenniidæ*).—Among these the only really marketable one is (1.) the CAT-FISH (*Anarrhichas lupus*†), also known as " Sea Wolf," and whereof a solitary example has been referred to by Dr. Laver (*op. cit.*) as captured at Walton-on-the-Naze, 29th August, 1885. It is truly a North Sea (and sub-Arctic) fish, enormous numbers being daily brought in to Aberdeen and Grimsby markets. Indeed of late years it has

---

* In January, 1901, several " Pocket Fish " were taken in the whitebaiters' stow-nets east off Southend Pier. A large one got by J. Noakes seized a pole pushed into the net, and holding it fast was thus lifted on deck. The fishermen have lately found out the value of their tail-flesh, and no longer despise pieces therefrom for home use. Thus a large Angler stranded in the Hadleigh Ray the end of January was quickly cut up by the oystermen. It was stated to be a female nearly ripe for spawning. (F. Bridge.)

† Consult McIntosh and Prince on its Development and Life-History. Trans. Roy. Soc. Edin. Vol. XXV. p. 874 (1890).

found its way to London and the provinces, where, retailed skinned, it frequently passes under the name of "Devonshire salmon." Its great teeth and fierce aspect have long stood in the way of its sale; so with head cut off it appears at the fishmongers, and customers then readily purchase it cut in thick slices. These are the "rock salmon" of Southend restaurants *menu*.

 (2.) The BUTTERFLY BLENNY (*Blennius ocellarius*), in contradistinction to the last, is a southern form, and seldom attains more than several inches in length. The eye-spot on its back fin is a characteristic mark. It has been detected by Mr. Horsnaill at Dover, the only locality in our District that we are aware of.

(3.) The GATTORUGINE (*B. gattorugine*) is another of the southern Blennies a rarity with us; indeed its presence is founded on two specimens in Essex waters. It is usually a deep water, rocky ground form, and locally named "Tompot" in Cornwall, being well known as a thiever of the crabpots. Larger than the last, it yet does not exceed 9 inches in length. One about half that size, supposed to be the first record of its presence in East Anglia, is noted by Patterson in the *Zoologist*, 1899, as having been caught on the 21st May by a shrimper near Yarmouth. But Mr. Fitch (*ibid.*) shortly afterwards pointed out the taking of one by S. Wright, off Stansgate, up the Blackwater, 19th August, 1898, this one being $5\frac{1}{2}$ inches long.

Such another example of the same size ($5\frac{1}{2}$ in.) was brought up in G. Gilson's trawl in deepish water S. of the Nore in the first week of September, 1899. It closely resembled Dr. Day's fig. Brit. Fish. I. Pl. 59, the darker cross-barring being more pronounced. It was a female, with undeveloped ovary. Food, comminuted shells and fleshy remains mixed with particles of sand and traces of seaweed, besides chalky granules like lenses of fish or crustacean eyes.

(4.) The BUTTER-FISH or Gunnel (*Centronotus gunnellus*) is so far appropriately named, for with its yellowish tint and slimy body, it is about as slippery as the eel in the hand when alive

i 2

It however goes by widely different local names in other parts of Britain. It is a common fish, apparently freely scattered about so far as the trawlers' catches are concerned. Numerous around the Brightlingsea shores and Mersea *Zostera* beds, up the Blackwater $4\frac{1}{2}$ to $5\frac{1}{4}$ inches long (Fitch), and various parts of the Thames estuary, where we get them from $3\frac{1}{2}$ to nigh 7 inches in length. Local name "9-eyes." The Gunnel is treated by the fishermen as among the rubbish, and swiftly goes overboard.

The Spotted Blenny of Boys' Sandwich Fishes, 1792, doubtless may be regarded as meant for the Butter-fish. But he also notices a Smooth Blenny in his list. We take it therefore as possible that this may refer to the Shanny (*B. pholis*), the Common or Smooth Blenny of some authors; though as to whether he had the Eel Pout or other form in his mind's eye we are left in doubt.

So far as is known the eggs of the blennies adhere in masses on the ground or are fixed to various submerged objects. There is one noted exception to this, namely, the form which here follows.

(5.) But perhaps the most remarkable of the family in our district is the EEL POUT, or Viviparous Blenny (*Zoarces viviparus*) ; this inasmuch as its mode of reproduction is concerned, as well as in numbers. At certain spots in the winter season it simply swarms. Ordinarily they are regarded as keeping near harbours, which to some extent is true; but we find them dispersed over the Thames and other estuaries, at times sparsely brought up by the shrimp and eel trawlers, or in the stow-boat-net or drag-net of the whitebaiters. The fish trawlers, however, do not get them, their large mesh of net easily allowing escape. So far as we know they are not much in evidence on the Kent coast, excepting up the Medway and creeks, including Queenborough neighbourhood and the Swale, where during summer they are met with in great quantities. We suspect they frequent Holehaven, at least on occasions they are found near the Chapman and down the Leigh middle and towards the Jenkins.*

But a great resort and breeding station, especially during the winter season, is in the Hadleigh Ray; whence in spring they obtain from the Low-way to Southend Pier. So plentiful are they in the Ray that it is recorded of one trawl-haul being almost entirely composed of Eel Pouts (literally thousands), the two smack hands with difficulty hoisting the net. In this case they were all thrown back alive into the water. Indeed this is the usual procedure, even if only single or few taken, for the Leigh folks make no use of them. Yet their flesh is wholesome, and elsewhere is used as food† or as crab bait. All during the summer small or medium sized fish are got in the Ray to a limited extent. As autumn wanes and colder weather arrives there appears to be an accession of large-sized breeders of both sexes. This congregation lasts till spring advances, when the old ones rapidly diminish in numbers, and seem to steer down the estuary, or otherwise disperse until renewal of autumnal meeting.

We have examined many hundreds of them in all stages of development, and for stomach contents, &c.; but below need only tersely summarize data of a few batches. The Eel Pout, unlike other food fish (irrespective of some sharks), does not shed its eggs, but instead retains them within the ovary where hatching occurs, and in due course the young are born alive full formed. Mr. Fitch (Essex Nat. V.) mentions finding on 8th November in the Crouch river an Eel Pout $8\frac{1}{2}$ inches long, containing 55 young, all lively, while they were very common in the Blackwater in the middle of September.

Those examined by us during summer were not advanced, only having diminutive eggs present; by October, however, the case was different. At this date in one catch of 117 specimens there were 71 females and 46 males. Among the females six had only small eggs in the ovary, these being young fish; whilst

* Yarrell mentions Greenwich as a locality for *Zoarces.*
† At one time sold regularly in Edinburgh (Parnell).

the 65 older ones all contained larval progeny fully formed, each 1 to $1\frac{1}{2}$ inches long. The shortest adult female Eel Pout was $4\frac{1}{2}$, the largest $9\frac{1}{3}$ inches. Of these pregnant females, containing well developed larvæ, the smallest was $5\frac{1}{4}$ inches long and contained 20 young, whilst one $8\frac{1}{2}$ inches in length carried 148 larvæ. Excluding a few females which had got rid of the bulk of their progeny, the general average of the others was 62 to a fish. It would appear also, though not an absolute rule, that increase of fertility bears a ratio to the age of the parent. For example: 195 larvæ have been found by others in a female a foot long and 262 in one of 13 inches. The male fish in this October series ranged from $4\frac{1}{2}$ to 8 inches, and the milt in the majority was only moderately developed. Passing on to mid-January, in a batch of 61 Eel Pouts 33 were females and 28 males. The shortest fish was 3·9 inches, the longest 8·4 inches. One female, 4·1 inches long, did not show any sign whatsoever of eggs; whilst in another 3·9 inches, and still others 4·1, 4·3, onwards to 6 inches, there were ovarian eggs the size of small pinheads; in those above 6 inches larvæ were present. Otherwise expressed, the sexual condition of the 33 were:—1 no ovarian eggs, 17 with eggs of varied size, 13 containing larvæ, and 2 spent fish. Among the males only a few had the milt in ripeness.

There are interesting matters concerning maturation of eggs and larvæ within abdomen, the early breeding of some, and the age of the young at period of expulsion, but these physiological subjects we here prefer to pass by.

Their food consists of crustaceans and annelids—thus Copepods, Isopods, Amphipods and Shrimps, &c., nereid or rag-worms and lug-worms were the chief fare, varied occasionally by molluscs, Tellina, young cockles and likewise small fish. While the Blennies (excluding Cat-fish) do not contribute directly to our fisheries products, yet they are of great utility in furnishing, both in their young and adult stages, a never-failing source of food supply to our more profitable fish.

Goby and Dragonet Families (*Gobiidæ* and *Callionymidæ*).— Gobies.—These fish though insignificant in dimensions yet play a certain rôle, if a minor one, in our fisheries. Their utility lies in becoming human food, as they get passed on among white-bait (to which reference has already been made) ; as nutriment to quite a host of marketable fishes ; and, like small crabs, they are among the best of littoral scavengers. A few species haunt the District's shores all round ; but it is in estuaries, creeks, swatchways, "guts," runlets and clay-pool flats where they revel in myriads.

The two species of the genus *Gobius* which are most commonly met with in our waters are :—(1) The Freckled, Yellow, or ONE-SPOTTED GOBY (*G. minutus*); and (2) The DOUBLE-SPOTTED GOBY (*G. Ruthensparri*). The local name for them among the Thames fishermen, irrespective of sort, is " Polywigs," or " Whitethroats," whereas in the Blackwater they are known as " Gobble-guts." The first form is the most prevalent in the Thames estuary. Its maximum size is $3\frac{1}{2}$ inches, but adults run between 2 and 3 inches. The second form is not quite so large, ordinarily about 2 inches long, though $2\frac{1}{4}$ inches is recorded.[*]

During the warm summer weather the fry or post-larval gobies at low tide hover in small batches at the drain mouths, eagerly devouring the minute particles of waste material. Others, again, left in shallow pools, where sea drift or algæ have collected, jerk about picking up microscopic creatures, such as foraminifera, ostracods, larval copepods, and molluscs. When disturbed they dart among and stir up the muddy sand, and in a second are lost to sight. Somewhat older ones gather in squadrons at the margins of the " guts " as ebb proceeds, and revel in the material floating off. As the water retires they follow to low-water mark, returning to the shallows as the tide flows. The adults are scattered about in the deeper water, some joining the whitebait brood as they approach

---

[*] Fitch, "Trip on Blackwater," 15 Sept., 1889, Essex Nat. II.

the shore when tide rises. They come up in the shrimpers' trawl, or are entrapped in the whitebaiters' stow-net. The adults consume such fare as sandhoppers, Amphipods, young barnacles, Mysidæ, minute shrimps, &c. These gobies little eggs do not float about, but adhere in flat layers on stones, dead shells, seaweeds and other objects. Each egg is of an oblong shape, and fastened at the base by an outspread network.* The young hatch out in spring, though spawning continues during summer.

(3.) The WHITE GOBY (*Aphia pellucida*), known also as the Slender Goby, is characterized by the transluccncy of its body, as its specific name implies, besides possessing other pecu-liarities. It is supposed to be rare in our District, but, on the contrary, it is astonishingly numerous.

Whether the White Goby is to be found on S. and E. Kent we cannot speak with certainty, but that it enters the Medway is not so doubtful. As regards Essex, Dr. Laver (*op. cit.*) had only seen a few chance examples caught in the Wallet, and therefore hesitates to express opinion as to its distribution or plenitude. According to our observations at Leigh station, as early as the first week, or from mid-February onwards, among the whitebait obtained by stow-netting, what are termed "heads-and-eyes" begin to appear. These are mainly sprats and herrings in their post-larval condition, but a few White Gobies are found among them. Throughout March and April the latter increase in numbers; at times 20, 30 to 50 or more may be picked out of a box of "bait." The extremes in length of those measured by us have been from 30 to 50 millimetres, or say about $1\frac{1}{4}$ to 2 inches. These are adults of the White Goby. Their extraordinary transparency, however, displaying all their internal organs, marks them off sharply from the similar-sized somewhat eel-shaped herring fry, the latter being of a duller coloured jelly-like consistence.

---

* For illustrations of Goby and Sucker families' eggs *see* Plate II., McIntosh's Brit. Marine Food-fishes.

During May specimens of *Aphia* are still got above and below Southend Pier-head, but somewhat irregularly, and by June they drop off—at least from the whitebaiter's catch, who now gets to shore with drag-net. Meantime, and later in the season, it appears, according to Albert Bundock,* that the White Gobies are found in shoals in the Lower Hope Reach to the Tilbury marshes, or even beyond. He believes he has seen them in spawning condition, and considers they breed thereabouts. Lower down they are lost for the season, returning in early spring as above narrated. We have examined adults of both sexes, as well as those of younger age, and can corroborate much that has been advanced by various writers.† Among other things their food in the Thames is nearly the same as in the Norwegian waters, viz., the minute Copepods and other crustacean larvæ, early stages of cockles, &c. We have not seen their eggs, but Holt and Byrne‡ describe them as of a fixed kind with thread-like attachment—a compromise between those of goby and blenny.

The DRAGONET (*Callionymus lyra*) in many ways is unlike the gobies, with which, however, it is regarded as an ally, though classed in a different family (= *Callionymidæ*). It is a common fish in our District, but particularly plentiful in the estuaries. They are got by the shrimpers and fish trawlers all over the estuarine area. In the winter not so plentiful, but all during summer and autumn they are taken, generally few at a time. In mid-June, 1899, on the West Oaze, one haul particularly brought up a perfect shoal of

---

* Previous to the Conservancy's Bye-Law, 1895, prohibiting stow-boating within their limits, he regularly fished up stream.

† Prof. Collett has made a special study of the White Goby obtained by him in the Christiania Fjord (Forhandl. Videns. Selskab., 1872, and Proc. Zool. Soc., 1878). In November he once netted as many as 4,000 at a single haul. Two species had previously been recognised, which he showed were only the male and female of one sort. The males at the breeding season develop long teeth, and this, with other characteristics, gave rise to their supposed separate identity. He reasons that the adults die after breeding, and therefore accomplish their life in the course of a year. This conclusion we have reason for doubting, but here need not dilate thereon.- (J.M.)

‡ Jour. Mar. Biol. Assoc., 1898, Vol. V., p. 338.

them. Nigh 40 of these were kept for examination, but this was only a tithe of the lot. Authorities do not regard them as gregarious, though in this instance the assembly was large.* The sexes are deemed to be in proportion of one male to three females; in our series there were 16 males to 21 females. The extremes of the sizes were $3\frac{1}{2}$-$8\frac{1}{2}$ inches, though they grow to a foot long. Their food consisted of worms, shell-fish (mussels, &c.), crustacea (shrimps, crabs and Idotea), one with fish remains and others hydroids.

The older males when in full dress are most remarkably gorgeous in appearance—orange, red, lilac and blue standing out in various stripes and spots, and a couple of the rays of the front back fin are of great length. The females, on the contrary, are rusty dull colour with short back fin. Add to this their sharp-nosed, broad, flat head and fore body, and their local name of " fox " is applicable. Their eggs float, thus differing from the gobies' adhesive ones. They are, moreover, quite peculiar in possessing an outside network egg-membrane. McIntosh assigns May to August as their chief spawning season in Scotland, while Holt found spent females in April on the west coast of Ireland, though their floating eggs were got from March to June†; but we were only fortunate in noting one with ripe spawn on 10th September below Southend Pier. They are not ordinarily used as food, though the flesh is well flavoured, hence, like the gobies, they alone serve as the prey of cod, whiting and other edible fish.

The Sucker Family *(Discoboli)* are fairly plentiful in our area, but have no mercantile value. They are of northern habit. The three British species are all with us. (1) The LUMP-FISH or LUMP-SUCKER (*Cyclopterus lumpus*) is the most pronounced member of the trio. We have not tracked the adult's movements

---

* As in Humber estuary, and W.C. Ireland, hauls, *see* Holt and Calderwood, Sci. Trans. Roy. Dubl. Soc., Sept., 1895, p. 424.

† Survey Fishing Grounds W.C. Ireland, in Rev. W. S. Green's Rep. to Council Roy. Dub. Soc., 1901. Append. C.

from deep to shallower water. Some seasons they are captured in numbers on the S. Kent coast, and the same applies to the opposite extreme near Harwich. Rather common in the Blackwater, especially on the Mersea shore. Specimen taken 24th April, 1897, length 16 inches, width 5 inches, weight $3\frac{3}{4}$ lb. (Fitch). In the Thames mouth the larger forms are got below the Nore, chiefly in the trawl, occasionally in the stow-net, peradventure a small one in the drag-net. In 1882 an order was received by an old Leighman, then resident in Southend, for young Lump-suckers. Quite a number were obtained from the whitebaiters, and taken alive in a tank to a German aquarium (Tyrrel). The biggest we have seen captured in spring in the neighbourhood of the Gilman and Girdler was close on 2 feet long, depth and thickness in proportion.* Another, a male 18 inches long, half that in depth of body, weight 6 lb., was caught in the stow-net 21st March above the Knock Buoy. Abdomen of rich red colour; milt in ripe condition. We took 100 whitebait from its stomach, besides several white gobies and others. Lump-suckers from 6 to 9 inches or a foot long at intervals are not infrequent.

The smallest, obtained in whitebaiters' stow-net 26th Feb., was under $1\frac{1}{2}$ inches long; another, $2\frac{1}{4}$ inches, in shrimp-trawl, on 30th April; this latter weighed $\frac{1}{4}$ oz. According to J. R. Tosh's reckoning† these would be about 10 and 12 months old. At these stages the general chubby form approaches that of the adult, and even then the rows of spinous tubercles on the body are quite a marked feature. The bright emerald tint and other peculiarities corroborate McIntosh's description of their

---

* Winter specimen of maximum size full of spawn, viz. :—A female received through Mr. Juniper, and caught near the Knock Buoy in whitebaiters' stow-net by W. Cotgrove, 15th December, 1900, was quite 2 feet long, 13½ inches deep, 3z inches girth, and 23 lb. weight. The ovaries weighed 2 lb. 12 oz. and the eggs were almost ripe for extrusion. Doubtless it would have spawned in January. A dozen whitebait were found in the stomach, besides 20 examples of egg-shaped jelly fish (*Ctenophora*). This female Lump-sucker was of the blue coloured kind, only the hinder fins reddish, thus contrasting with the bright red-bellied breeding males. We cooked a portion of the ova and a bit of more solid muscular flesh, and both ate well; but the thick layer beneath the skin became a jelly-mass on cooking. (*See* Buckland's note, *Land and Water*, 1879, p. 188.)

† 12th Ann. Rep. S. F. Board for 1893.

early stages.* As to spawning places, these are evidently spread about, for oyster dredgers and others have got great bunches of their pinkish eggs from the Margate sands westwards along the Kent shore, and ova are found on the partly sunken wrecks on the Maplins. The Leigh fishermen reject the Lump-sucker as useless ; but in the Blackwater and presumably Colne mouth neighbourhood Dr. Laver says (*op. cit.*) the fish is exposed for sale as food. The males, "red lumps," are those only eaten (Fitch).

(2) The SEA SNAIL (*Liparis vulgaris*) and (3) MONTAGU'S SUCKER (*L. Montagui*) never attain the dimensions of the preceding. They are browny, plump, soft, greasy-skinned fishes. The largest we have met with when with trawlers in the Thames mouth have been 5 inches the former and 3 inches the latter. The fishermen throw them overboard among the rubbish. Mr. Fitch has found these little " purple wrigglers " sometimes so abundant when trawling in the Crouch river that he has got bushels of them in a day, and such a case occurred to him 6th November, 1900. They are in no-ways so plentiful in the Thames, at least got in much fewer numbers during our many fishing trips at all seasons. Of their presence around Kent we have no information.

The **Lepadogaster Family** or Flatheaded Suckers (*Gobiesocidæ*).—One member of these curious diminutive fishes, viz., the TWO-SPOTTED SUCKER, Donovan obtained in Kent nigh a century ago. We also learn there is a specimen at the Brightlingsea Marine Station which was obtained in the waters adjoining 21st July, 1894 (Fitch).

Sundry Families.—We include under this heading a few odd fishes, most only lonely accidental stragglers within our Kent and Essex waters, but their mention rounds off our sea-fish fauna.

Fam. Xiphiidæ.—The SWORD - FISH (*Xiphias gladius*).—

---

* Brit. Mar. Food-Fishes; and Ann. & Mag. Nat. Hist., Aug., 1886, on "Paternal Instincts of *Cyclopterus.*"

Though got around Britain, their numbers are far too few to be of economical importance; but they form extensive fisheries on the American seaboards, and likewise in the Mediterranean. In our country the interest attached to the sword-fish has chiefly hinged on pugnacity, viz., attacks on whales, or cases in Court where polemical evidence has arisen for and against the penetration of their swords through the planking of ships.* These we need not enter into; but, instead, refer to records of sword-fish capture on our Kent and Essex coasts.

The earliest notice of the Sword-fish in Kent is in Boys' list, 1792 (*op. cit.*). One 10 ft. long was captured 20th October, 1843, in the neighbourhood of Deal, viz.:—" a little way to the South of the outer beacon leading to Sandwich Haven." It had got stranded in 4 ft. water, and a crew in a six-oared galley managed to noose its tail and secure the prize. (Yarrell, Zool. 1843.) In Wood's Nat. Hist. one is referred to seven feet long as taken off Margate. There was a cast of a specimen over eight feet long in Buckland's Museum of Economic Fish Culture, South Kensington, captured by the Ramsgate fishermen, 1870. In October, 1888, a bargeman successfully secured an example in the Long Reach, Milton Creek, Sitting-bourne. It measured 5 feet 2 inches from the tip of the sword to tail extremity. We find mention of a dead one which came ashore on the coast of Essex in 1834 (Zool. 1847); again on 23rd October, 1862, some oystermen discovered a Sword-fish alive in a creek on the river Roach near Potton Island. In plunging about trying to get to deep water it had driven its sword into the mud. The length of the fish was 9 ft. 1 in., the sword 3 ft.; weight about $2\frac{1}{2}$ cwts., and girth 46 inches. The tip of the sword was broken off, and supposed to be an injury of old standing—(C. Parsons, Zool., 1862). In the beginning of November, 1866, an unusual fish was observed by the Leigh fishermen hanging about for several days. Latterly it got into the creek and was there captured. It was sent off to London,

---

* Ann. and Mag. Nat. Hist., XIII. (1844); *Land and Water*, II. (1866); and Rep. U. S. Fish Comm. (VIII.) for 1880.

and became the property of a fishmonger in the Strand. The Duke of Argyll called Buckland's attention to it, who made a cast, intended for his museum. This fish measured in extreme 8 feet 8½ inches, the sword being 2 feet 9 inches long.

Fam. Sciænidæ.—The MAIGRE (*Sciana aquila*) has been compared not inaptly to a huge bass, though it differs in several respects from that family. The only authentic record within our District is of one taken off Margate in October, 1843. We have also been told of another supposed Maigre brought into Folkestone some years ago, but no particulars were vouchsafed. Several have certainly been got on the Sussex coast, one such, 3½ feet long, was examined by Dr. Murie 40 years ago. They are of tropical extraction, and wander up the English Channel, a few being taken annually.

Fam. Labridæ.—Two species of this family are known to frequent our District—both are rare. (1) The BALLAN WRASSE (*Labrus maculatus*). Under the name "Antient Wrasse," Boys records it in his list, 1792, without exact locality other than Kent. Henry Lee saw two got by the Margate fishermen in February, 1870. Dr. Laver has also shown us one, the green variety, obtained by the Brightlingsea boats a few years ago. Mr. Fitch has two preserved in formalin got by S. Wright in the Blackwater off Stansgate 23rd June, 1898: each 7 in. long.

(2) BAILLONS WRASSE or Goldsinny (*Crenilabrus melops var.*). Two Essex specimens have been described by Dr. Bree in *The Field*, December, 1866. Another example of the variety *Norwegicus*, 8 inches long, body depth 2½ inches, minus fins, was caught by a Leigh trawler 7th April, 1900. It proved to be a female with ovary about two-thirds ripe. Nature of food somewhat doubtful, being pulpy in condition though probably semi-digested annelids.

Fam. Gasterosteidæ.—The Sticklebacks, although chiefly inhabiting fresh waters, nevertheless have a species, No. 1, a true marine form, while varieties of the other two have been recorded from our estuaries. (1) The 15-SPINED STICKLEBACK

(*Gasterosteus spinachia*) is of common occurrence around Dover and other spots iu Kent. They have been got 3 to 4 inches long in the Blackwater by Mr. Fitch; and by Dr. Laver, in trawling for eels among the *Zostera* beds. We have also found them in the Thames estuary widely distributed, at Leigh sometimes known as "sawback," which is its common name in the Blackwater. (2) The THREE-SPINED STICKLEBACK (*G. aculeatus*) we have already stated gets into the whitebaiters' nets, as occasionally do both in the shrimpers' hauls.

Fam. Coryphœnidœ.—The OPAH, or KING-FISH (*Lampris luna*) is notable for being a North Sea form of most gorgeous colouring and great size. Its body is deep and laterally compressed. It runs to several feet in length and weighs over 1 cwt. in full-grown specimens. Its bright scarlet fins and tail and body stripe, its purple back, emerald sides, yellow belly and silver spots throughout the body give it a most striking aspect. It is a casual visitor to Kent, being at rare intervals brought in to Ramsgate, Dover and Folkestone. It occurs in Boys' list (*op. cit.*).

Fam. Sclerodermi.—A specimen of the FILE-FISH or TRIGGER-FISH (*Balistes capriscus*) was captured in a trawl 27th September, 1884 (by the Dymchurch men), in the bay between Folkestone and Dungeness Point. It was dull slate coloured, $10\frac{1}{4}$ inches long, $4\frac{3}{4}$ inches deep, excluding fins.[*] This very rare fish is remarkable for its armoured compressed body, its strong chisel teeth, which act like pincers on shells to extract the soft-bodied mollusc, and for its long file-like fore dorsal spine, which only acts when in unison with the shorter second spine—triggerlike fashion. It is a southern form and mere wanderer to our coast.

Fam. Gymnodontes.—The Sun-fishes, two in number, are spread world wide, those straying to our shores evidently coming from the Atlantic. They are quite peculiar in several respects. Their body outwardly resembles a fish cut short and

---

[*] Tegetmeir in *The Field*, Oct., 1884, and Harting, Zool., 3rd Ser., Nov., 1884.

tailless, with back and belly-fin stuck vertically at the end; internally their gristly spine, the flesh, and internal anatomy are characteristically different from ordinary fish.

(1) The SHORT SUN-FISH (*Orthagoriscus mola*) is oval shaped and laterally flattened. Specimens have been got several feet in diameter, such enormous ones weighing several hundred-weights; but their flesh is valueless as food, becoming of jelly (starchy) consistence when cooked. Several examples have been taken both on the seaboard and estuaries of our District.

Among others we may enumerate Boys' Sandwich specimen, 1792. It has also occurred occasionally near Harwich, Essex coast (Dale and Lindsey). In the beginning of December, 1868, the Folkestone fishermen captured a specimen, which Buckland made a cast of for his museum. It measured, nose to stern, 3 feet $5\frac{1}{2}$ inches, and vertically from tip of back to tip of belly-fin 4 feet 8 inches—weighing close on 1 cwt. A large example is recorded from Margate in August, 1867. At intervals it is not unusual on the Dover coast.

Fig. 15.

SUN-FISH
(*Orthagoriscus mola*) as it appears at the surface of the water, extremely reduced.

Mr. Fitch has noted the case of a female $4\frac{1}{2}$ feet long, taken in the Crouch river near Battles Bridge, above Burnham, 21st October, 1874. This was afterwards exhibited at Rayleigh, Rochford and Chelmsford. A second was seen by him in the same river some years after. It moved slowly, and the boat got near before it sank and made off. One weighing 196 lb., a total length of 4 ft. 3 in., depth 5 ft. 2 in., was caught by the shrimpers off Southend at the end of September, 1872. It was exhibited at Messrs. Groves, Bond Street, London. At Leigh-on-Sea, September, 1897, J. Frost and R. Kirby, returning to harbour, espied an unusual fish, or rather high fin, sticking out of the water near Canvey Spit. They rowed to it, and gently approaching, suddenly seized the fin and whisked the big fish aboard. Never having seen the like, it was brought to Dr. Murie for identification. This male measured 24 inches long by 16¼ inches vertical depth; thickness, 3-4 inches; weight, close on ½ cwt.; gill-slit, 1½ in.; no true teeth, but turtle-like mouth, with hard gum-plates; rough leathery skin of a dull brownish hue.

(2) The OBLONG SUN-FISH (*O. truncatus*) is brilliantly coloured, never attains the dimensions of *O. mola*, is not so deep, and is encased in a coat of mail, composed of minute, close-set, bony, button plates. Our only authorities for its Essex authenticity are Dale and Lindsey, who incidentally mention that at Harwich it is rare.

The Pipe-fish Family (*Syngnathidæ*).—Several members of this family are residents and very numerous pretty well everywhere in our District. They are known locally as "Snake-fish," no distinction being made between the different kinds. As a rule they are cast away when caught. If kept they are stringed together, garland fashion, as a mantelpiece ornament. Formerly dried and pounded, the powder was re-garded as a sure cure for whooping cough. Five species obtain, which naturalists class into almost as many genera. Those are:— (1) The GREATER PIPE-FISH (*Syngnathus acus*) and (2) the BROAD-NOSED PIPE-FISH (*Syphonostoma typhle*), which two are the most common. The big ones occasionally come up in the shrimp and eel trawls, frequently are trapped in the stow-net or captured in the drag-net. (3) The OCEAN or SNAKE PIPE-FISH (*Nerophis æquoreus*) and (4) the STRAIGHT-NOSED PIPE-FISH (*N. ophidion*) have a more tapering, whip-like, almost finless tail, and fewer are taken, especially of the latter, which is rare.

Pipe-fish are interesting in their singular habits rather than of their benefit to fishermen, for even as bait they are valueless. For instance, the male (*not* the female) hatches the eggs in a kind of belly-pouch or scaly flap covering; both sexes progress

K

or move about body vertical, head either up or down, and their
tail is prehensile, or grasps the reeds and weeds, while the body
sways to and fro. Thus, on the south coast of Kent, they are
charged with feloniously visiting the lobster pots, and are
brought up swung fast by their tails to the bars. We have
found the Greater and Broad-nosed species carrying ova during
summer and autumn, though seldom fortunate in seeing young
in the pouch. Young fish, like darning needles, $2\frac{1}{2}$ to ?
inches, are plentiful in late autumn, winter and spring. These
keep company with the whitebait and other small fish, particularly sojourning in weedy ground. The maximum length
of *S. acus* obtained by us has been $17\frac{1}{2}$ inches (in Blackwater
16 inches, Fitch), but 15 inches down to a foot are frequent
Those examined appear to have fed on minute crustacean:
(Copepods).

There is still another exceptional form in the family, viz.
(5) The SEA-HORSE or HIPPOCAMPUS (*H. antiquorum*), which mus
be more frequent on the Essex coast than hitherto supposed
Dr. Bree records two as very rare fish at Brightlingsea, Nov.
1866, while Dr. Laver has not
met with them. A good sized
one was taken by J. Cotgrove
off the Shoebury sands in his
shrimp-trawl, 1876. His wife
was offered 10s. for it, but it still
remains an ornament in the
parlour. A small one of size
represented in Fig. 16 was got
in the drag-net by A. Bundock,
May, 1900. He kept it alive in
a dish of sea water for some
days, afterwards presenting it to us. Some twenty years ag
two Leigh men (J. Little and J. Tyrrel) had an order from
London to procure specimens. So when shrimping at Harwic
during the summer season they procured altogether five or si

Fig. 16.

SEA HORSE.

(*Hippocampus antiquorum.*)

score. These were caught chiefly in the E. Swin and neighbourhood of the Sunk Light. Moreover, Yarrell mentions one that lived three weeks in confinement at Harwich. Then Dr. Sorby found *Hippocampus* in the *Zostera* beds at Colne Point, 1897. Lastly, J. Avery got a specimen at Clacton, 1900. (Fitch).

The **Eel Family** (*Murænidæ*) are represented by (1) The CONGER (*Conger vulgaris*), a salt water resident, and (2) the COMMON EEL (*Anguilla vulgaris*), a fresh water sojourner, which annually migrates seawards. Bearing considerable likeness to each other, their most conspicuous distinctions are :—Congers, dorsal fin commencing well forward, and snout projecting ; Eels, back-fin starting mid-body, and lower jaw in advance of snout. Colour forms no sure guide, and other so-called varieties of both kinds of Eels depend rather on age, locality, sterility, and other variable conditions than on specific differentiation.

The Conger.—Along our southern border, for example, the Ridge and Varne shoals, the neighbourhood of Dungeness, Folkestone and Dover, Congers are very numerous, and many of enormous size. Buckland mentions capture of a Conger 8 feet long and 26 inches girth, at Folkestone, and he saw another there 5 feet 7 inches long and 24 inches girth. This last had a flounder and two soles inside it. A third he records from Folkestone, 6 feet 4 inches long, girth 21 inches and weight 50 lb. Thirty and more are got at a haul near Dungeness. Some of the Folkestone men follow Conger-Eel fishing the greater part of the year, sending the bulk of their catch to London. The Conger, however, is widely, perhaps irregularly, distributed in our Fisheries District, though not specially sought for at many of the stations. They occasionally pay visits to the brackish waters, nay, even ascend rivers. For instance, several were caught in the Thames, as high as Woolwich, in 1869. They now and again have been taken in the neighbourhood of Sea Reach, or captured by the shrimpers near the Chapman Light and in the Leigh Roads.

Here usually they are got in the autumn or beginning o
winter, and seldom are above a foot or 18 inches long. W(
know of one case, in the spring of 1870, where a specimen o
3 to 4 feet long, and thick in proportion, was foun(
floundering in a tidal pool on the south side of Canvey Island
About the Knock Buoy or from Southend Pier down strean
the whitebaiters annually get some in their stow-net during th(
course of the winter season's fishing. Among others we ma:
allude to one caught in 1875, 5 feet long and from 30 t(
40 lb. weight; another, a female, 4 feet long, with the ovar:
apparently ripening, 24th November, 1899.

More seawards, mention is made by Donovan (Brit. Fish
of a Conger weighing 130 lb. captured at the Nore. One wa
shot, of 30 lb. weight, from the seawall, Foulness Island
February, 1894. Another, 6 ft. and quite 40 lb., was found hig]
and dry on the Saltings, Foulness, after the great storm 27t]
November, 1897. Those fishers who frequent the Shoebur:
Swins and Guts say they have not come across Congers; but a
the Maplin Lights a smack spratting there caught one 9 f(
long = 60 lb., in mid-December, 1887, which they sold to ;
Clacton boatman (Mr. Gregson). Nor are the Congers infrequen
on the North Kentish coast, a well-known spot being the rock
near Broadstairs. They also visit the Blackwater, to wit on
6 ft. = $\frac{1}{2}$ cwt., and a second upwards of 30 lb., both caugh
mid-December, 1887. Just previously, on the 26th October, :
Conger of 37 lb. weight was secured up the river at Beeleigh
Maldon. One weighing 20 lb. was found on the hard leadin;
to Northey Island, December, 1897. Another, about the sam(
size, was caught in the brackish water at Beeleigh the sam(
week (Fitch). At Clacton-on-Sea a specimen of 40 lb., an(
one $31\frac{1}{2}$ lb. were found beached in January, 1885, and December
1887, respectively. The above cases show they are at interval;
to be met with in these neighbourhoods, the same being the cas(
on the rocky ground near the Naze (Harwich).

As to their food, those we have had an opportunity of ex

amining contained small fish, chiefly Clupeoids; other observers elsewhere have found quite a variety of round and flat fish, besides squids, crabs, and soft parts of whelks, &c. On the S. Kent coast Congers are caught by long bulter-lines, tough wire hooks, strong "beckets" (snood-fastenings), which oft-times have to be cut when hooks are difficult of extraction. The large fish are landed by gaff.* Congers' air-bladders are remarkably susceptible to get blown during heavy frost and snowy weather, and cases have occurred at the Thames mouth, and off Kent and Sussex, where enormous quantities of these fish have fallen an easy prey to the fishermen. Among others, a Folkestone boat in January, 1855, brought in 800 thus affected by the cold, and at this date some 80 tons fell to the lot of the Hastings fishermen. (Buckland.)

We reserve remarks on their breeding till treating of the next form.

(2) The River, Common or Silver Eel of Leighmen is said to be exceptionally numerous on the Blyth in spring and early summer. Presumably they are then migrating up stream, or congregating preparatory to ascent from the marshy Egypt and St. Mary's Bays (Kent) or other brackish water inlets on the opposite (Essex) bank. Those then caught in the trawl chiefly range 4, 6 to 12 inches long. The whitebaiters take some in their stow-nets, seldomer in drag-net.

There are no regularly employed eel fishers at Leigh, but a few individuals go a-fishing in flat-bottomed punts, partly for sport. Some of their catch they sell, the remainder they use at home. Up river eel fisheries are well known; the Thames, indeed, has always been celebrated for its eels up to London and far beyond.† The Dutch eel "schuyts" make Holehaven their headquarters, and send to their boats, moored off Billingsgate,

---

* Big Congers are most powerful and by no means easy fellows to tackle. Buckland's version runs :—"terrible things to bite sure-ly," and the Folkestone 8 ft. one *supra*, kicked up "mags' diversion" in the boat and nearly got out again. An old fisherman assured Mr. Fitch they at times would fiercely rear up on deck and "bark" at you.

† *See* "Gleanings in Natural History," articles by Jesse, Dr. Roots and Yarrell.

such quantities as market needs require. The Hadleigh Ray, the Swatchway, the Run—and the Rye—guts, &c., near the W. Shoebury Buoy, are all attractive eel haunts. The same may be said of the Medway and the Swale, as well as the opposite shore, viz., Foulness creeks and channels connecting therewith from Havengore to the Burnham river. They are so plentiful in the Blackwater that, as Dr. Laver remarks, " Trawling for eels is there quite a paying business." Within the Hamford water is also said to be good eel ground. Buckland states* the common eel is numerous in the mud of Folkestone harbour, and he gives reasons for believing they breed there, likewise in the military canal near Hythe.

We have only imperfect information regarding eel migration, their reproduction and rate of growth in the Leigh neighbourhood. It would seem the adult breeding eels that descend the river in the autumn do not all pass seaward as conjectured, at least in so far as the following case illustrates. In the fall of 1896 two Leighmen (Kerry and Outing) suspected eels lay in a hole at Scurry's Gut (Blackpoint Piles), east end of Canvey Island. The spot in question was where the great storm of 1881 broke down the sea-wall ; afterwards it was daily overflowed at high tide, the pit being remnant of the old inner ditch. During ebb, neap tides, the men proceeded to bale out the water with buckets, and at last came to quite a colony of eels. Some were large, others smaller, but 2 feet and over was a common length. Suffice to say some 3 cwts. were obtained and carried off in sacks. These were disposed of in Leigh and London. Altogether £5 was made out of the transaction. Most of those sold in Leigh fetched 6d. per lb. Infilling of sand has since partially destroyed the pit. Mr. B. Baxter has told us his father, in 1875, obtained some 10 to 12 gallons of large (breeding ?) eels out of a gut-hole below Southend Pier. He himself once came across a similar congregation in a hole near Shotley, River Orwell, not far from Harwich. Query—might these form breeding holes or are spawning grounds hard by ?

---

* "Curiosities of Natural History," 2nd Ed., 1860.

Concerning dimensions, about 2 feet 4 inches has been the maximum length within our ken in Leigh catches, though there are many records of their attaining twice that elsewhere. The minimum has been 4 to 6 inches in the "bait" boxes. But the

FIG. 17.

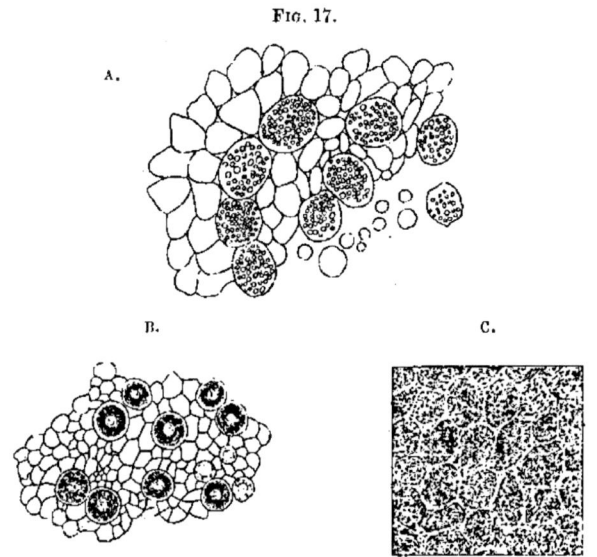

A.—Thin slice of an immature ovary of the Silver Eel as seen under the microscope. B.—Similar section of that of the Conger.

In A. the layer of fat-cells (shown in white) form the main mass, and distributed among them circles dotted within represent the unripe eggs. In B. the same structures are shown of the Conger. (Both reduced after Cunningham's figs. in Jour. Mar. Biol. Assoc. II. for May, 1891.)

C.—Thin slice under the microscope of the male organ (testicle) of the Common Eel. The dark portions are the dotted sperm cells surrounded by white lines, which indicate the blood vessels. (Reduced after Syrski's fig. in Biol. Sec. Adriat. Sci. Nat. Trieste, 1875.)

average size most commonly taken are 1 to $1\frac{1}{2}$ ft. long; the weight of the latter $6\frac{1}{2}$ oz. or thereabouts. Here it may be noticed that the male eels seldom grow larger than the last mentioned size, the big ones hitherto having been all found

females by authorities who have studied the question. They are
not very fastidious in their diet. Shore crabs, fish eggs, small
fish, even their younger brethren or garbage of any sort, all
come alike. Instance, one caught 23rd May, 1891, outside the
locks, Heybridge Basin, near Maldon, which contained nine perch
and a rat. This eel weighed $2\frac{1}{2}$ lb.

Most persons having to do with fish and fisheries are still
under the impression that nothing is yet known of the procreation of the eel. It is assumed there is only belly fat where
the roe should be present. It is true that only within comparatively recent years has a flood of light been cast on the
subject. No wonder therefore it has not yet penetrated into
every nook and corner of fishing communities. The matter is
interesting as pointedly marking the slow progress of scientific
inquiry on what might be thought one easy of solution.*

Taken in a general sense the sexual organs of the Conger and
Common Eel are so similar to each other that separate notice
may be dispensed with. Usually in biggish eels there only
seem long strips of belly fat. Notwithstanding, the less prominent right and left ovary or the milt are present. The amount
of fatty tissue certainly is apt to deceive, particularly as a
matter of fact that the eggs themselves are so small as barely
to be perceptible to the naked eye, and in the immature fish
best demonstrated under the microscope. The accompanying
illustrations, Fig. 17 (A, B, C), may help to an understanding of
how the mass of fat cells (spaces in white) prominently surpass
the eggs (circles dotted within) in quantity. Hence comes it to
appear to ordinary vision that there are only long pieces of fat
in the eel's belly. The eggs themselves in the Common Eel are

---

* To those interested it may be enough to refer to data and summaries of the whole
problem by English writers, viz. :—Brown Goode, " Life Hist. of Eel," Bull, U. S. Fish.
Commiss., 1881 ; " Nat. Hist. of Aquatic Animals," in Fishery Industries of U. S., 1884 ;
Cunningham in Jour. Mar. Biol. Asso., Vols. I., III., IV., 1891-97 (several articles), and
his vol. " Market. Mar. Fish," 1896 ; McIntosh's " Brit. Mar. Food Fish," 1897 ; and
Williamson, "Reprod. of Eel," in 13th Ann. Rep. S. F. B. for 1894. With a few exceptions in England and America, it is to Continental workers belongs the main credit
of investigations thereon. Italian, German and French *savants* alike come to the fore,
among whom Benecke, Calandruccio, Delage, Grassi, Hermes, Jacoby, Möbius,
Mondini, Müller, Pauly, Rathke, Robin, and Syrski may be mentioned among a host of
others who have taken part in the elucidation of the puzzling question.

only $\frac{1}{4}$ to $\frac{1}{3}$ of a millimetre in diameter, and therefore little more
than pin-points. The Congers are somewhat larger, nearly
1 millimetre, or equal to pin's-heads in size. A Conger which
died in the Berlin Aquarium weighed $22\frac{1}{2}$ lb., the ovaries alone
8 lb., and it was calculated the eggs numbered over three
millions. The eggs of the Common Eel are given approximately
from five to ten millions by different authorities.

Fig. 18.

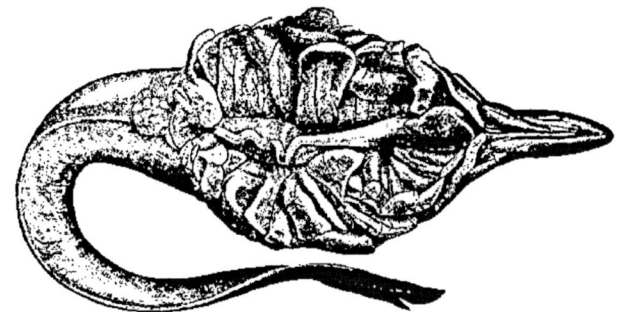

Silver Eel opened, at period well towards spawning condition. It
shows the liver, stomach and gut lying along the middle line, and the
belly flaps turned aside, covered by large lappets of the ovaries. (From
specimen 19 inches long when fresh, now preserved in the Hunterian
Museum, preparation No. 2,660 C.)*

To make out the sexual organs of the eel distinctly we have
found it best to examine a lean specimen, say over a foot long—
such a one as the whitebaiters take from mid-October to mid-
November. The absence of fatty tissue renders clearer defini-
tion of the parts. In the female the ovaries then appear as
long, flat, gelatinous-looking strips, sometimes somewhat scol-
loped. They pass back from opposite the liver, on either side
of the stomach and gut, to beyond the anus. The male sexual
organs lie in a similar position, but have more resemblance to

---

* This example of a nearly ripe female was originally described and figured by
Tegetmeir in *The Field*, 12th Dec., 1895. *See* also Cunningham's remarks " Maturity
of Common Eel," Jour. Mar. Biol. Assoc. IV, (1895-97)

a knotted string, or are lobed, and they are firmer in consistence and more shiny surfaced than are the ovaries. In the ripe or well-nigh mature female eel the ovarian fat is in a great measure absorbed, and the enormous ovaries then stand out as little more than a dense mass of eggs, forming great sinuous or frilled bands, almost filling the abdomen, the alimentary canal lying between them. Our Fig. 18 represents such a condition.

So far satisfactory that eels and congers do produce eggs and milt, and that their sexual apparatus to some extent conforms to that of other fishes. When we come to shedding of their spawn, whether that takes place in the sea, or whether, as others maintain, in the shallow, brackish waters, or in the sand, like the sand-eel, then the subject becomes obscure. Further, the development of eel and conger from egg to larval and post-larval stage still lacks desirable completeness.

Again, the translucent elvers and darker coloured young eels that migrate up the rivers in spring are perfect eels in their way ; but it has been suspected their earliest stage differed. *Leptocephalus* was the naturalist's name given to a small thin diaphanous fish (supposed adult) discovered in 1763, near Holyhead, afterwards elsewhere in Britain, the Mediterranean, and even Mid-Atlantic. Bearing considerable resemblance to the eel tribe, these Leptocephali, after much speculation and research, have been traced to be preliminary developmental conditions of the eel, conger and allies. The remarkable thing is that the thin, deep-bodied Leptocephalus decreases in dimensions ere acquiring eel and conger characters (*See* Fig. 19, A, B, C). This subject we need not pursue, but refer to the literature in preceding footnote.

Finally, it seems to us that our District, with its many eel haunts, affords ample facility to ascertain still dubious points. *Exempli gratiâ* :—What follows eels or congers spawning—their destruction or otherwise ? Opposite views have been expressed by experts. Yarrell states two eels from Sheerness, 18th May, appeared spent. Are there Leptocephali in our estuaries ? H. Wilder acknowledges more than once coming across little, transparent, ribbon-shaped, eel-like fish in the Thames mouth.* Whether congregation of eels in holes points to hibernation or breeding purposes ? *Antea* Kerry and Outing's incident. Are there eel-spawning grounds within our area—where ? These doubtless are scientific queries, but they tend towards more practical matters connected with our fisheries, of which more hereafter.

FIG. 19.

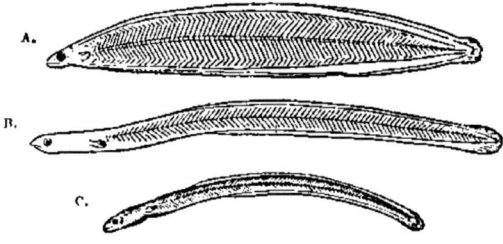

Assumed development of the Eel.

A. So-called *Leptocephalus.* B. Transition stage or half-eel. C. Young eel (or elver). All natural size. (McIntosh after Grassi.)

The Sturgeon Family (*Acipenseridæ*).—Within Kent and Essex waters the COMMON STURGEON (*Acipenser sturio*) once had high repute, the Thames and Medway being then noted for the frequent visits of this Royal fish.† When these rivers became polluted its advent slackened. It is rather rare around S. and E. Kent, the nature of the ground less suiting its

---

* Here special reference may be made to A. Scott's interesting " Observations on the Occurrence and Habits of *Leptocephalus*," in Rep. Lancashire S. F. Laboratory for 1898. He clearly establishes their presence in numbers in the mud-flats at Rod Island (Piel Sea-Fish Hatchery) near Barrow. Our Thames grounds closely resembling the above gives strong probability of Leptocephali being about.

† The Corporation of the City of London's claims of jurisdiction over the Thames fisheries to its mouth goes back to 1197—when Richard I. sold the rights to the citizens on their raising money to enable him to enter on the Crusade in Palestine—excepting the interval when the power temporarily was delegated to the Company of Free Fishermen of the River Thames, 1680–1780; but the Corporation retained their rights up to 1856, when these were passed by Act of Parliament to the Thames Conservancy. The subjoined is an edict early issued by the Corporation : " You shall further inquire what Royal Fishes have been taken within the Jurisdiction and Royalty of the Lord Mayor of London, as namely, Whales, Sturgeons. Porpoises, and such like, and to present the Name and Names of all such persons as shall take them to the Lord Mayor of London for the Time being."

proneness for rummaging in muddy spots. But a few ascend the smaller rivers and inlets from the Thames to the Suffolk border.

At Thorpe-le-Soken, which has a narrow communication with Hamford Water, a small-sized one was taken in July, 1864 (Bree). One is chronicled as taken in the Colchester Channel, May, 1700, being 8 feet 4 inches long and weighing 194 lb. The Blackwater seems a favourite haunt, witness a specimen secured near Beeleigh Mills, Maldon, and figured by Donovan ; this weighed 131 lb. Another, conjectured to be 1½ cwt., was captured alive at the Point between Heybridge Basin and Maldon, 9th May, 1886 ; afterwards exhibited in the Basin lock with a rope round its tail and hauled up to view at 1d. a head. Still another, a female scaling 212 lb. and 7 feet 11 inches long, was hauled out of the "Smack Hole," directly opposite our Chairman's residence, close to Maldon, 15th May, 1890 (Fitch, Ess. Nat. IV.). A. Sexton caught one very near the same spot, 6th June, 1898. Seen alive (by Fitch), length 7 ft. 6 in., weight 192 lb. In the Cronch river, August, 1891, a dredgerman spied a Sturgeon near Cliff Reach, Burnham. A loyal subject in 1879 sent to Her Majesty the Queen, 21st June, a Royal fish 7 feet 9 inches long, and weighing 132 lb., which he had shot in the Medway above Maidstone Bridge. Dr. Day (Brit. Fish) figures a specimen 5 feet 4 inches long obtained by the Margate fishermen.

The smallest Thames one we know of was only 9 in. long from eye to tip of tail, and was caught by T. Howlett while angling at Charlton, near Woolwich, June, 1880.* Near Westminster Bridge in May, 1867, two boatmen landed one 7 feet long and 60 lb. weight. At the International Fisheries Exhibition, July, 1883, we saw a Sturgeon which had been captured by some workmen off Erith as it floated down stream in a stupified condition.† H. Mellish captured in Limehouse Reach, Medway, Rochester, a sturgeon weighing 130 lb., and

---

* *The Field*, 9th April, 1881.   † Harting, Zool., August, 1883.

measuring 7 ft. 6 in. in length, 17th April, 1868 (Zool., 1868). Many Thames fish of 5, 6 and 7 feet have been noted at various times. Two Leigh whitebaiters say they have come across small sturgeon-looking fish which others called sterlet ; but their meagre account leaves the matter in doubt.

As to their migrations, they seem most often to go right up the rivers during early summer to autumn, some being in spawning condition. Hence the estuary trawlers seldom come across them. What they feed on in our waters is not certain, the stomach being often empty, though minute crustaceans have been found. In captivity they freely eat lobworms. The finding of diminutive fish made Dr. Bree inquire whether they bred in our rivers rather than migrate from the Danube. As they are found in the North Sea, Elbe and Baltic, the presence of young with us receives easier solution. Fishmongers make a show of Sturgeon ; how few have tasted their flesh. Truly the taste of the populace has altered since Kings and Aldermen gloated over Sturgeon and Porpoise. Valuable indeed are the Sturgeon fisheries of Russia, their great home. As sole living representatives of the thick armour-clad Ganoid Order of fishes in our country, with shark-like tail, sucker for mouth and gristly spine, they are well worthy of inspection.

The Shark and Ray groups (*Plagiostomata*).—Although some families in these groups are met with at times in numbers within our Committee's District, yet neither group, as a whole, yields so much, in a mercantile sense, as might be anticipated from the amount of catch. Several of the Sharks are but rare visitors, and the Rays are seldom got in such profusion as permanently to engage the attention of the fishermen with profit. Still the Dungeness, Folkestone and Margate fishermen make good hauls in the summer months.

The Sharks.—Among these strange forms suffice first to mention the remarkable—

(1) HAMMER-HEADED SHARK (*Zygæna malleus*) which was captured by the Dover fishermen in that neighbourhood in

1887 (Webb). Its priority of a Kent visit appears in Boys' "Fishes of Sandwich," 1792. (An Ilfracombe specimen, 1865, contained two thornbacks and a bass.)

(2) The long-tailed THRESHER SHARK (*Alopias vulpes*) has been captured several times around Kent (Boys noted it 1792). One was taken off Folkestone in October, 1867. It measured 13½ feet, the tail alone 6 feet 10 inches, and it weighed 3¾ cwt. It contained 27 mackerel. A second, 4 feet long, was secured by the Folkestone fishermen in June, 1868, and still a third got entangled in their herring-nets in October, 1869, which measured 14 feet 10 inches long. Nineteen mackerel and two herrings were found in its stomach. A 12 feet long example the Walmer fishermen were successful in taking, 24th October, 1882. Tales of its great fights with enormous whales have been often told; but some authorities are inclined to think there has been error of observation, and credit the Killer Whale (*Orca*) as the more probable deadly aggressor.

(3) Another species which attains considerable dimensions when fully adult is the PORBEAGLE SHARK (*Lamna cornubica*). This in fact is a pretty constant annual summer or autumn visitant to the Kent coast, and more irregularly off Essex. A very fine example was exhibited on a barrow in the streets of Dover, October, 1889. The crew of a Folkestone fishing-boat had secured it with difficulty after doing great damage to their nets. It was 9 feet 3 inches long, and weighed 4½ cwt. This and the Long Sand specimen *infra* must have been nearly full-grown.* In September, 1867, a specimen, 8½ feet long, was caught by the Margate fishermen in a mackerel-net. In 1874, some Essex fishermen took one 8 feet 2 inches long and nigh 20 stone weight. Again, 20th October, 1892, near the Long Sand Light, a Shoreham boat fishing for mackerel took to their surprise instead a Porbeagle nigh 10 feet long and about 5 cwt. This they exhibited at Harwich. On 8th December of the same year a male 7 feet 10 inches long was secured in the Colne estuary, opposite the Martello Tower.

---

* South-Eastern Naturalist, Vol. I., 1890.

In the above cases of the Porbeagle the second mentioned was mounted for the British Museum; but as a rule nothing is made of the body other than as a show by the fishermen. These sharks are fierce, and appear to have a partiality for their brethren, the dog-fishes, though not loth to other booty, such as the cod-fish family and large cuttle-fishes.

(4) The Common Tope (*Galeus vulgaris*) is an example of the Shark tribe, which may be said to be widely distributed in our District, and always with us. When full grown it may reach 6 or 7 feet long or over. Generally speaking such magnitude is now rare in the Thames estuary, though when Long-lining in the Deeps was in vogue large fellows were by no means infrequent. In Essex they are known locally as " Dogs " or "Sweet William,"* in South Kent as "Rigs," in Sussex as " Penny Dogs." The Varne Bank is said to be a favourite and noted locality by the Folkestone fishermen, who use hooks and long-line, and capture a great many.†

In past times the Leighmen hooked them mostly in the E. Swin and from the Sunk Light, south-west along the Black Deep. Though the Long-liners pursued their cod and skate fishing through the winter, yet it was not till the end of March or beginning of April that they were troubled with the "Dogs." Then there seemed a wonderful lot of them, and it was an everyday occurrence to hook some of all sizes.‡ When hauled in the big ones especially had their throats cut, the liver extracted, hook disengaged, if possible, portion of skin kept to make deck scrubbers, and the fish then thrown overboard. Within later years the Topes' head-quarters aforesaid are seldom fished, and the old hook and line tackle being out of date with Leighmen the larger " Dogs " seem scarce. Nevertheless

---

* Pennant (Brit. Quad.) thus accounts for this name :—Its skin and flesh have an offensive rank smell, therefore we suppose Mr. Dale (Hist. Harwich) gave it ironically the title of " Sweet William."

† *See* Buckland's droll account of Folkestone fishermen's experiences with " Rigs " when fresh caught, and a number lying in the bottom of the boat.

‡ R. Johnson, senr., mentions their capture was not always confined to spring, he himself having caught as many as a hundred between November and December in the neighbourhood of the Swin.

the trawl perchance brings one up now and again, more often small-sized specimens.

Thus we find them in the Crouch mouth, the entrances of the Blackwater and Colne, and up the Thames to about Southend Pier. One 16 inches long a shrimper netted in the Leigh Roads, 12th September, 1898; it had a belly-full of crabs. Such another was taken in the Crouch, July, 1890; shrimps and crabs being also its diet. About 1847 a 9 feet long specimen was caught in Mayland Creek, Blackwater, which fetched only 3s. 6d. The brothers Wright secured one off Stansgate, 3rd June, 1898; it was 4 feet 10 inches long, and weighed 84 lb. Still another was taken by them only 1 inch shorter on 20th August, 1898. (Fitch.) On 23rd October, 1886, a large one was taken by a trawler in the Wallet, and thereafter exhibited at Colchester. (Laver.) A female 4 feet 9 inches long was captured in the Colne mouth, near Brightlingsea, August, 1888, and another female $5\frac{1}{2}$ feet near Clacton Pier, 1st November, 1888. At irregular intervals small ones from 1 to 3 feet long turn up in the neighbourhood of the Gunfleet and E. Swin. The fishermen are well aware of its producing young alive. It is not usually eaten as food among the estuarine populace; but a small one caught by a Leigh trawler just before the August Bank Holiday, 1899, we traced to a fried fish shop in the outskirts of Southend.

(5) The Smooth Hound (*Mustelus vulgaris*) or Skate-toothed Dogfish bears considerable resemblance to the Tope; differing however in relative position of the fins and in dentition. The teeth are flat, forming a tesselated plate, as in the skate. It is a ground feeder, like the Tope, and consumes crustacea and shell-fish, to which the rasping nature of the teeth peculiarly fit it. It is chiefly found in the Channel and Kent coast; we have but seldom met with it in the Thames estuarine area, and then only of small size. Full-sized, it reaches a length of 4 or 5 feet; so far as we are aware, not used as food in our District. It brings forth its young alive.

There are several of the smaller Dog-fish which the fishermen in a general way distinguish as " Nurses." The three best known are :—(6) The Picked Dog-fish (*Acanthias vulgaris*), notable for possessing a spine in front of each back fin ; hence the sobriquet " spur-fish " and " bone dog " of Kentishmen. (7) The Small-spotted Dog-fish (*Scyllium canicula*) called " Huss " or " Hussie " by the Folkestone fishermen. Boys (*op. cit.* 1792) names it " Cat-fish " or " Bounce." (8) The Nurse Hound or Large-spotted Dog-fish (*S. catulus*), the " Bull Huss " of Folkestone, and to which Buckland and Day also give " Bounce " as a local name.

These three species of Dog-fish appear chiefly to frequent the two extremes of our District, more particularly the neighbourhood of the rocky ground and deep water thereabouts. At Dover it is said the fishermen only bring them in when other saleable fish are scarce. " They command a price of a few pence amongst the poorer community, whereas forty years ago they were seldom eaten, but simply destroyed as enemies of the mackerel and herrings " (Webb). " The small fish-dealers (hawkers) may be seen cutting off their heads, tails and fins, and splitting them into halves ; they are then salted and hung out to dry, and taste when broiled like veal chops " (Buckland). Even " Folkestone Beef " has become a byeword for the flesh of the Huss and the Rigs.

The Leigh people never seem to have used them as food ; when caught, if of fair size, they were skinned and the carcass " chucked " overboard. The skin was afterwards used for polishing various objects. Occasionally a fish might be taken to a friend or sold at Harwich. These dog-fish pestered the fishers during the long-line fishing season, which lasted from spring to autumn. The places where generally obtained were in the neighbourhood of the Cork Light, or towards the north end of the E. Swin and from thereabouts towards Harwich. But they seldom came across any from the above area south to the Thames mouth, though sometimes extending their fishing close

L

to the Queen's Channel or tracks around. Some days the trawl would bring up a few, others without any, or again an odd one at intervals. The Harwich local line-fishers, equally with the Leigh men, would occasionally be sorely troubled with them on their hooks.

They seemed to feed chiefly on the Pink Shrimps (*Pandalus annulicornis*), though fish and worms found a place in their dietary. The sizes of these large and small Spotted Dog-fishes most often met with varied from 6 to 18 inches, seldom more, though these fish grow to twice that size. These last three Dog-fish are oviparous (egg layers), and do not produce live young. About midsummer the horny egg cases, or "pixy-purses" have been observed floating about, and ofttimes are carried by the currents or driven ashore at Herne Bay and other parts of the Kent shores.

There are two large species of Sharks which we mention with considerable reserve as visitants of the Kent coast. First, the Basking Shark (*Selache maxima*), which Boys names in his "Sandwich Fishes, 1792;" but as he omits the Porbeagle, which makes its appearance yearly, we doubt his identification in this instance. The same may be said of a supposed White Shark (*Carcharias lamia*), taken August, 1867, near the Reculvers. What this last may have been we cannot say.

(9) The last to mention of the Shark group is the ANGEL-FISH (*Rhina squatina*), which only is known at Leigh as the "Fiddler," though in S. Kent (and Maldon*) it goes by the name of "Kingston," elsewhere as the "Monk-fish," &c. While combining attributes belonging to the Shark tribe, its squat, broad form and various other characters resemble much those of the flat skates and rays, hence it may be regarded as a bridge joining the latter with the former.

The "Fiddlers" are got all round the Kent coast in moderate quantity, but Webb regards it as somewhat of a rarity just at

---

* "Kingston Fish" is an old Maldon name, *see* Salmon's Hist. of Essex, 1740, p. 426. "Kingston" also appears to be a local Sussex name, *cf.* Day, Brit. Fish, II., 327.

Dover. It is not a common fish in the Thames estuary, in one sense, though there are seasons when it is very frequently got in the trawlers' nets. In 1893 they were unusually plentiful during the summer months in the neighbourhood of the Oaze, Girdler, Gilman, and so-called S. Channel generally. From June till August there were few boats but had examples among their other catch, and some of the specimens were of large size. For instance, C. Kelly, in June, obtained a female quite four feet in extreme length, and there escaped from this nineteen young live full-formed fish, each nigh a foot long. On 17th August, J. Noakes procured several in his few hauls, these ranging from 3 feet to 4 feet long. On the same date R. Johnson took a male measuring 2 feet long and 13½ inches diameter where broadest. Again, he got another smaller female specimen on the 26th August when shrimping near the Oaze. In short, at various times Monk-fish have been taken from 1 foot to 5 feet long, the longest of which were reckoned as weighing considerably over half a hundredweight—their breeding season (as above mentioned) apparently occurring about midsummer. They seem not to visit the estuary during winter or early spring, and apparently take more to Kent side; some have been got as high as the Jenkins (W. Nore Sand Buoy), never beyond the Yantlet. In 1899, and again in 1900, they have been quite as numerous; the latter year most frequent during August, September and the first weeks of October.

Those examined by us showed decidedly their preference for fish, the staple forms being whitings and whiting-pout. Even in some, where the alimentary canal contained apparently only yellowish-brown glutinous substance, the presence of innumerable lenses of fishes' eyes revealed the true nature of their diet. A few people use their flesh, but not many, for the hawkers, though they try, cannot always dispose of them. Dr. Laver considers it too rank in flavour for his taste, but something depends on the age of the fish and mode of cooking. Undoubtedly there is a strong ammoniacal flavour from the fresh fish, especially the large ones.

The Skates and Rays.—These together come under the family *Raiidæ*, whereof the first comprise the long-snouted species (= Skates) and the second the short-snouted series (= Rays). In addition, there are two other allied families, the *Trygonidæ* and *Myliobatidæ*, whose representatives will be mentioned in due course.

Long-snouted Group (= Skates).

(1) The SKATE (*Raia batis*), true or typical Skate, is widely distributed in our District, but there are places where the adults seem to congregate in greater numbers during certain seasons. The large-sized, marketable fish, as a rule, keep to the deeper water. Among the most fertile grounds for them on E. and S. Kent are the off-shore channels and sandbanks. some of these even beyond the international limits. In shore, however, lesser and moderate-sized fish pertain, *e.g.*, near Ramsgate, Deal and Folkestone to Dungeness.

On the Essex borders there is considerable similarity of the on-and-off shore distribution ; but there is this to be said, that the numerous estuaries, the multiplicity of shifting sands, the number of swins, and altogether shallow water, may have a modifying influence on migratory habit. At all events, the fact remains that, half a century ago, even less, an important Skate. Ray and Cod fishery obtained from Leigh, which finally was abandoned as unprofitable, it being affirmed that the fish became sensibly diminished in numbers. This long-line fishing lasted from the beginning of November till March. At the commencement of the season it began in the Wallet, the boats gradually working northwards to abreast of Harwich, and afterwards southwards by way of the Deeps. For remarks concerning the failure of the Leigh Skate fishery *see* " Long-lining," sect. vi. At the very start Skates only were taken, and very rarely indeed thornbacks. The former continued to be hooked throughout the season, the great majority being far and away larger than the latter. Roughly speaking the biggest Skate would be 3 feet across, while the smallest might range about half that size. On rare occasions a bigger fish would be obtained; one exhibited at Gravesend in December, 1881, being 5 feet across (Day).

Whether the Skates migrate to deeper water during summer, after breeding, we may leave an open question, data to substantiate such a movement not being forthcoming. The same applies as to whether their numbers have again increased during the winter season, seeing there is now no long-lining from Leigh to judge by. Apart from the area above mentioned, and taken in a general way, a line drawn from the vicinity of the Knock John, south and westwards, whence Skate of smaller dimensions, young and otherwise, are spread irregularly over the estuary to near the Nore. As, however, Skate are purely ground feeders and sand burrowers in their way, whilst hook and line are discarded, it follows that fewer are now captured by at least the Leighmen. The better class of fish indeed escape, for they are never taken in the stow-net, and only the smaller sort in the trawl-net. Such places as the neighbourhood of the Margate Sands, the Spaniards, or about the Oaze seem where they are most often met with. We may instance a day's fishing on the Oaze, mid-August, 1898, where skate were found, numerous but small. A few over a foot or so long, but the average 7 to 9 inches, body a little over half that, and proportionately broad.

The long-liners used to distinguish the Skate sexually as " he- " and " she-fish," and considered the latter (females) as much outnumbering the males. Their horny purses or egg-cases were now and again observed floating about during the early summer, whilst spawning was supposed to take place in the spring among the deep channels. The flowing tide and easterly winds would doubtless account for egg-cases up the several estuaries.

As to their food, the juveniles examined by us had chiefly shrimps and diminutive crustaceans, though the more adult besides had crab and fish remains. The Gravesend specimen (*supra*) had devoured a dog-fish 2 feet long, a young skate

and a lobster. When long-lining was pursued the big Skate
were despatched to Billingsgate by boat, or in the first of the
season sold at Harwich. Such Skate as are now got are
disposed of at Sheerness and Chatham, or Leigh, to the
hawkers, or are used by the fishermen's families. Off Margate
Ramsgate and Dymchurch neighbourhood eastwards are said
to be good Skate grounds.

(2) The rare FLAPPER SKATE (*R. macrorhynchus*), an intermediate form between the last and that which follows, is
recorded from Dover, but no memorandum of date or other
particulars are given (Webb).

(3) Of the WHITE SKATE (*R. alba*) Dr. Laver refers to
Lindsey as indicating its presence at Harwich. This may
be the case, although authorities acknowledge its extreme
scarcity on the S.E. coast, while it is more frequently found in
the English Channel, especially westerly. When old it is
allowed to be the largest form of British Skate. Its white
belly is a marked feature in contrast to the grey or bluish
colour of the abdomen of the Common Skate (*R. batis*). In its
young stages its back is orange tint, with a dark rim, hence
Couch called it the Bordered Ray; and it also goes by the
name of the Burton Skate.

(4) The LONG-NOSED SKATE (*R. oxyrhynchus*), whereof its
name denotes its prominent character, Webb mentions as among
the Dover fish fauna. This species appears to be entirely confined to deep water, and is reputed not to be taken during
winter. Nos. 2, 3, 4 it has not been our fortune to meet with
in the Thames area.

Short-snouted Group = Rays.

(5) The THORNBACK (*R. clavata*), familiarly known as the
"Roker" in our District, is a much more common species than
any of the preceding. As a rule it haunts the shallower waters
more than do the skates in general. Hence often captured in
the shrimpers' trawl almost at all seasons; this especially
during its early stages, so that apparent abundance may have

some connection with habit. In every nook and corner of our seaboard is it to be met with, and at times and places even swarming, notably where crustaceans and young fish overrun. In the Thames estuary its distribution is somewhat akin to that of the skate. It is scarcer on the Essex side, seeming to have a preference for the eddy currents towards Kentish Flats, Spaniards, so-called South Channel, &c.

As referred to above, when long-lining in the Wallet, &c., Rokers were few at the beginning of the fishing season, but as the sprats came about so did the Rokers multiply. They would then be from 18 inches to 2 feet wide, length in proportion, and more big than small ones. As an instance of a good catch, some 30 years back (1870 ?) in the Barrow Deep one morning, on 28 lines 190 great Rokers were hooked, besides several lines being lost through weight of fish on them. Most unfortunately "they fetched *no* money" (Tyrrel). As in the case of skate, females are in excess. Males from 1 foot broad upwards were spoken of as "Bashaw Rokers," a term in use at other fishing ports. The young till nigh half grown are recognised as "maids." These and the very small sort are got in considerable numbers below Southend Pier, where the brood of other fish congregate ; likewise on middle ground, Nore Sand. At these places they come in plenty in spring and early summer. On 10th May, 1898, when shrimping from the Girdler Buoy and Lightship back to the Gilman, quite a lot of Rokers were obtained. They ranged from 12 to 30 inches snout to tail end (the latter less than half the length), and breadth from 8 to 20 inches. As winter and cold weather approaches they hie to the deeper water seawards.

We have found their food to be similar to that of the skate. The men's statement is they feed "on all manners of things," *i.e.* sprats, plaice, dabs, crabs, &c., but not often shell-fish. The egg-cases are seen in summer, the quite young fish chiefly in autumn, the "maids" and fully adults

in the spring time. The spawning grounds seem rather in
the deeper waters. In the earlier times the marketable fish
were sent to London with the skate and cod. Nowadays
none go there. The larger ones are taken by the fish
trawlers to Sheerness and Chatham, and others with the
" maids " dressed or crimped are sold in Leigh and neighbourhood. The latter are reckoned quite a dainty. Indeed,
when the " wings " (pectoral fins) are fried, with egg and
bread-crumbs or batter, in boiling fat, they truly are delicate
sweet eating, very easy of digestion yet nutritious. What
the shrimpers capture and keep are brought to Leigh, and
either passed over to the hawkers or reserved for home
consumption.

(6) The HOMELYN or SPOTTED RAY (*R. maculata*) is got in
goodly numbers on E. and S. Kent, viz. : off the Goodwins,
Dover, and along Dymchûrch Bay, &c. It has not been
mentioned as among the fishes of Essex by Laver. But undoubtedly it inhabits the Thames estuarine area from the
Maplins eastwards amongst the Swins and Deeps, as also the
sands bearing towards Margate and the Kentish Flats. It was
well known to the Leighmen when long-lining, and regularly
hooked along with the skate, thornback and cod. There can be
no mistake as to its identity, for old hands have accurately
described to us its roundish shape, smooth and dusky spotted
back and other characters. Besides, it was and is still distinguished by name among them as the Homelyn. Those then
hooked varied in size from a foot to 18 inches wide or thereabouts ; therefore generally inferior in size to the skate and
" rokers " caught at the same time. Only the large ones were
sent to Billingsgate, and these altogether were not many. Of
the small ones the " wings " only were kept as a tit-bit for
the fisherman's family.

Young examples are reported as at wide intervals having
been got almost as high as the Nore ; but we have only seen
an odd small one in corroboration of their estuarine catch.

Evidently it is not so plentiful as the thornback and true skate. Our information as to the Homelyn's movements, food, reproduction and growth are meagre.

Fam. Trygonidæ.—The STING RAY (*Trygon pastinaca*) is known at Leigh as the " Fireslower," and in the Blackwater as " Festlaw " or " Fierce-claw," or " Fire-flare." The fishermen give it a wide berth when brought on board. The expression is, " It flies about terrific," and will dab its tail-spine through your boot—hence take care to stand clear. The first thing the men do is to chop off its tail. This fish is not eaten as food, but the liver is taken out and boiled for oil, the body being cast overboard. Occasionally the tail spine is cut out and used as a netting-needle, or for stringing flat fish together. The Sting Ray is not abundant in the Thames estuary, those taken being more frequently of small dimensions. These last in the spring months are no bigger than half to a palm's breadth, exclusive of tail. Around the Kent coast and at Burnham specimens $1\frac{1}{2}$ to 2 feet and more in diameter are not uncommon. Tho Leighmen are of opinion that they have decreased in numbers, but the evidence is not convincing, as tho fishing is now conducted differently.

At present the chief place where this Ray is found is among the Maplin Swins or in the Blackwater. It has been observed that ordinarily they are more numerous on the Essex rather than Kent shore of upper estuary. But its capture at Herne Bay and elsewhere shows they are not entirely absent on the Kentish side of the water, and we find it is represented about Dover and southern coast. Besides, Boys recognised it among his Kent fishes more than a century ago.

Fam. Myliobatidæ.—The EAGLE RAY (*Myliobatis aquila*) has a certain resemblance to the last, in having a tail spine, and long whip-shaped tail without terminal fin. The " wings " (pectoral fins) however extend out more wedge-shaped, and the head is distinct from the disk. Occasionally small specimens have been captured nigh Dover (Webb); it is got on the

Sussex coast; and Buckland (Brit. Fish) describes the purse or egg-sac of an Eagle Ray, obtained by the Margate fishermen. We are not aware of records of this fish from the Essex coast. A dead one was got on Lowestoft beach, June, 1867.

The **Lamprey Family** (*Petromyzontidæ*).—Of these we deal with two kinds—the sea and the river forms. Regarding Dover, "We have no Lampreys, or their allies," so says Webb. Whether this applies to the Kent seaboard generally we are unable to answer, but at least Boys, 1792, notes the Lesser Lamprey in Sandwich area, and most certainly they ascend the Medway.

(1) The SEA LAMPREY (*Petromyzon marinus*) seems more prevalent in the Essex waters. Dr. Laver* mentions two in the Colne to his knowledge. One, a fine specimen, was captured near Hythe, Colne river, close to Colchester. They are often taken at Fullbridge, Maldon, especially in spring. They go far up the Thames, Yarrell noting one taken in June, 1834, and another in June, 1835, near Sunbury Weir.

In early spring, as they leave the sea and ascend the river to breed, they are now and again met with in the Thames mouth by the trawlers and stow-boat fishers, but the period of their descent has not been observed. In 1878 a specimen 18 inches long adhered to an individual when bathing at Margate, the species being identified by Dr. Day. A white-baiter (Ben Emery) caught one over 2 feet long in his stow-net in April, 1899, below Southend Pier. He remarked that they had been pretty numerous for some weeks before then, though, unfortunately for our purposes, all were returned to the water, for the fishermen eschew them as food and do not use them as bait.

Albert Bundock, who formerly fished much up river towards Gravesend, states that they are very numerous beyond the Lower Hope later in the season, and that they, as well as

---

* Fishes of Essex, 1898, and Essex Nat. V. (1891).

examples of the River Lamprey, are there frequently taken in the drag-net.

(2) This latter, best known as the LAMPERN EEL (*P. fluviatilis*) among the Leighmen, or sometimes as the Silver Lamprey, is a common fish, though hereabout there is no Lampern fishery, and those accidentally caught are seldom landed. They are most frequently procured by the whitebaiters, presumably in their spring migration up river; for instance, among several got in 1899, one, a female not fully ripe, measured 13½ inches long; others a quarter that length the succeeding spring. But they are also taken later in the year, for example one caught in the stow-net by B. Bundock on 7th December, 1900, had a length of 14¾ inches, weighing 3½ ounces. The ovary was in a "pinky" stage of development, its food doubtful. Others about the same date were 12 and 13 inches long. Even bigger ones of both sexes got near Southend Pier, which were supposed by the fishermen to be in full breeding condition? Mr. Fitch says they are often seen in the Chelmer above Beeleigh Mill, after floods.

In the Thames they are found much more numerous higher up the river, and formerly there was quite a prosperous Lampern fishery to the west of London. Lampreys from the Thames and elsewhere are a prized bait of the Grimsby and other North Sea line fishers. Pennant (Brit. Zool. 1812) states that 100,000 had been sent to Harwich as bait for the cod-fishing, at that period in its zenith there. Yarrell considerably later (1841) mentions that "formerly the Thames alone supplied from half a million to twelve hundred thousand Lamperns annually." In the evidence before the Parliamentary Committee on Fresh Water Fish, 1878, reference is given of an individual securing 130,000 Lamperns in the upper Thames during one winter. In a single season a party received £400; and as much as £4,000 credited for annual numbers sold generally—the Dutch being the chief customers, using them for turbot bait, &c. In 1881-82 the Thames Lamperns were unusually abundant; but complaints were made (*Field*, January, 1882) that the fish seldom got further than Teddington, the fishermen there having a complete monopoly in numbers and prices, to the disadvantage of their Chertsey brethren. Females have been said to preponderate in mid-April; fish ready to deposit roe the end of that month, and all spawned by the middle of May.

Finally, we have observed in the Buckland Museum, S. Kensington, a bottle labelled Lampern Oil. This appears of a dark amber colour, but there is no information of whence obtained or of its use and market value.

SHELL FISH (MOLLUSCA).

The marine molluscan fauna of our District to a considerable extent bears relation—to the nature of the shore, to whether within the influence of the English Channel tidal phenomena or that of the North Sea, and to the amount present of brackish water in the estuaries. Contrast the chalk-cliff and seaweed rock pool shore of S.E. Kent, say with the Shoebury and Maplin Sands, and distinction is apparent. Even the muddy estuarine reaches present their quota of special residents. Among the innumerable invertebrate animals, *i.e.*, mollusks, crustaceans and other lower forms, including plant life, of our shores, it is deemed expedient in what is to follow only to refer to such few of them as directly bear on fishery questions.

EDIBLE SHELL FISH.

Oyster Family (*Ostreidœ*).—The OYSTER (*Ostrea edulis*) deservedly takes front rank as the bivalve of most importance within the Kent and Essex Sea Fisheries area. The Thames estuary's fame for its oysters still holds good, though the original natural beds have at times dwindled to the vanishing point. Probably the bank of oysters at the mouth of the Blackwater, so-called "Pont," dredged chiefly by the Tollesbury and Mersea fishermen, and the large area known as the

Kentish Flats, represent nearly the last of the freely fished natural beds. Even these may diminish in supply, for they are almost continuously worked on, and good spatting seasons are not too many.

FIG. 20.

OYSTER DREDGERS AT WORK ON NATURAL BEDS IN THE NEIGHBOURHOOD OF THE PONT.
Original Painting by HENRY A. COLE, 1897.
Reduced from Pl. X., "Essex Nat.," by permission of the Editor.

Small patches of self-sown native oysters may possibly here and there exist in the Swin or the Deeps; but if known no special dredging for them is carried on so far as we can learn. Occasionally a living oyster or oyster shells come up in the trawler's net, and the empty shells are not uncommon in the neighbourhood or outside of Margate sands; otherwise there is scant evidence of the oysters flourishing (other than in the cultivated beds) in its ancient haunts within the Thames estuary. The fact is like what has been proved to have happened in the once wonderfully productive Firth of Forth oyster scalps, where depletion has run so far that there is not abundance enough of full-grown oysters to multiply sufficiently and recuperate the destruction of spat and loss of young brood, under the ordinary or the untoward conditions which frequently arise.[*]

[*] "The Past and the Present Condition of the Oyster Beds in the Firth of Forth." Dr. T. Wemyss Fulton in Rep. F. B. Scot. for 1895 (sep. cop. 1896).

It is well known that after such seasons as have been deemed favourable for oyster spatting, a multitude of young brood and halfware are obtained in the neighbourhood of the cultivated oyster layings. Thus, for instance, the last few years back along the foreshore above Southend young oysters have been plentiful. Even on the pier piles there, and old wooden pier, Herne Bay, they have been found sparsely. Still more strangely, an oyster was met with developed in a sea-water tank, used for flushing, placed high up in the buildings at the end of Southend pier. Nor is this a solitary instance, for spat and young oysters have been found in the Hospital Tank, Roy. Sea-Bathing Infirmary, Margate, and in a large bath at Herne Bay.* In these cases the spat doubtless had been pumped up with the sea water, and the free-swimming larva, on finding a clean surface, settled and grew accordingly.

It may be added that the public grounds at the mouth of the Blackwater (= Pont), notwithstanding constant dredging, appear to continue fairly productive, rather by the timely floating thither from the cultivated Tollesbury, Mersea and Blackwater layings, and those of the River Colne and Pyfleet Creek, than entirely depending on the spawn shed within the natural oyster bed itself.† Again, around both east and west of the Whitstable Company's layings, and in particular on the Kentish Flats, young and matured oysters are obtained; and when a heavy fall of spat takes place, as it has done recently, it gives employment to many hundreds of fishermen. Some of these oysters in question are within easy distance of the cultivated layings, others much further off, a good deal depending on the state of the weather and tides at the time of the parent's spawning. Something similar on a smaller scale, with modifications, obtains on the Burnham River and elsewhere. These

---

* Henry Lee in *Land and Water*, May, 1871.

† An opinion also held by Fulton, Report cited. Buckland mentions conversely that the natural beds seaward of the Isle of Ré (France) furnish the spat which floats shorewards and enriches the oyster parcs.

scattered offsets of cultivation in the majority of cases grow and mature into a fine native oyster.

Varieties.—The oyster inhabiting the estuary of the Thames, or original native, is the *O. edulis*; but conchologists admit several varieties, differing in the nature of the shell. That known as var. *Rutupina** is distinguished by the neatness and regular oval shape of the shell. It was the oyster the Romans prized, and it is said still sparsely exists in a semi-cultivated state near Reculvers and towards Margate. There is a small shelled flat variety of a greeny-brown colour which is found occasionally on the backs of crabs or on shells—the var. *parasitica* of naturalists. Its stunted growth is doubtless attributable to defective nutrition from being carried about by its host and food consequently curtailed. Another larger variety, with coarser, thickened shell—conchologists var. *hippopus*—is little else than the deep-sea oyster of commerce. These two latter varieties are relatively rare at the Thames mouth, the last indeed trending beyond the territorial limits of the estuary.

Distribution.—Let us take a brief survey of the oyster's former distribution on our coasts, temporarily discarding the great oyster farming centres. Even at present there are beds of deep-sea oysters in the English Channel, to wit, near the Ridge and Varne Shoals. These are extra-territorial, but still furnish occasional dredging grounds for S. Kent fishermen.

The genuine Rutupian natives of the modern Pegwell Bay neighbourhood are a matter of ancient history, for Richborough and Sandwich no longer are sea-washed or oyster-bearing grounds. Seldom more than dead " valves " are now met with on the Shellness beach. Off the Margate Sands about the Wedge Buoy and Queen's Channel, small patches of natives now and again turn up. Here in 1870 a rather nice oyster bed was found ; but the news no sooner spread than 75 smacks from all

---

* Named from Rutupium (= Richborough), which during Roman occupation was the eastern fort guarding the then broad navigable channel leading into the Thames at the western fort Regulbium (= Reculvers), Thanet then being truly an Isle. *See* sketch maps, Gattie, " Memorials of the Goodwin Sands," 1890.

quarters flocked thither, and *presto* left the ground bare. On the flats more westerly of this, near the Spile, the Spaniards, and towards the Columbine, there formerly were spots where goodly numbers of genuine native oysters came up in the Leighmen's old form of shrimp-net. This latter dug more into the ground surface than does the beam trawl now in use. B. Baxter recalls times when he and his father went shrimping thereabouts that four gallons of prime natives would on occasions reward their toil. That the Kentish Flats in early times were quite natural and fruitful oyster beds is pretty certain, and what is now spat and grown there quickly assume the habit and flavour of the indigenous or true natives : for they are without a doubt the offset from the Whitstable beds.

The Cant edge, inside the Nore Lightship, even yet is strewn with old oyster shells, remnants of a prolific race once living there. So valuable was this shelly material for culch elsewhere, that at one time quite a fleet of smacks could be seen fishing it up. The amount may be conceived when each vessel would load with 150 to 200 tubs, and this continued daily for a considerable period. There was another oyster bed discovered about 1860 between the Cant and the Cheney Rocks (Sheppey), but this lasted a very short time, which sufficed to clear them out. The oysters at this place did not seem to be of native breed, but were composed of small Jerseys and stunted deepsea kind. Hence it was suspected they were derived from droppings of the Messrs. Alston's Channel fleet, which for a time had their headquarters hard by. The newly opened free oyster field was worked when these bivalves were unusually high priced, so a tub or so a day (= 3 pecks) worth from £1 1s. to £2, amply repaid the dredger's labours (Baxter).

Though coadjacent, we have the ancient Queenborough*

---

* We are indebted to our colleague, Mr. George Baxter, for the perusal of an elaborate but interesting report of a legal case (oysters) at Maidstone, 1823 : "The Mayor, Jurats, Bailiffs and Burgesses of the Borough of Quinborowe, in the County of Kent, *versus* Edward Skey" (Lond., 8vo, 1828). Therein evidence of the early rights and bye-laws as to oyster dredging, &c., and later troubles arising therefrom between the corporation and fishermen are given in full detail. The whole shows the great difficulty of satisfactorily adjudicating in fisheries questions. In this instance the defendant Skey gained the case.

fisheries between Swales Spitt and King's Ferry, whose Charters date 14th and 15th centuries. Adjoining (mid-Swale), the once celebrated Milton native beds, of repute since the time of King John. Eastwards, the Faversham grounds—these even going back to King Stephen, 12th century. Thus doubtless the Swale throughout was here and there the natural *habitat* of *Ostrea edulis*, the laying of brood and cultivation on restricted beds being subsequent in time.

What the natural oyster beds of the Medway may have been in early times we have no explicit data at hand to go by.

On the Essex side of the Thames, some of the oldest oyster-men recall in mind when self-raised native oysters were regularly taken in fair numbers inside the old Leigh-Middle, and on the Marshend side (Canvey) of the Channel. Within the Hadleigh Ray (during Mr. Plumb's lifetime), and before the latter was cultivated and worked as it now is, several old Leighmen managed to eke out a living by picking up at times four to five pecks of very saleable native oysters, from small self-reared brood, the whereabouts of which the men themselves only knew. Outside the extremity of the old Southend Pier there were within memory plenty of shells and live natives to be got. Now all this ground has silted. Again, from the Knock Buoy to almost as far as the Blacktail Swin, according to Baxter, were long strips of oyster shells, his inference being that these were the remains of former worked-out beds.

There are no records whatsoever of oysters living or thriving shorewards beyond the Blacktail Swin—say to Whitaker Spit—the clean sands on the coast there being inimical to them. There are those among the fishermen who also well remember native oyster patches in the Barrow Deep and around the Goldmer Gat and the Sunkend. At this latter spot, about 1860-70, the late Geo. Baxter's crews of his oyster craft are credited for clearing out a small bed accidentally hit upon there. Another find of self-reared oysters was inside of the Stone-Banks, betwixt the Naze and Harwich.

M

These, however, were described as altogether a poor lot, of little value. The neighbourhood of the Wallet has always been reckoned as every now and again, after good spatting seasons, to be a sure place to find small areas of indigenous native oysters. As to the Pont at the Blackwater exit, its constancy and prolificness have been phenomenal.

In 1900 there was a wonderfully great fall of spat inside (shorewards) of the Buxey, and some 50 sail were there in the autumn hard at work. It was reckoned they got about a "wash" to a man. A "wash" is equal to 4 gallons. Three men and a lad to each smack would earn say about 7s. 6d. each daily.

To sum up, it can be pretty surely affirmed that our indigenous oyster at one time was spread in banks here and there over all the area of the Thames estuary—taking this in its broadest sense (N. Foreland to seaward of Harwich)—besides holding once upon a time a footing in the now much altered Sandwich district. Its locations one by one unfortunately have been rooted out, till at last the Pont and Kentish Flats are about the only survivals. Thus, therefore, it behoves our Fisheries Committee to investigate their condition closely at intervals and carefully safeguard their utter destruction, alike in the interests of dredgermen and oyster cultivators. Most fortunately, meantime, several well known cultivated beds in both counties produce without a doubt the finest oyster in the world, and thus retain a perfectly legitimate hold on the mercantile public by their rearing under more favoured conditions the product of the Fisheries District itself.

Size.—Concerning the dimensions of our Native Oysters, we may take these as they are sold in Billingsgate, say 3 inches (or to be more accurate $2\frac{3}{4}$ inches by 3 inches) in diameters, represents an average size of the trade Natives. Primes range from 3 inches up to $4\frac{1}{4}$ inches in diameter, any larger may be reckoned rare in the ordinary market stock.

The public, however, demand a large full-grown oyster. Still, at times, odd ones do crop up, said to be nigh 5 inches length and breadth. These latter are quite old shell-fish which have got into nooks seldom dredged. Such examples the Thames shrimpers at rare intervals formerly routed up in their trawls in proximity to the Spaniards.* Genuine natives, doubtless offsets of the Whitstable layings. The very smallest of the marketable natives are $2\frac{1}{2}$ inches diameter, and seldom many of these; though a $2\frac{1}{4}$ inch one we have come across after much searching—a deep shelled little fellow full of meat and delicious in flavour.

Growth.—The annual rate of growth of oysters in the Pont natural bed is not known. Those on the cultivated layings around Kent and Essex may thus be summarized. Say spawned in July, in five or six months after they equal $\frac{1}{2}$ inch in diameter; the "brood" next season (first year) run from an inch and over; the "$\frac{1}{2}$-ware," or second season (17 or 18 months), $= 2$ to $2\frac{1}{4}$ inches, some more; "ware," or third season, $= 2\frac{1}{2}$ to 3 inches diameter, when many go to market; "full grown," or fourth season, fit for market, but more fit at the fifth or sixth year. But such calculations are liable to considerable fluctuations in their accuracy. This inasmuch as the temperature of the season, whether hot and calm or cold and stormy, with other subsidiary circumstances, have to be taken into consideration as to whether there be advance or retardation of growth conditions. Like other higher animals, constitutionally unequal, some of the sedentary oysters grow quickly, others slowly, or some may be more advantageously placed towards food sources. Even whether spatted early or late in the season tells considerably on their primary start in life. Besides, frequently a small but deep oyster will contain more flesh than a larger flatter shelled one. Hence size of shell is not always the criterion of goodness.

---

* In 1860, when with shrimpers in this neighbourhood, a monster oyster was brought up—one almost sufficient for a single meal.—J.M.

Food.—As to this, the contents of the alimentary canal presents quite an assortment of substances. The water currents simultaneously carry in sandy mud and extraneous matter along with the nutrient particles. These last are chiefly diatom and desmid-plants, seaweed spores, infusoria, foraminifera, along with minute larvæ of hydroids, worms, mollusks and crustacea. Most of these are so broken up as to be difficult to determine, but the diatoms and foraminifera with their hard silicious crusts are more readily identified. Such at least was the case in our examinations of oysters from Hadleigh Ray layings, diatoms being a prominent feature under the microscope. Indeed, nigh 60 years ago the Rev. J. B. Reade* found the oyster's stomach to contain (besides other material) close on 20 different species of diatoms. Many of these latter are forms of common occurrence in the Thames estuary.

As mentioned before, p. 15, in connection with Whitstable Bay and its matchless fattening grounds, our Thames mud flats swarm with lowly plant and animal organisms, fit food for the oyster family, and the sea water and shallow banks to the estuarine limits receive their quota of brackish water forms every ebb tide. The Mersea and Blackwater shores, Shenstone and Benham have shown, are equally fruitful of oyster food.† Sorby even goes further, and essays to prove in the case of Pagelsham and Brightlingsea that the variance in the growth and flavour of the oysters at those places bear relation to the amount of diatoms in the former and infusoria in the latter.‡ Previously he had pointed out the most extraordinary abundance of minor life in the Swale, Queenborough, the Medway generally,§ as well as the Lower Thames reaches. Shrubsole, a shrewd naturalist (formerly resident at Sheerness), regarded the oyster food of the Medway grounds as mostly diatomaceous;

---

* " On the animals of the chalk still found in a living state in the stomach of the oyster." Trans. Micros. Soc., Vol. II., 1849 (read Dec., 1844).

† Essex Nat. III. (1889). ‡ Essex Nat. X. (1897). § Rochester Naturalist, Oct. 1883.

though Dowker's* examination led him to think it chiefly foraminiferous in character. One thing stands out clear, viz., that there is no lack of pabulum for the oyster within our waters.

Resting Position.—This in oysters has been a keen source of controversy (*Field*, 1864). Some have maintained the right or flat valve downwards is their natural position, others hold an opposite opinion. Again, observers have found on natural beds the oysters sunk hinge down and the gaping free edges of the valves upwards. Furthermore, it has been asked—Does it matter which side they lie on? This is the experience of the oystermen of Southend foreshore and the Hadleigh Ray: that ·in 19 out of 20 cases the oysters are found resting on their flat shell;† but after boisterous weather —especially wind on-shore—many of the oysters may be seen thrown over, lying with the curved valve downwards (Baxter). F. Bridge further remarks that when noticed flat valve uppermost his men very often turn them the other way. Their notion is that when the curved shell is downwards, this more readily fouls by catching up the weed and other stray substances borne along by the ebb and flow of the tide. As to the Portuguese oysters, these as a rule bed themselves in the muddy sand hinge down, so that the gaping valves are alone freely subject to the streaming tides. Mr. Sibert Saunders, of Whitstable, a keen observer of marine creatures thereabouts, substantially endorses the Leighmen's views. He gives good reasons wherefore the opposite opinions of Huxley, of Cunningham and other authorities may each be so far correct under certain conditions. We may further add that Ryder assures us that in the natural banks of American oysters in the Chesapeake, they there "assume an approximately vertical position "—*i.e.*, similar to what occurs with the Portuguese breed in the Ray as above noted. This fact is interesting, inasmuch as the American *O. virginica* and

* *Land and Water*, Sept., 1880.
† Fulton's dredging in the Firth of Forth supports this view.

Portuguese *O. angulata* are bisexual, *i.e.*, male and female separate; whereas our natives (*O. edulis*) and deep-sea oysters (*var. hippopus*) are unisexual (=hermaphrodite).

Query—has this any relation to the difference in their habitual positions ?

Greening.—With regard to Green Oysters a good deal has been written, but we cannot do better than refer to Professors Herdman and Boyce's interesting compendium of the subject up to date, and their own researches, chemical and physiological, with deductions therefrom.* There is also a good repertory on Greenbearded Oysters given by Dr. Bulstrode in the Local Government Board Report.† The Roach River, as many are aware, is the most noted locality for the greening of oysters in our Fisheries District. Still, there is another place less known, Holchaven Creek, where Portuguese and East Rivers have greened remarkably the last two seasons, of which more hereafter (Chap. VI.—Oyster Dredging).

Weather influences.—Oysters laid in our shallow waters, creeks and flats are very sensitive to wind and weather. In dull, cold days, or rains and strong winds, they soon get out of order. Atmospheric changes, doubtless, affect their vitality. Besides, these conditions equally react on their microscopic provender, and, this diminished, the bivalves are impoverished. On the more exposed parts of our coasts, during storms and especially strong easterly winds (such as 1881), with low tides, like results ensue. In the beginning of 1879, and still more so in 1891, fatal frosts occurred ; nearly all stations lost heavily. In 1879 the seconds or inferior class oysters suffered most, particularly on the Kentish side and Colne, but " natives " and their brood held out fairly well.‡ In the Hadleigh Ray and at Whitstable Bay, February, 1895, the water froze right round

---

* Lancashire Sea Fisheries Memoir No. 1.—" Oysters and Disease," Lond. 1899, with coloured illustrations.

† 24th Ann. Report for 1894-5 Suppl., "On Oyster Culture in Relation to Disease," Lond. 1896.

‡ Coleman in *Land and Water*, February, 1879.

the oysters, and as the tide ebbed, many were carried right away down stream in the ice blocks. Then, with the unusual arctic winter, the loss was appalling everywhere on the Kent and Essex oyster grounds.

Though warm temperature has usually a beneficial effect on the fattening and generation of oysters, yet intense heat under certain aspects is sometimes the reverse of desirable. For instance, during midsummer "dog-days," with neap tides, those oysters long exposed on dry banks to the burning sun get out of sorts.

FIG. 21.

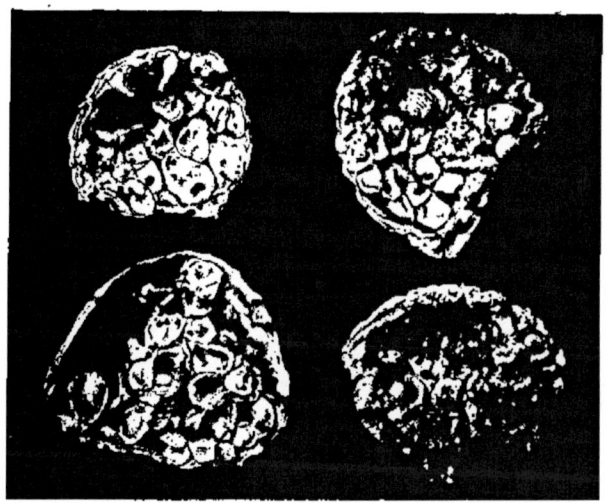

Specimens of fixed spat on oyster culch taken from the Whitstable beds, season 1900. Supplied by Captain Anderson, of Whitstable.

As to the bugbear organic pollution, there is this to be said, that without the bacteria therein developed, the "floating-spat" would have less chance of food, and the tiny oysters fixation. Living foes to the full-grown oyster are many, some of which will be noticed under their separate headings further on.

Fertility.—The breeding of the oyster (*O. edulis*)—whether indigenous natives or imported—within our Kent and Essex area presumably is of regular annual occurrence. No one we know of though has verified the fact of reproduction in the same individual oyster for several successive seasons. Such observation or experiment might be worth trial. Still, those oysterculturists of both counties who have given attention to the subject affirm that the great body of the adult oysters do spawn every summer. Some reckon that in favourable seasons 90 per cent.* " sicken "; but under adverse conditions consequently fewer. Intermissions of procreative capacity however are quite feasible. A constant annual fertility seems inconsistent with the long serial succession of complete failures in spatting seasons. Yet the two statements are not antagonistic, for breeding may be regular, counteracted sometimes by vast destruction of floating spat.

The prosperity of the Kent and Essex native oyster industry, particularly Whitstable, Burnham and Colchester, depends on the supply of native brood from the natural beds before mentioned, as well as the favoured spatting grounds of the Roach River and the Kentish Flats.

Spatting Seasons.—The irregularity and inequality of oyster spatting seasons within our District for the last half century is worthy of consideration. To this end we have searched through a number of sources,† in some only eliciting scraps of information, in others obtaining more definite data. It was sufficient though to indicate the uncertain distribution of fall at different places. For example, it might be fairly abundant in the Roach, less satisfactory in the Colne or in the Blackwater; and generally a good season on the Essex coast is a bad one on the Kentish side, and *vice versâ*. Omitting places and

---

* Prof. Möbius calculates on more accurate data, that in the Schleswig-Holstein beds only 44 per cent. bring forth broods of young oysters in the course of a summer. "Die auster und die Austerwirthschaft," 1877—transl. Rep. U.S. Fish Commis. for 1880 (1883).

† Among others the long series of *The Field, Land and Water, Fish Trades Gazette,* Board of Trade Reports, Parliamentary Papers, &c.

quantities, we have reduced the complex matter and a lengthened table to the simpler form given below.

TABULAR VIEW OF 55 OYSTER SPATTING SEASONS WITHIN KENT AND ESSEX WATERS.

Year.	Spat.	Year.	Spat.	Year.	Spat.	Year.	Spat.
1846.	Moderate.	1860.	Bad.	1874.	Moderate.	1888.	Moderate (?).
1847.	,, (?).	1861.	,,	1875.	Good.	1889.	,, (?).
1848.	,, (?).	1862.	,,	1876.*	,,	1890.	,,
1849.*	Good.	1863.	,,	1877.	Moderate.	1891.	,,
1850.	,,	1864.	,,	1878.	.,	1892.	,,
1851.	Bad.	1865.	Moderate.	1879.	Bad.	1893.*	Good.
1852.	,,	1866.	,,	1880.	Good.	1894.	,,
1853.	,,	1867.	,,	1881.*	,,	1895.	,,
1854.	,,	1868.	Good.	1882.	,,	1896.	,,
1855.	,,	1869.	Moderate.	1883.	Moderate (?).	1897.	Moderate.
1856.	,,	1870.	,,	1884.*	Good.	1898.	,,
1857.	Moderate.	1871.	Good.	1885.	Moderate (?).	1899.	,,
1858.	Good.	1872.	Moderate.	1886.	,, (?).	1900.*	Good.
1859.*	,,	1873.	,,	1887.	,, (?).		

The asterisks indicate the very good, unusual years; the notes of interrogation where information has been defective or contradictory. This table may be regarded as only of a tentative kind, not meant as absolutely correct. It is to be hoped defects may be remedied, for the archives of the oyster companies and notes of private individuals may supply information not accessible to the reporter.

Taking these data for what they are worth, it would appear that during 55 years, 12 of them were seriously bad spatting seasons, either very poor falls or amounting to little short of a total failure at nearly all the stations. With an intercalation of three years 11 ran in succession. Hence occurred the alarm and wail of dredgers, merchants and companies, even the public generally, during the fifties and sixties. Of moderate years there were 26. Among these at some stations the fall was better than at others, that is to say unequally distributed. The really good years numbered 17. Those of 1849, 1859, 1876, 1881, 1884, 1893 and 1900 were quite remarkable almost at every station in both counties.

Why variations in Spatting Seasons.—This abundance and scarcity only partially fits Buckland's cycles or periodicity in the fall of spat. It demonstrates, however, that the moderate years (nigh half) far and away preponderate ; besides that, the good seasons are in excess of the bad ones. Those persons interested in the oyster industry some time ago justly harped in the press on the terribly distressing years between 1851–64, with ofttimes allusion to the bright interval 1858–59. Excepting for 1879, there has been annually fair falls of spat in some portion of our District, and even a dozen good ones, equivalent to a third of the interval. All this may be interpreted that, despite the outcry of the run of bad seasons 1851–64, spatting more often takes place with tolerably regular recurrence and on the whole favourable.*

That overfishing has been a prime moving force in the production of poor spatting, which some have maintained, hardly tallies with the course of things. So far as we are aware, the dredging for brood within our District has not materially altered for over a century. This doubtless does not apply to the English Channel natural beds of adult oysters, which were mercilessly swooped clean up by great fleets of smacks from all quarters some 50 years ago. Even Buckland and Wiseman's theory of " heat and tranquility " only partly accounts for poor spatting seasons. For example Dr. Bree mentions that in 1869 and 1871 (*The Field*), at Mersea and elsewhere, with one of the coldest of Junes, fair spat ensued.

Most probably a combination of agencies, and not one cause alone, determines the oyster's fertility, and more essentially the quantity of spat that gets fixed. That meteorological conditions at the time of spatting is one, may be taken for granted. Though, as Möbius (*op. cit.*) has pointed out, something may also depend on the condition of the parent oyster at the time

---

* Curiously enough in France the spatting between 1851–56 was at its lowest ebb. The well-known successful experiments of Prof. Coste, 1858–59, happily coincided with good spatting seasons, there as in our District. Then a few succeeding years there was temporary decline and bitter disappointment, when the trial artificial beds of St. Brieuc were virtually destroyed by inclement weather. This corresponded nearly to our bad spats 1860–64. Since 1865, with a long run of passable seasons, better results have followed in the French endeavours, though, as admitted by M. DeBon,* the artificial breeding of oysters can scarcely be successful excepting in the neighbourhood of the natural spawning beds. (*Ostreiculture en, 1875—Revue Maritime et Coloniale. Paris, 1875.)

of sickening. If poorly nourished prior to the generative act, the result will be less productiveness, irrespective of the weather at the immediate spawning time, and *vice versâ.* In our District tides have to be accounted for. Whilst the flow carries "floating-spat" shorewards, our ebbs being stronger conversely carry quantities of this to sea, beyond chance of fixation on the natural beds, and therefore to be totally lost.

The Roach layings have long been noted as in advance of our other stations for the successful deposition of spat. This we are inclined to believe comes about by the Crouch mouth spat being sent up flood tide into the Roach. Exit at Havengore, however, is delayed until the tide has swung round the Maplins, and this latter finally nigh stops out-current of Roach branch. A reverse action at ebb drains northwards with greatly weakened current, and thus much spat is trapped. Again, the Kentish Flats receive the spat of the Whitstable layings, and the eddy current of ebb from the North Foreland first sufficiently checks or modifies the north-easterly ebb current to favour deposition of spat on said Flats. The Pont natural beds gets its spat partly from its own stock, and, as previously hinted, great additions from the layings of the Colne, Tollesbury, Blackwater and Crouch, according to circumstances of wind and weather. Modifications may arise with heavy rains and freshets bearing mud seawards.

The conditions favouring the oyster's breeding are precisely those for abnormal increase of various enemies of the "floating-spat." It is a case of action and reaction between complicated natural phenomena, and a toss up which should overcome.

With all the above, human efforts avail little. The practical outcome of the question is to watch and regulate, as far as circumstances permit, that these natural oyster beds do not get too much depleted, and that sufficient breeding adults and plenty of culch be left. On how this is to be accomplished, there doubtless may be divided opinion. The dredgermen have interests in these free fishing grounds, and our Committee, as a matter of public policy, are bound to uphold them. This, of course, without losing sight of the public duty of protecting, and improving if possible, the chances of obtaining a steady supply of brood. The companies, needless to say, are anxious to see these natural beds kept in a good state of preservation, and not depleted, otherwise the supply of the genuine native might in time share the same fate as other famous oyster centres, and become extinct. It would come to be a nice adjustment of how best to serve both. It is not, however, a matter of mere *ex parte* opinion, for investigations of the actual state of the natural beds is a primary necessity. At all events, it is hardly likely that the Oyster Bye-laws of 1697 be revised *in extenso.**

Dates and Age of Breeding.—With us oysters as a rule become " sick " chiefly in June and July. On occasions, with a premature spell of hot weather, this may even occur in early May. On the other hand there are numerous instances of spatting in September and October; moreover, a Whitstable oyster has been found full of spat on Lord Mayor's Day, 9th November (Buckland). This latter of course is quite exceptional. Dilnot† has recorded spat in oysters taken off Herne Bay in January, no bigger than a pinshead, and Fryer‡ has seen similar specimens at Whitstable in December. Buckland has even supposed there were two falls of spat in the River Roach in 1868, one early June the other late September. Oysters are regarded as commencing to breed in their second year, but at Reculvers specimens 1 and 1½ inches diameter, inferred to be only a year old, have been observed in the " white-sick " condition. This, how-

---

* This contains some 17 Bye-laws and Ordinances. It was issued by the Company of Free Fishermen, and applicable to the area from London Bridge to N. Foreland and on to Harwich, embracing " waters, rivers, creeks and places " within the bounds of their charter. Among other items it put restrictions on oyster fishing at certain seasons and places, and was severe on encroachments of oyster layings, &c. Only by permission of the Company could any river, creek or fleet be dredged which did not naturally stock itself. Apprentices must serve seven years with a freeman, and no outsiders were allowed to dredge for oysters under any pretence. Unlawful nets and engines were to be destroyed, and resistance to officers on duty to be severely dealt with.

† *Land and Water*, January, 1869.   ‡ 8th Ann. Rep. Inspectors for 1893.

ever, is a most unusual case. Mr. Kemp, of Whitstable, states[*] he has seen oysters there with two rings of growth in a year, thus throwing doubts on Buckland's idea of one ring of growth taking place annually.

Spat on odd Places.—It is a matter of everyday experience to the oystermen that the " floating-spat " seems to prefer clean surfaces whereon to fix itself. Some of these are certainly quaint. In the Buckland Museum, South Kensington, there is a collection of such, most of them having been obtained in Kent and Essex waters. Among others we may notice—on a parasol, on and within a bottle, on a housemaid's flat-iron, on a thermometer, on a clay pipe, and on the back of a live crab, &c.

Meat to Shell.—Probably the last of Buckland's observations on oysters was a short contribution[†] on relation of meat to shell. We extract a few of his figures relating to the Thames estuarine production.

The Royal Whitstables	} Meat to shell
Colchesters (including Pyefleets ?) ...	} as 1 to 4.
Roach Rivers and Herne Bays (sorts not stated)	} Meat to shell
French and Portuguese laid at Brightlingsea	} as 1 to 5.

Other oysters from various sources, home and abroad, he enumerates as ranging from 1 to 6, grading upwards to 1 to 20.

In what precedes, with a few exceptions, we have confined remarks to natives (*Ostrea edulis*). But Portuguese and American oysters (*O. angulata* and *O. virginica*) now claim considerable attention on some of our oyster grounds. This brings up subjects connected with oyster culture and artificial propagation, which we here refrain from entering into. For the oyster industry methods in vogue at our different stations, and as compared with continental ones, this has been critically sum-

---

[*] *Land and Water*, Oct., 1880.

[†] *Land and Water*, 16th Oct., 1880—he died two months after.

marized, among others by Bashford Dean,[*] and Anson and Willett[†] have supplied much information thereon. A neat abstract is also to be found by Dr. Balstrode in the Local Government Report for 1894–95. We may incidentally allude *en passant* to the great hopes that were raised on the introduction of French methods into England.[‡] They, however, did not revolutionize the trade, and to-day are extant nowhere. Our colleague, Mr. George Baxter, we understand, has been experimenting at Pyefleet and at Colemonth Creek, and Captain Prettyman, we believe, has pond culture at work on the Orwell, besides others at Felixstowe. We are not aware of these having resulted in what might be deemed a profitable issue.

Crow-oyster Family (*Anomiidœ*).—Closely allied to the preceding are small, flat, oyster-looking mollusks, sometimes known as " crow-oysters " or " silver-shells." The naturalists' name is *Anomia ephippium.* They fasten themselves by a fleshy foot or plug to stones, shells, seaweeds, &c., or at chance times are even found adhering to an oyster. In their early stage they are sometimes taken for oyster spat. At Herne Bay some 486 young crow-oysters were counted, fixed to a cork slab $8\frac{1}{2}$ inches square—part of a fisherman's buoy (Hunt). In Buckland's museum there is quite an illustrative series of these " crows," ranging in size from pin-heads to 2 inches or $2\frac{1}{2}$ inches in diameter. They are widely distributed in our District, being found in shallow and deeper water at Deal, off Margate, Thames estuary, Blackwater, Harwich neighbourhood, &c. Their fisheries interest only lies in being confounded with young oysters.

Scallops or Pecten Family (*Pectinidœ*).—There are at least four species (with varieties to boot) of Scallops or Escallops or Fan-shells found in our District's waters. In a general way they may be regarded in the light of the big and small scallops.

* Report on the European Methods of Oyster Culture. Bull. U.S. Fish Commis., Vol. XI. for 1891 (1893). † Prize Essay, Fisheries Exhibition, Vol. XI., 1884. ‡ Lobb, Pamphlet on " Successful Oyster Culture," Lond., 1867.

(1.) The LARGE SCALLOP (*Pecten maximus*) is that of most commercial value to the Kentish fishermen. It seems to inhabit the Kent off-shores, especially those of the English Channel, rather than those of Essex. So far as we can learn it seems to thin out and be lost northwards of Dover—dead shells, however,

FIG. 22.

Scallop Shell.

have been picked up on the sands in the neighbourhood of the Sandwich Flats. On the contrary, it is common near Hastings. The average size of *P. maximus* for sale in the Billingsgate Market is $4\frac{1}{2}$ inches in height with a breadth of 5 inches, though a few may be less, while larger are rare. An 8 inch diameter specimen has, however, been recorded, as well as one only $\frac{1}{25}$ inch in length. We have not come across any example of this species even so small as in the wood cut (fig. 22).

For long the scallop has been justly esteemed as an article of diet in the counties bordering the western parts of the English Channel, and searched for accordingly. The taste for it travelled westwards later on. About 1850-55 three boats were engaged scallop dredging, some 11 miles south of Worthing, on beds there found at a depth of 14 fathoms. By 1860 15 to 20 boats were at work in the same neighbourhood.* In 1877 about 40 craft from Dover, Folkestone, Rye and other Sussex ports were actively employed ; even a few Brightlingsea smacks joined in the occupation, for oystering was then in a depressed condition. Hundreds of bags of scallops were then sent to London every week, besides a large quantity sold along the coast.† Folkestone and a few Dover fishermen still find spring employment scalloping, but dredge towards the Varne and Ridge shoals, and, as we understand, land fair quantities at the former port. The Government Inspector's Report for 1899

---

* Merrifield, Natural History of Brighton (1860).
† Polley, on Scallop Fishery, *Field*, April, 1877.

credits Brightlingsea with 10 first class smacks scalloping January to March inclusive.

(2.) Under the ordinary name of "QUEENS" comes the *Pecten opercularis*, otherwise "Frills" of S. Devon, "Squins" of Dorset, *alias* Common Scallop and "Clam" of the Scotch fisheries. This appears to range with us from the Channel along E. Kent (*e.g.* Deal, Shellness, common near Margate) and the entire seaboard of Essex (*e.g.*, E. Swin, the Deeps, and near Harwich plentiful on the Landguard Fort Beach). It is got of $2\frac{1}{2}$ inches in diameters, not infrequently of lesser size. It comes up in the dredge along with the large scallops and deep-sea oysters, and passes current with the former, both being used for food, as well as a taking bait for the deep-sea fishers.

(3 and 4.) The small-sized VARIEGATED SCALLOP (*P. varius*) and the LITTLE SCALLOP (*P. pusio*) are seldom above $1\frac{1}{2}$ inches in diameters. They, like the Operculate Pecten, are spread round our coasts, and more generally are found nearer shore than are Nos. 1 and 2. *P. varius* has been obtained in the Blackwater, and in rare instances may turn up near the Red Sand and Girdler, though none of the scallops are strictly shallow, brackish, estuarine forms.

The habits of all the scallops in most senses approach those of the native oyster. They dwell on the same grounds, are hermaphrodite, and in their ciliated embryonic condition they whisk about freely. They do not, however, usually in our area, fix themselves to solid objects for good by their shells, as does the oyster, more often in numerous groups being partially inserted in the muddy sand. They may be likened to the mussel, inasmuch as in their juvenile stage they spin, temporarily, threads (byssus) of attachment. They even possess a certain power of jerking locomotion by flapping their shells together. The shells of the adults are regularly ribbed, the Channel specimens often exhibiting flourishing bunches of waving hydroids(the fishermen's whiteweed plants, fig.11, p. 77). Their food is like that of the oyster. Of their periods of spatting on our southern shore and annual rate of growth there is yet much to learn. According to Fullarton,* in the Firth of Forth a few *P. opercularis* may be found in breeding condition the end of February and beginning of March; by July and August the maximum is reached, the great mass having spawned by mid-September.

As scallops bear removal from the water badly, this considerably detracts from them as a market commodity. Their shells, however, are fashioned into fancy ornaments, which meet a ready sale at our seaside resorts. Polley (*loc. cit.*) rather prides himself on the fishermen's mode of cooking them. The flesh is left in the hollow shell, placed on a gridiron over a slow clear fire, thus well stewed in its own liquor, with butter and bread crumbs and seasoned to taste, it becomes a tempting fare.

The Mussel Family (*Mytilidae*).—Some half-dozen species, with a few of their varieties, of this family are residents around Kent and Essex. Excepting the Common and the Horse Mussel, the former of which simply teems in the brackish estuaries, the others are found scattered sparingly. The mussel has been suggested as the poor man's oyster, a feature however shared by the cockle, as evinced by its sale at many of our seaside resorts.

The COMMON MUSSEL (*Mytilus edulis*).—*Distribution.*—Referring to its natural distribution—as in the case of the oyster excluding the temporary cultivated grounds—we may note their presence from Dungeness to the North Foreland. On this stretch of coast they are not so numerous or aggregated into such great assemblages as in the muddy and brackish river mouths of N. Kent and Essex. They are freely scattered about, however, more frequently seen within harbours, or on piles, &c., Folkestone to wit. Nor are they wanting off shore. For example, the iron Light Vessels of the Trinity Corporation on

---

* "On the Development of the Common Scallop (*Pecten opercularis*)," 8th Ann. Rep., S.F.B., for 1889 (1890).

the Goodwin Sands got so crowded with mussels (var. *pellucida?*)
as regularly to destroy the vessel's efficiency. Hence every two
years they had to be taken into harbour to be cleaned. In consequence a return had to be made to the old style of wooden
vessels. (Gattie, "Memorials" already cited.)

Along the N. Kent shore, from the Margate neighbourhood towards Birchington, Reculvers, Herne Bay and Whitstable, they increase in numbers. In the case of the old pier at
Herne Bay, its tumbledown piles are a great rendezvous for
mussels and other marine objects, where they hang in clusters.
On old wrecks everywhere in the estuary there they make
lodgment, grow and multiply amazingly. On the Kentish
Flats to the Margate sands are great beds, at least all around
there they are annually sought after during the season for
brood stock to the cultivated layings, and even for manurial
purposes, so plentiful are they at times.

The Swale from east to west, here and there come in for
full share, and Queenborough and Sheerness have their quota.
They run up the Medway as far as Upnor. In places mid-stream
(Medway) they can be brought up in dredgefuls ; indeed,
formerly they were regularly worked for outside of Colemouth
Creek. Sheppey foreshore, particularly about Cheney Rocks,
is another spot for them. There are sparse beds of small-sized
mussels in the Jenkin Swatch. Their diminutive size B.
Baxter attributes to their partial but continuous destruction by
the bargemen and others, the sailing craft hereabouts being at
times very crowded. Furthermore, the shrimpers at times
work this ground, and may give them little chance of growing
large.

The Nore Lightship, like those of the Goodwins, is also
pestered with mussels in masses. Even copper and zinc is not
sufficient protection to their deposition, for within a short time
the accumulation is extraordinary. In fact, in Thames, Medway
and other estuaries, wherever buoys are, to those mussel spat
clings, and the Trinity have to keep a sharp look-out, and

frequently renew them. On " Bell's Hard," near the Yantlet, and at Egypt Bay, mussels are of common occurrence.

On the Essex side the Mucking Flats are here and there good mussel ground. Some are found near the Chapman Light, and also among the weeds and stones of the sea-wall, Canvey Island. Leigh Ray and Swatchway to Southend, and the whole foreshore of the latter, from earliest times have been noted as rich, muddy, sandy, natural mussel areas. Indeed, in former years at Southend mussel heaps bestrewed the shore, and were quite a feature. In 1898, at the recommendation of our colleague, Capt. Anderson,* the Town Council made a clearance; yet still they come, wherever there is the slightest chance of object to fasten on. The original wooden pier, which stood for some 60 years, prior to and at its demolishment, had its seaward posts at their bottoms perfectly crammed with them, for quite half-a-mile in length. When the pier was removed (1894), and an iron one erected, its pillars, especially those outside low-water mark, were very soon colonized and covered with mussel brood and acorn barnacles innumerable. At present the landing pier steps, as well as pillars up to and beyond low-water mark, are everywhere carpetted and festooned with *mytili* of all ages and sizes, the young ones packed in semi-solid, dense cushion masses.

Between Southend and the Knock Buoy everywhere mussels have asserted dominion over the oysters close by. On the Shoebury Sands, in the pools created by the whirl of the tide around wrecks, and target ranges, or other extraneous flotsam and jetsam, the mussels gather in quantity. Clementine Gut, near the Blacktail Spit, the inner part or " Land of Blacktail," and other nooks inside the Swin, are favourite spots for them. The Burnham river has been infested with mussels for long years. In the Blackwater and Colne estuaries, avoiding repetition, similar conditions to those of Thames and Medway

---

* Report to the Corporation on the Foreshore Fishery, Oct., 1898.

prevail. Hamford Water, Harwich and the river mouths thereabouts, all have scattered mussel collections.

Redundance in our District.—It will be readily understood then their numbers are far from few. Thus, as in the case of the indigenous oyster, the mussels keep company, even predominate, in the muddy places, and wherever they are, there is abundance of minor life and brood fish hovering hard by. At the same time, as Coleman has remarked (*Field*, 1869), a heavy fall of mussel spat is sometimes dangerous to oysters, by gathering mud and otherwise smothering them, besides competing for food—a view corroborated by Anderson, Baxter and other practical oyster growers.

Quite contrary to what is the state of things on the N.E. English and Scottish shores—where mussels can hardly be obtained in sufficient quantity for bait to the line fishers—Kent and Essex could willingly spare, and be the gainers thereby. Yet Wilcocks,* evidently only on theoretical grounds, suggested as desirable places for mussel bouchot culture, Sandwich Haven, Swale, Medway, Crouch, Blackwater, Colne, Stour and Orwell; giving his diagram-plans of proposed wattled palisadings on the French system for Hamford Water, Colne, &c.

In discussion of a resolution for a uniform close time for mussels, brought forward at a Fisheries Conference by Superintendent Dawson† (of Lanc. Sea Fish. Comm.), our colleague, Capt. Austin, then forcibly put the Kent and Essex case thus:— "The oyster beds are being destroyed by the accumulation of mussels, therefore to make any bye-laws for the whole coast of England would be, to put it mildly, absurd." Coleman followed by assuring those present that "We should be glad if some of our North Sea friends would come and fetch them away." He had, it seems, about 1876, sent mussels for bait to Scotland from the Thames estuary, but the expenses of carriage nullified

---

* Prize Essay, Internat. Fish. Exhib., Lond., 1883 (Vol. XI., 1884).

† Rep. Proc. Conference, Nat. Sea Fish. Protect. Assoc.,1893. Bye-laws prohibiting taking of mussels from May to August inclusive are in force in the Eastern, Western and Lancashire Districts ; and from May to July inclusive in the Glamorgan District.

the transaction, and there the matter rested. Similarly the late Mr. George Baxter made a fruitless venture. Those therefore who decry and would prohibit the Kentish men's dredging for mussels, to be used as manure for land culture, would do well to ponder ere too pronouncedly expressing opinion thereon. Certainly it would go hard with our fishers if "made a penal offence to use mussels for manure," as recommended by Robertson Carr.*

In connection therewith Prof. McIntosh's report on the Yorkshire beds† possesses much interest and information. The condition of things there is, however, on a different footing, and defective local supplies are imported from Germany, the Netherlands and elsewhere. But how comes it mussels do not pay in exportation from the Thames estuary? We are not prepared to answer; rather at a loss to understand wherefore there has not been more persistent business efforts made to secure a trade among the north-eastern fishermen, who crave for them as bait. Thus we are driven to the supposition that the cost of labour in this country is the initial drawback, not altogether the want of energy in our merchants.‡

Sex and Spawning, &c.—In the early stages of the edible mussel, distinction of sex is rather obscure to the naked eye; but as the generative organs ripen differentiation into male and female becomes apparent. The male then is characterised by paler coloured tracery of sperm-sacs, whereas the female has

---

* Prize Essay, Fisheries Exhib., Literature, Lond., 1883 (Vol. IV., 1884).

† Rep. on Mussel and Cockle Beds, Estuaries of the Tees, the Esk and the Humber, 1891. *See* also several short notices in Reports Northumberland S. F. Comms. by King, Wilson and Meek; besides Herdman and Scott's articles in Lancashire S. F. Laboratory Reports for 1892 on to 1900.

‡ We have elicited the following from an old hand, who can recollect batches of seed mussels being forwarded to Scotland. He puts it thus, without vouching for the accuracy of the figures :—"In our estuary at the time referred to the buying price of the mussels in question would be (say) 1s. per tub or bag. Men were employed to ' set them out,' then 6d. per bag was paid to pick them up. The bag itself cost 3d., and the carriage to London by sailing boat was 6d. Hence each bag cost the vendor 2s. 3d., for which his return from the buyer (who paid steamboat carriage from London north) was only 2s. per bag, or at a loss of 3d. on each bag. This strange mercantile transaction was pursued for the reason that it was more economical to lose 3d. per bag and thus get rid of certain over-stock than otherwise to clear and clean the beds."

more uniform scattering of eggs among the tissues of the
mantle, and these are of a ruddier orange tint. An appeal to
the microscope settles the difficulty. Thus it follows that the
common and the horse mussel are not hemaphrodite like our
native oyster, but rather resemble the Portuguese and the
American oyster in the sexes being separate.

In our haphazard examination of a series of specimens of
the common mussel, the sexes seemed to be tolerably evenly
divided. McIntosh inclines to think females preponderate.
But Jas. Johnstone* has shown, by a more extensive research
to determine this point on the Lancashire mussel beds, that
there the ratio of sex stands as six males to five females, or
thereabouts.

The period in which mussels usually spawn in the Kent
and Essex waters is reckoned by the growers to be from spring
till midsummer. As in the case of the oyster, much depends on
weather conditions. There is no hard and fast date of their
commencing or ceasing to emit spawn. This appears to be the
case equally whether self-sown colonies or among those laid on
the beds under semi-cultivation. In cold and wet springs the
mussel men expect them to be later of breeding. Speaking in
a general way, with us April, May and June may be regarded
as when the great bulk of the mussels are " sick " and out of
order, and then their floating spat (*i.e.*, stage, with ciliate
swimming fringe) is to be obtained in numbers in the tow-net
in the neighbourhood of the mussel and oyster beds. By the
close of June, even occasionally some weeks earlier, the growers
notice many mussels to be already spent or fast losing flesh.
By mid-July some are already steadily recovering from the
thinning effects of procreation, and begin " putting on flesh,"
as the phrase goes. Meantime, and till August, there are still
a very few late breeders, but the great majority are fast
getting into sound condition, fit for market, that is if the

---

* " The Spawning of the Mussel (*Mytilus edulis*)," Rep. Lanc. Sea Fish. Labor.
for 1898 (1899).

weather remain favourable. If it should be cold and wet less food is about, and the mussels then thrive more slowly.

The result of search for young, shelled, fixed spat from May till end of June has been rewarded in finding plenty in the Hadleigh Ray layings (both among those mussels that have been there from spring-time and fresh lots brought in summer from the Kentish Flats) as well as those free-growing ones fixed on the Southend Pier piles. These tiny mussels are found among the entanglements of the foot-web or byssus of the adult forms. Some on the broken shells and weeds are inextricably bound up with the mussel lumps. Their size has ranged from $\frac{1}{25}$ to $\frac{1}{13}$ (transparent pin heads) to $\frac{1}{4}$ or $\frac{1}{2}$ an inch in length—like to a bean in appearance. Others of larger size are likewise got on the stones or attached to the oysters or to the boats' bottoms. The very smallest are undoubtedly summer spawn, but those of longer dimensions may be the spring or the previous year's brood? This seems simple and, so far, clear, if there is only a single summer spawning. But a complication arises, and leads us to think that a moderate percentage of mussels breed much earlier, and even a few others possibly later than the period given above.

Our attention was called to this in finding in the beginning of April among the Southend natural colonies at the Pier-head, young mussels as diminutive as any of the above-mentioned midsummer series. There was also quite a consecutive series in sizes. Their age might be therefore several weeks and some as many months old. Now this tallies very well with McIntosh's* observations at St. Andrews, where sexual maturity is arrived at in April; by May and early June ova fast diminishing and in July spent. He assumes the brood of May-end ($\frac{1}{2}$ inch long) are early year products or slow growths from the year before. His later report on Tees (N.E. Sea Fish. Distr.) mussels, already cited, sustains his previous conclusions above enunciated.

* Ann. and Mag. Nat. Hist., February, 1885.

Wilson's[*] researches at the "Gattie" Marine Station strengthens the view of maturity being in March and April, though swimming embryos are abundant in June. Herdman and Scott (Liverpool Laboratory)[†] found ripe mussels in January and February. Dawson[‡] says that in April "mussels are, however, now fast going out of condition." Yet Johnstone (in paper quoted) holds strongly that June and July are the maximum spawning months on the Lancashire mussel beds. Notwithstanding, he admits, by way of assumption, that it is necessary some may spawn early in the year, otherwise how are larvæ in January and February to be explained? It seems to us that, presumably as a side issue, there is a kind of half-hearted support given on his part to the Lancashire District Committee Bye-law of a four months closure. At all events, judging from Johnstone's reading, by contrast the East Coast mussels are in full swing breeding, and are spent and "making flesh" somewhat earlier than in the case of the Irish Sea group.

Howsoever it be there still seems somewhat of a discrepancy in the statements of the Lancashire authorities. A possible explanation may be that the mussel has a more lengthened spawning period than hitherto accorded it, and not two separate spawning times in the year. A variety of circumstances may advance or retard spatting. May and June being the chief spawning months. So far as Kent and Essex are concerned, at present and in prospect there is no sign of warning of diminution of mussels, therefore no necessity for restricting their collection. At the same time, as in the case of oysters, it is well, nay, the duty of our Committee, at intervals to inspect and report on the condition of the natural accumulations of these mollusks. To be forewarned is to be forearmed against any untoward changes likely to happen.

Early and After Growth, Size, Food, &c.—The consecutive rate of the mussel's growth is less accurately known than is that of oysters. We gather just a bare notion of the quite

---

[*] In 4th and 5th Ann. Reps. F. B. Scotland for 1885 and 1886.
[†] Rep. Lancashire Sea Fish. Labor. for 1894 (1895), tabular statement.
[‡] Lanc. Sea Fisheries, Superintendent's Report, 30th April, 1894.

young stages from various scattered observations. For instance, specimens reared from fertilized eggs, in 12 days were then 0·134 millimetres; though they lived for 40 days they made no further progress in development (Wilson). Other samples 0·27 mm. to 0·45 mm. have been assumed to be about 1 month old (Johnstone). Some examples ⅛ inch long, which appeared in the well of a Tees steam-dredger, were supposed to be about 2 months old—but queried by McIntosh. A series each under ¼ inch obtained from barrel buoys at St. Andrews were conjectured to be 5 months old. Mussels on "Roosebeck" Scars (near Piel Laboratory) are known to have grown ¾ of an inch in 5 months (Scott). At Montrose it is reckoned that seed-mussels on the best ground attain 2 inches length in 3 years, in other parts of the beds up to 5 years is required (Fullarton).

According to mussel culture in the Thames estuary, the smallest sized laid in February and March are from 1 to 2 inches long, and are reckoned to be about 1 to 1½ years of age. When 6 months on the bed, that is to say from 1½ to 2 years old, they as a rule will be about 1¾ to 2 inches in length, some being over. The very biggest of not less than 2½ inches will then be fit for market. At 3 to 3½ years of age they may be nigh 3 inches in length, if in low-lying ground and covered by water. If inclement weather their growth is not so quick, but given an extra spell of warmth, with favourable tides, this stimulates them with a spurt. Supposing the mussel's development is divided into four stages, the first makes slow progress in growth, the second and third are much accelerated, whilst in the fourth, nigh full-grown, there is, other things being equal, retardation of increase in dimensions.

As to the mussels on sale at Billingsgate, their average sizes on the stalls generally are from 2½ to 3 inches. The former usually predominate; a few only 2 inches in length find their way to the dealer among the others. Larger than 3 inches are a rarity. The big Horse Mussel (*Mytilus modiolus*) is here excluded. It only perchance in a desultory manner forms part of a consignment despatched to market. The smallest we have met with in their living habitat have been (*supra*) almost microscopic, or little more than visible to the naked eye. There are abundance of seed size—bean length to an inch upwards to the other sizes above given. The very largest—and not many of them—seldom more than $3\frac{1}{2}$ to 4 inches. Wilson (*l.c.*) says : examples measuring $4\frac{3}{4}$ inches are commonly dredged near St. Andrews.

The mussels which are raised in our District, be it observed, are chiefly intended and ostensibly sent to London for culinary purposes. Only to a very limited extent are they used as bait for local line fishing—say, at Margate, Deal, Dover, Folkestone and Harwich. London is the principal market for the matured mussels, though we understand that considerable consignments of seed mussels at times are sent to Holland, the fresh produce of the Whitstable dredgers on the Kentish Flats and the Blackwater. As already indicated, hundreds of tons are dredged, mostly by the Faversham and Rochester boats in the Thames mouth and sold to the Kentish farmers for manure. In like manner, Brightlingsea craft supply Essex's agricultural wants.

Concerning the food of the mussel, it is nearly similar to that of the oyster; but, possibly, at least in our Thames examples, there seems to be more comminuted vegetable material and sandy mud in the former than in the latter. Otherwise expressed, the mussel is the grosser feeder of the two. Whilst sand is not infrequently fatal to the oyster, the mussel doubtless possesses a greater power of getting rid of it,[*] while accumulating mud around.

Species and Varieties.—So far as our fisheries are concerned, the (1) COMMON MUSSEL (*M. edulis*) is the all-important one. But there are several other sorts, recognised by naturalists, which are found here and there, and some of them ordinarily

---

[*] *See* "Researches of Viallanes," quoted by Ascroft, "Mussel Beds and Mud Banks," Rep. Lancashire S. F. Labor. for 1898.

pass current with it. The more delicate kind of the edible mussel, distinguished as *var. pellucida*, has already been mentioned as often fixing itself to the buoys and wrecks in our deeper channels. But examples have been picked up at Margate, and we have found some at Southend Pier-head and elsewhere even settled among batches of the common sort in the cultivated beds, and sold accordingly, delicacy of flavour being notable. Its tenuity of shell, as compared with the ordinary mussel, its light browny colour, and longitudinal purple streak-lines, are quite diagnostic.

(2) The so-called HORSE MUSSEL (*Mytilus modiolus*), from its large size (often twice as big as the common sort) and other features, is as easily recognised. Their local name in Kent is "squibs." They are far from being so numerous as the trade mussel, though in suitable places in all our estuaries it occasionally comes up in the dredge. We have come across a good many in the cultivated beds, doubtless brought thither with the mussel dredgings obtained on more seaward localities—Kentish Flats for example. Unlike *M. edulis*, with its deep bluish-black coloured shell, that of the horse mussel is of a rich orange and dark-brown tint. In shape it is more oblong, and not usually so triangular as in the common species. The flesh is of a darker orange and the foot ruddier than in the edible kind. When in the fresh state the epidermis (outer shell-skin) is seen to possess rows of cross-fringes, and there are other characters unnecessary to mention. Suffice to say the horse mussel in due course is sent to market without scruple. As food it is said by some to be coarser-fleshed and tougher than its congener, while others who have partaken of it in the north give it preference. It stands heat and removal from the deep water badly. When transferred to the beds that dry up it often is killed by the sun's rays.

(3) The BEARDED MUSSEL (*Mytilus barbatus*), and (4) the ADRIATIC MUSSEL (*M. adriaticus*) are two small-sized, yellow-ruddy, unimportant forms, somewhat rare in Kent and Essex waters. There are three other still smaller mussels belonging

to an allied genus, *Modiolaria*, wherein the mantle is folded
into a tube; but they are not food products. Regarding (5) the
small-sized MARBLED MODIOLARIA (*M. marmorata*), this finds its
way into the skin of the tunicates (or sea-squirts); (6) The
Modiolaria discors is a nest weaver among the seaweeds; (7)
The BLACK MODIOLARIA (*M. nigra*), said to reach no further
south than the Dogger Bank (Jeffreys), though specimens have
been obtained in the Crouch River.*

Sundry Subjects.—(a) Variations in colour and shape.
Concerning these, and speaking in a general way, mussels do not
bear that marked stamp of local character met with in the
oyster. The latter the dealers will instantly tell to a nicety
whence the district derived. Usually mussels assume a tolerably uniform appearance wherever bred. In lots spread over a
given restricted area, however, the cultivator knows fairly well
from what parts of the ground they may have been procured,
from their general appearance. In certain spots some are much
barnacled, others clad with weed, hydroids, worm tubes, &c.,
and elongation or relative breadth, and otherwise style of
growth, well fed or stunted state, gives a clue to whereabouts
their localization.

(b) McIntosh and Herdman have called attention to the
absence of "greening" among mussels as compared with
oysters. We can corroborate this as applicable to Kent and
Essex; that is, we have neither seen nor heard of the occurrence
among the vast numbers under constant supervision.

(c) The manner in which mussels group themselves into
bunches, and how it arises that these so collect mud in such
abundance, deserves a few words.† Oysters in their early
stages get soon irrevocably fixed. Whereas mussels at a similar
age are to some extent wanderers, actively employing their
elastic foot to drag them hither and thither. Afterwards, by
chance or choice, they take to settled life, often in near
proximity to each other. Then comes their spinning and throwing out of foot-webs (byssus) and complex entanglement of

---

* "Trawling and Dredging in Crouch, 1891," Essex Nat. VI., 1892.
† *See* Ascroft's remarks, L. S-F. Labor. (1898), already referred to.

same. In this get included gravel, broken shells, barnacles, sea-weeds, hydroids, &c., and frequently diminutive mussels themselves. These entrapped, the latter grow and flourish, and soon arises a colony of all sexes and ages. But the detritus heaps—altogether a rough sieve, no wonder mud collects— though in some senses deleterious, say near or among oyster beds, yet are not without a benefit, for they foster and give protection to a vast colonial life of all kinds of the lower creatures—many microscopic, fit food for the mussels and oysters themselves. Möbius (*l.c.*) has well shown the importance of such social communities, and this has been emphasised by others, and can be witnessed daily on our shores. The net result is that the congregation of the infinitesimal and larger sized fauna is of immense importance to the fisheries at large as fish and shell-fish food, &c.

FIG. 23.

VIEW OF COCKLE BEACH, LEIGH, AT LOW TIDE.

Cockling craft in foreground, men with "yoke" and baskets (two sorts), &c. In distance and to right are cockle sheds and cockle-shell heaps, and beyond row of fishermen's dwellings.

The **Cockle Family** (*Cardiidæ*).—*Different Sorts.*—Several kinds of the cockle tribe inhabit our sands. (1) The COMMON COCKLE (*Cardium edule*) ranks primarily in numbers and mercantile value. (2) The SPINED COCKLE (*C. echinatum*), sometimes called the Horse Cockle, is a large sized form, nigh three inches in diameters when full grown. This has been recorded as got sparingly from several places in both counties, viz., in the neighbourhood of Deal, Pegwell Bay and Margate, and also in the Crouch and Blackwater estuaries. It is of a roundish form, and, as its name implies, bears short spines. Unless by naturalists, who distinguish differences, it is regarded among the cocklers and others as only a big common cockle, and passes current accordingly in their gatherings. (3) The NORWEGIAN COCKLE (*C. norvegicum*), some $2\frac{1}{2}$ to nearly 3 inches diameters when adult, has the shell only faintly ribbed, and to the eye is altogether more elongated in shape than is the *C. edule*. We only know of it from Shellness (Cockerell); it may be found elsewhere, though hitherto passed over so far as we are aware. (4) The LITTLE COCKLE (*C. exiguum*) is, broadly speaking, a common form in the oozy ground of the Blackwater, the Crouch and in the Thames estuary (off Margate, &c.). Possibly it otherwise may be more numerous than hitherto credited. It is seldom above half an inch in diameter, and is markedly triangular in shape. If obtained by the cocklers among an ordinary gathering it seldom or ever is brought back by them, for its small size enables it to pass through their sieves. Hence it does not come under usual food product; its chief use doubtless being as fish-food.

The COMMON COCKLE (*C. edule*)—*Distribution*—has a wide distribution with us, somewhat similar to that of the mussel, but with this difference that it is chiefly confined to the expanse of sands which, dry or otherwise, constitute so prominent a feature of part of our coasts. Take for example the great sandy bay stretching at least from Romney considerably eastward of Dymchurch. Again, Deal to Ramsgate, or Margate to Whitstable, besides the south side of the Isle of Sheppey, all over which in places is the cockle to be found at home. Or along Essex, *e.g.*, the Maplins, Buxey, Dongie Flats, and beyond the Naze towards Harwich, everywhere cockles can be got in fewer or greater quantities. But the fact is that ordinarily the cockles lying hidden in the sands precludes accuracy of their presence in the live conditions, whilst here and there only is it sought for to be disposed of as food locally in a limited way. On the other hand, from the great cockling industry in the Thames estuary it might be supposed there to be in greatest abundance.

Quite truly where fresh mingles with the sea water, as in the estuaries, there the cockles flourish, and become most valuable commercially; but they are by no means restricted to such places, or the drying sands, for they exist in the deeper water. There profitable fishery, however, must necessarily be under favourable circumstances of proximity to market, &c.

As Leigh is the chief centre of the cockling trade in our District, consequently convenience necessitates the cocklers searching for them in localities nearest home. The more notable places for cocklers in the Thames then are Shoebury Sands, and the Maplins, the sands facing Leigh and towards Southend; the Grain Spit and places in the vicinity of the Spaniards, and the Gilman; the Pollard and sands round the east end of Sheppey. At rare intervals within the Swale towards Elmley Ferry, and "the Hole," near Queenborough. There are also small collections made at times by some of the older men on Canvey Spit, Chapman Sands, and the Marsh-end Sands, &c.

Size, Numbers, Food.—The largest cockles which have come under our observation were brought from the Pollard (inside the Columbine, Whitstable Bay). Taking one as a sample—the united shells of one dried after cooking—its measurements were $1\frac{3}{4}$ inches (over) transversely, and $1\frac{1}{4}$ inches long diameter, and

1½ inches thick.   This was not a solitary example, for there were very many such, and quite a pile only a trifle smaller.   They were eight or nine years old as indicated by growth marks; supported by the men's statement that it had been eight years previously since cockles were gathered on the same ground. Search in another cockler's shell-mound for the most diminutive that had underwent cooking, we discovered a very few of these dimensions : ¾ inch across, ½ inch long, and a trifle over ¼ inch thick.   But the ordinary smallest size in this lot were barely 1 inch crosswise, just over ¾ inch long, and somewhat less than ¾ inch in thickness.   The most of these last were two and three years old.   The batch were from the Grain Spit, solid, meaty little fellows.   From this ground all the cockles, however old (like the mussels in the channel outside), are never known to attain any considerable size.   Probably the average size of the summer cockles, when the men are pressed for quantity to meet sales, may be taken as 1¼ inch across, 1⅛ inch long, and above ¾ inch thick.   Of course there are many above this.

Compare samples from Lynn (The Wash) procured by us, on sale at Billingsgate.   The maximum was 1½ by 1¼ diameters and 1 inch thick.   The minimum was 1 by ⅞ diameters and ¾ inch thick.   This last very nearly corresponded with a longish series from various parts of the Lancashire coast taken throughout the year (*see* Rep. for 1894, L. S. F. Labor.).   According to the Lancashire District bye-laws, the official gauge as a minimum breadth (*i.e.*, thickness *supra*) is of ¾ inch in the fresh living state.   But as Johnstone (*l.c.*) has observed, and his words are strictly applicable to our Thames cockles, " the ratio of length to lateral breadth in the cockle is of course variable within certain limits."   Hence the standard of size is purely arbitrary, oldish specimens which have freely bred being no bigger than many their juniors.

Taken in a broad sense, cockles around Kent and Essex are abundant on the whole.   Nor does there seem to be any falling off in numbers. Sometimes, through inclement weather or other cause, the cocklers (who frequently " hunt in a pack ") will considerably diminish the produce of a particular ground, and fishing for them there becomes unprofitable, but after an interval of a year or more, when the men return to the spot, they find well grown material fit for market. Seldom indeed has there been decided scarcity from over-fishing. Moreover, it should be taken into account that the numbers of the cocklers have been on the increase.

As to the food of the cockle, of that there is no stint in our District. Though not such a grazier as is the periwinkle, the cockle nevertheless seems to live fully as much on marine plants as on animal substances, sand likewise is not infrequent. Herdman and Scott have found the cockles' stomachs often empty.* In our examinations relatively not many were in this condition. Some of ours were examined on the spot, others shortly after they were taken off the sands. Their digestion is active, so before long the alimentary canal exhibits scant traces of food. This latter in many respects resembles that of oysters and mussels, viz., fragments of algæ, diminutive crustaceans (ostracods, &c.), diatoms, foraminifers and so forth. Scott mentions a copepod (*Lichomolgus agilis*) as resident (a messmate) within cockles and mussels; we cannot say whether this is the case in the Thames specimens.

Sex and Growth.—Separation of the sexes occurs as in the common mussel, but the Norwegian cockle is said by Lacaze Duthiers to exhibit a hermaphrodite condition. On this score we can give no information personally.

The cocklers in our District find traces of spawning from spring till end of June. By July in good seasons the adult breeding cockle gets flabby, and by the end of this month shows signs of recovery, and from August onwards they think it is in best condition. We have not examined their repro-

---

* Rep. Lancashire Sea Fish. Labor. for 1891, tabular statement.

ductive condition so closely as to be certain of the exact dates,
but end of April through May and June there is no doubt of
their being in a breeding state. Their very minute condition
we have not had full opportunity of studying, but competent
authorities aver that, having its short escapade as a tiny
swimming creature, it settles down to a creeping life about a
millimetre ($\frac{1}{25}$ inch) long. With us ordinarily a cockle "trayle"
on the sands is first noticed when the animal and its delicate
shell has attained nigh $\frac{1}{4}$ inch or so. When the men see this
in quantity they take heed, and a year or two after expect to
find some better evidence of a future fishing ground.

As to growth of cockle, at say a year or more old, it may be
$\frac{1}{4}$ inch in diameters, or over this. At 2 years and above, from
$\frac{1}{2}$ inch to $\frac{3}{4}$ inch diameters may be roughly the estimate.
Rising three years onwards they are of marketable size, and
the old ones range from $1\frac{1}{4}$ to $1\frac{1}{2}$ inches; those of many years
age, as above stated, seldom passing $1\frac{3}{4}$ inch in greatest breadth;
a 2 inch cockle is a rarity in our District.

Habits and Use.—Concerning their habits during the breeding season, the cocklers find great congregations of them
crawling about and disporting themselves on the sands.
Should stormy weather intervene they are driven about pell
mell by the waves, and vast numbers then perish; and remains
of cockle shell heaps attest their destruction. The cockle's
great muscular foot enables it to hop about with ease.
Doubtless they betimes shift residence, and even on occasions
may be met with among the shallow pools, feeding on the sea-
weeds, &c. Ordinarily, out of the breeding season they are
pretty much stay-at-home individuals. Unlike the mussel,
which as we have shown moors itself by byssus threads, the
cockle hides himself just below the surface of the sand. To
those accustomed to search for them, small holes in the sand
or a bit of seaweed partly drawn in generally betray their
whereabouts. In rare instances juvenile cockles either creep
into or get entangled among the network foot-threads of the

mussel, where they grow and develop freely without being buried in the sand.*

Apart from their usefulness as wholesome, nutritious, human diet, and even as bait and as food for some fish (plaice, &c.), the empty shells of the boiled cockles at Leigh find a ready sale in barge loads to be used in garden walks, and for a variety of other purposes.

The Clam Family (*Myidæ*).—All the three British species of Clams or Gapers are found in our District:—(1) BINGHAM's CLAM (*Mya Binghami*) is a puny shell-fish, in rare instances more than $\frac{1}{2}$ inch by $\frac{1}{4}$ inch in diameter, and of no account in our fisheries. (2) The TRUNCATE CLAM (*M. truncata*) is a much larger gaper, 2 inches by $2\frac{1}{2}$ inches in diameter being an average size of adult. In many respects it is like the common clam, except that the shell is cut short (truncate) at the hinder end, where the (foot-like) syphons protrude. It is to be found at a number of places in both counties, but especially at the seaward parts of the estuaries, there lodged in the ground from 6 to 9 inches deep. It is said to be a fine flavoured shell-fish, and in some instances may do duty for the next species. We are not aware of any exclusive search for it within our area for domestic purposes, though in northern countries it is relished as food.

(3) THE CLAM (*M. arenaria*), for by this name alone is it spoken of in Kent and Essex. The clam of the Scotch people, as we have already shown, is one of the scallops. In America, quite a string of clam names are given to entirely different kinds of shell-fish, our clam being their soft clam or long clam.† *M. arenaria* is very common, and has an extensive distribution and is plentiful in our District.‡ It seems to

---

* Darbishire in Rep. "Fauna of Liverpool," Vol. I. (1886).

† Browne-Goode, U.S. Fishery Industries, 4to, 1884.

‡ Therefore clashing with Harding's statement "there were few clams in England," Conference Paper "Mollusca . . . . used for food or bait," Internat. Fish. Exhib., Lond., 1883.

prefer, however, the mud soil of the estuaries, where the water is brackish. In walking along the sandy mud in many spots they abound, and their biggish holes, with an ejection of water from them, tell of their residence. They usually are sunk from a few inches to a foot deep, according to age, and with their rugged leathery water-tubes or syphons occasionally stuck up close to the surface.

The average size of the adult forms dug up for food or bait is about 4 by 2 inches. The largest we have met with have been 5 by 2¾ inches and 1¾ inches thick. An extreme case mentioned to us by a clammer was between 6 and 7 inches greatest diameter. The smallest clams got by us have been little over 1 by ⅝ inch in diameter, and we have a series running upwards. Young shells lying about are usually only 2 by 1½ inches and much worn and eroded. As a rule, only dead shells are got on the surface mud, but in the guts and muddy runlets we have now and again come across an adult living specimen of full size.

Our examination of early stages and growth is scanty. The clammers say they are in best condition late in the autumn, and believe they are early winter breeders, though others aver June and July to be the spawning season.

The clam is a scavenger by trade, and feeds on varied waste surface material, infusoria, algæ, diatoms, fragmentary hydrozoa, &c. The layer of clyty London clay in which they reside is too surely black and filthy, and when the clams are dug up their appearance is anything but inviting ; but kept for a night or a day in pure water they soon cleanse themselves, and tone down wonderfully in colour.

Clams are not a favourite diet, though well washed and properly cooked they are not to be despised, and they form a cheap and wholesome food, besides being good bait, fresh or salted. At odd times one finds men of the labouring class having a clam hunt in view of home consumption; otherwise few persons follow clamming as a matter of profession for selling them to the public. (*See* Sect. VI.)

The Periwinkle Family (*Littorinidæ*).—The Periwinkles, or "winkles," are of considerable economic value in our fishery industries. They are well known browsers of algæ, hence as vegetable feeders, wanderers for pastures new, and even somewhat gregarious in habit, they represent the ruminants among the shell-fish. Three kinds, apart from varieties, inhabit the littoral of the District quite up to, or even beyond, high-water mark. The sexes are separate, and one species (*L. rudis*) brings forth its young alive, like the eel pout among fishes. They, often together, frequent nearly the same grounds, and to the fisher one and other pass without distinction as " winkles " for edible purposes. They are spread less or more all round the coast, equally grazing among the sea-weeds in the rock-pools from Sandgate on towards Dover as on the flatter grounds in other parts of Kent and Essex. In all the estuaries they are very plentiful, particularly the common " winkle." On the Thames and Blackwater especially there are numbers of " winklers " kept busily at work during various times of the year, and this sometimes when other occupation is temporarily suspended by inclemency of weather and other causes. (*See* further, Sect. VI., " Winkling.")

(1) The BLUNT PERIWINKLE (*Littorina obtusata)* is the scarcest and smallest of the three, being little more than half-an-inch in diameter. It is nut-shaped, big-mouthed, squat spired, hence its name, and only accidentally gets mixed with the common periwinkle as food product. (2) The ROUGH PERI-WINKLE (*L. rudis*) is got much more frequently. Like the last, the female is largest, and what is most unusual among mollusks, it bears living (viviparous) progeny, as Boys fully a century ago showed was the case in Kent specimens. It breeds during summer and far into the autumn. They seldom overstep 1 in. by ¾ in. in diameters, are variously coloured, and may occasionally get amongst market produce.

(3) The COMMON PERIWINKLE (*L. littorea*) is by far the most numerous, and *par excellence* furnishes our staple " winkle "

industry. Moreover, it is a useful animal to the oyster-culturist. When the latter's grounds are subject to weed, advantage is taken of its grazing habits, and numbers of them are regularly laid down to clean the pits, which their rasping tongues effectually do.

The average dimensions of the trade "winkle" is about 1 by ¾ inch, first class being 1¼ by nearly ¾ inch. Among consignments sent to Billingsgate from the north of Scotland still longer ones occur. Of those bred and reared in our District, they seldom run more than an inch long; though occasionally there are larger fellows found near or on those beds where winkles are brought from market to be deposited only temporarily.

The common periwinkle, in contradistinction to No. 2, deposits eggs (therefore oviparous). Their patches of eggs, loosely stuck together by gelatinous substance, as well as diminutive, crawling, shelled fry, here and there, are in profusion on weeds, zostera, stones, &c. The adults are found in breeding condition all summer, occasionally even up to November, weather exercising an influence as to early or late procreation. The eggs hatch quickly. We have not followed the rate of their early stages of growth; but those of half-an-inch are supposed to be a year and some months old. At two up to three years they attain a marketable size.

Usually "winkles" are scattered about singly on stones, gravel, posts, shells or zostera, and among the oysters and mussels, or on weeds in the shallow muddy pools in the brackish water, even on rocks high and dry. At other times during the season they congregate, and even are said occasionally to take to travelling or shifting of feeding ground *en masse*. On the Essex shore, Leigh and Southend neighbourhood, some are worn and roughened, chiefly at the spire end. This erosion may be due either to the sand wash of the tides or other cause.*

---

* Shrubsole in Conch. Jour. II., ascribes this erosion to an excess of lime in the water—calcic. carb. giving off carbonic acid. *See* also Jeffr. Brit. Conch. I. Introd. Erosion.

Otherwise as a rule they are tolerably clean shelled, and fleshy bodied. Unlike the whelk, reversed shells are of extreme rarity. To our knowledge, "winkle" is the only local name with us, but "Pin-patches" is a colloquial in N. Essex and Suffolk. There is a small, short-spired sort (*var. brevicula*) found at Southend. As a rule periwinkles are not so much run upon as other shell-fish by holiday-seekers at the coast. "Trippers" seem to prefer picking up a few fresh ones as they wander about. London is the great centre of their consumption.

The Whelk Family (*Buccinidæ*).—The first to mention is the Dog Whelk or Whelk Tingle (*Purpura lapillus*), of bad omen to the oyster-culturists. The whelk tingle is notoriously a dire enemy to the oysters and mussels. Its manner of attack is simple, for it squats on its prey, and steadily, with workman-like fashion, proceeds to bore through the shell, and finishes by extracting and devouring the soft body contents. They are a perfect nuisance on some oyster grounds, Whitstable as else-where; the owners in the Blackwater vicinity willingly pay for their destruction. Prolific summer breeders, their clusters of flask-shaped egg-sacs get stuck on to oysters, barnacles, stones, &c.; the young, as soon as they are able, following the habits of their parents. An ordinary size of the adult is about $1\frac{1}{2}$ inch by 1 inch. With us it is not used as food, though palatable notwithstanding.

The Common Whelk (*Buccinum undatum*) (White Whelk of Billingsgate) in Kent and Essex holds a very subordinate position as an article of diet. Nevertheless, there is a large return commercially for whelks to be used as bait at home and abroad, and for the London market. Harwich, Ramsgate and Margate, Whitstable and Faversham, are the chief centres of the trade. Their fishing from the first three ports is pursued mainly seaward, but the fishermen of the two last ply their vocation on the Kentish Flats. The whelks are mostly caught by "trotting," some by dredging, and a smaller share in pots.

For description of methods *see* Sect. VI. In 1899 there were twenty second class boats fishing all the year round from Harwich (Inspect. Ann. Rep.), and about as many from the other ports taken together. The sum thus derived from the whelk fishery may be roughly estimated at £25,000 per annum, possibly considerably more.

Though the whelk inhabits our entire seaboard, the estuarine mouths are its principal location. A limited number, however, come up in the shrimper's trawl-net almost to the limits of the brackish water; these usually are thrown overboard. That they are abundant on the areas regularly fished for may be surmised from the net proceeds mentioned.

Reversed shells are not altogether scarce, and there are several named varieties (by naturalists) of monstrous shells. It is a carnivore and scavenger in the true sense of the word. Most dead animal bodies, and also many living ones, are subject to its voracity. Even the oyster is said to have an enemy in the common whelk, though the evidence thereon is not wholly satisfactory.

The dimensions of the marketable whelk are variable, for we have seen both small and large among tub-fulls in the Billingsgate stalls. The usual sizes there are 3 by $1\frac{1}{2}$, $3\frac{1}{2}$ by 2, and up to 4 by $2\frac{1}{4}$ inches. We have a series before us of 25 collected in the Thames area, beginning with $\frac{5}{8}$ by $\frac{3}{8}$ inch (inhabited by a hermit crab) the next 1 by $\frac{1}{2}$ inch, the rest graduating steadily and successively to the market sizes above given. A few have their surface partially covered with serpulæ tubes and acorn barnacles, though most are tolerably clean, the skin (epidermis) peeling off as they dry.

Honeycomb masses of whelks' eggs are familiar objects washed on to the sea shore. In the adult the sexes are separate. They are winter and spring breeders, October and May being the extremes. The young are forward, tolerably well formed, with shell and operculum, ere leaving the egg. Their rate of growth would seem not to be very fast, so that the larger market specimens are at least several (presumably not less than five to six) years old. It is common knowledge that whelks are a taking bait, and much used in the North Sea cod fishery. As an esculent, curiously enough they are less partaken of at the seaside than in London—their consumption at the East End, boiled and pickled, being something enormous.[*]

The RED or HARD WHELK (*Fusus antiquus*).—We place this under the Whelks, for as one of such it is known commercially, although *ipso facto* it belongs to an allied but different family, namely, the *Muricidae*. The Billingsgate name is Almond or Red Whelk; at Liverpool, Hard Whelk. Conchologists know them as Spindle Shells, and class them apart from the whelk on account of slight structural difference, though to the ordinary observer they are very like each other. Much of what has been said of *Buccinum*, its fishery, habits, even size, &c., applies to *Fusus*. The latter, however, are more a deeper sea dweller, and their egg cases do not exhibit identity with the former. A large percentage of the Ramsgate and Harwich catch of whelks are of this species (*F. antiquus*). A slender kind, *F. gracilis*, has been got sparingly on our coasts, and perchance sent to market, though said to be frequently rejected there. Males of it are said to be the most numerous.

MOLLUSKS AS BAIT, FOOD OF FISHES, &c.

The presence in multitude of certain minor shell-fish on our stretch of sands and mud is one of the piscine attractions to our waters. Subjoined is a passing notice of a few of them and others used as bait, &c., or otherwise destructive in habit.

Sand and Mud Dwellers.—(*a*) The SOLENS or RAZOR SHELLS, *alias* the elongated double-shelled Spout fishes, are represented by three species. These are *Solen ensis*, *S. siliqua* and *S. vagina*: size, straightness or slight curvature of shell chiefly distinguishing them. They seem to prefer sea margin rather than estuary, or only quite at mouth of latter. Lodging in the sand, on the slightest tremor of footstep near, they give a squirt, and disappear quickly and deeply. They make an

---

[*] Witness, Mahew, "London Labour and London Poor," Vol. I.

effective bait for long and short lines. Plaice and dabs have a strong partiality for them. The difficulty of securing the live razor fish more often limits their use as bait, for their celerity of escape is remarkable. A barbed wire thrust quickly into the sand is commonly used for their capture. Kent and Essex folks don't usually value them as food, but in Yorkshire they are much liked as a culinary adjunct. Boiled razor fish are regarded as delicious eating.

(*b*) The TELLINAS are another set of bivalves whereon plaice and dab revel in crunching them for food contents. Taken generally they are small sized, most $\frac{1}{2}$ to 1 inch in diameters, the largest under 2 inches. They are residents in muddy sands, of oval or somewhat triangular shape, and laterally compressed.

The BALTIC TELLINA (*T. balthica*) is probably the most abundant in the estuaries, equally of Thames, Crouch, Blackwater, Stour and Orwell. But it is also found in the neighbourhood of Margate, Pegwell Bay, and various parts of S. Kent, Dungeness beach for example. On the cockle grounds it is numerous. In some places, *e.g.*, Blyth Sand, there are great banks of dead shells ; and hereabouts, as already mentioned, is a favourite concentration area for flat fish at certain times of the year. Its flatter shelled ally, the THIN TELLINA (*T. tenuis*), burrows scarcely so deep. During our strong easterly gales this, the *T. balthica*, and at intervals the biggish *T. crassa*, get surged into the shallows, an easy prey to the aforesaid mollusk-eating flat fish.

FIG. 24.

Diagram to illustrate a sectional view of the mud, exposing a family congregation of the Scrobicularia in various positions. The central one is shown with fleshy foot extended below, and the pair of long syphon tubes stretched upwards to the water.

(c) The SCROBICULARIA (various sorts) within our District constantly contribute provender for plaice and dab, and in season are preyed on by the flounder, while in the North Sea haddocks and cod are particularly fond of them. Outwardly to a certain extent they resemble the Tellinas; like them, bed gregariously, and are residents of mud, sand and clayey soil.

The PEPPERY SCROBULARIA (*S. piperita*), relatively a large form (1½ by 2 inches diameters), is of common occurrence at Walton-on-Naze, Harwich, Felixstowe, &c. (Crouch), though not found by him in his dredging in the Burnham river.* It has been got at several places on the Kentish shores, Pegwell Bay, Reculvers, &c. In digging for clams (*Mya*) on the fore-shore clyty-mud close to Leigh, we have come across great batches in family groups. These occupy the top layers, 2 to 3 inches from the surface, whilst clams lie below them, but much more deeply situated. The syphon tubes of Scrobicularia, like those of Tellina, are separate, and at times stretch out and are thrust upwards to the water (*see* sketch, fig. 24). Other much smaller, more delicate species, *S. alba*, *S. prismatica*, and *S. tenuis* with varieties, are numerous on our shores, the last one supposed to become the food of the grey mullet. "Butterfish" is a local name given to specimens of Scrobicularia and Tellina indis-criminately.

(d) The MACTRAS, of stouter build and shaped something like Scrobicularia (but with united syphons as in the clams and other likenesses), only furnish food for fish in our area, though elsewhere they are used as bait, and occasionally partaken of as edible product. *M. solida*, *M. subtruncata* and *M. stultorum* are freely distributed on various parts of our littoral and estuaries. The last named turned up in enormous quantities when dredging the harbour of Newhaven (Sussex) in 1861. Barges trans-ported the dredgings outside, whither flocked flat fish in such multitudes that the trawlers reaped a golden harvest close in shore (Jeffr., Brit. Conch., Vol. II.).

---

*Essex Nat. VI. (1892). Yet this does not imply its absence in the marginal muddy sands there.

When examining fishes' stomachs as to nature of their food, we have very frequently detected fragmentary shells of young cockles (the fishermen's "trayle"); at chance intervals also other diminutive shell fish, of less account from fisheries point of view, such as species of *Nucula, Tapes, Odostomia, Rissoa*, &c. Indeed, our Zostera beds and seaweed, rocky pools, besides the hydroid clusters on the covered sand banks, are natural rendezvous for the fry of a variety of mollusks and other lower marine organisms. Thence resort the shrimps, and accompanying minute crustaceans, followed by brood and adult fish, as thick as hops.

The Wood Borers—(*e*)—of which the SHIPWORM (*Teredo navalis*) is a notable representative, yet cannot be claimed as useful for bait, though in a limited way it may be reckoned as provender for small crustaceans and diminutive fish. We here introduce remarks on it as a silent worker, a foe whose hidden presence fishermen and others have to keep a sharp look out for.

A worm only by name, and shape of lengthened body, nevertheless its organization is that of a bivalve mollusk. Its ravages in ships' timbers, piers and landing stages, &c., are notorious and need not here be dilated on. It is destructive at Ramsgate, Broadstairs (fishermen's elm-stakes), Herne Bay (Old Pier), Sheerness (harbour piles), and Queenborough. It is found in the Medway and Thames generally, especially among stationary watch-boats, and such craft as have been moored for a long period. The Medway neighbourhood gets the credit of being the most fraught with danger from Teredo. We may exemplify its occurrence by one instance. When with a shrimper at the Medway mouth, adjoining the Nore Sand, suddenly the "Bawley" was brought up sharply, something had gone wrong with the trawl then down. Only after much manœuvring and injury to net was a barge's great leeboard hoisted in. This was riddled with live Teredo. Such instances are not uncommon. Again, the fishermen's craft, though frequently cleaned and tarred or covered with patent chemical compositions, are still liable to weed and worm. When the boats are left high and dry for some time, if in hot weather, then the Teredo dies; or if there is a hard or long continued frost (as in 1895) this likewise kills them.

Notwithstanding that the wooden piles of old Southend Pier were protected by closely-set broad-headed nails, yet on their final removal we observed that Teredo had found entry into a few of them. Such timber piles as were afterwards required in addition to the iron ones and framework were of greenheart. Whether these will ultimately resist Teredo remains to be seen. Various penetrating re-agents* have been recommended and tried elsewhere, but, though beneficial in some degree, yet hitherto they have not proved perfect checks to the creatures' ravages.

The *Xylophaga dorsalis* is a shorter-bodied wood perforator, intermediate in characters between Teredo and Pholas (*infra*), probably nearest the latter. The only instance and locality we know of adjoining our District is a record of its occurrence at Gravesend (Jeff., Brit. Conch., Vol. III.).

Chalk and Stone Borers (Patella and Pholas).—(*f*) The COMMON LIMPET (*Patella vulgaris*) may be taken as an example of a shallow excavator in our chalk cliffs. It is probably most numerous in S. Kent, where the shore is rocky in nature. They are not much partaken of as human aliment in our District; but in the N.E. of England they are consumed in great quantities by the populace. They are with us southern folks rather serviceable as bait, notably for pout and codling among rod and line sea-fishers. Their fleshy body gets tougher and holds better to the hook when partially sun-dried.

The true stone borers belong to the genus *Pholas*, all four British species inhabiting the Kent shores. The SMALL PHOLAS (*P. parva*) and the CURLED PHOLAS (*P. crispata*) are rarer; but

---

* Such as Bethell's Creosote, or oil of coal tar, Burnett's Chloride of Zinc, Tryan's Corrosive Sublimate of Mercury, Margary's Salts of Metals, Payne's Chloride of Lime and Sulphate of Iron. *See* Paton's paper on Old Southend Pier-head and Ravages of Teredo, in Proc. Inst. Civ. Engineers, Vol. IX., 1850.

the FINGER-SHAPED PHOLAS (*P. dactylus*) and the WHITE PHOLAS (*P. candida*) are quite numerous in some localities. The two last excavate deep holes at low water mark—the base of the chalk cliffs near Margate, and in the Dover neighbourhood from St. Margaret's Bay westwards to Shakespeare Cliff. The blocks of stones forming the Folkestone pier are likewise pierced and tenanted by Pholas. The animal has an elongated plump body and foot. It is not infrequently removed from its hole to furnish fish-bait. On the French coast opposite it is a common market mollusk, and cooked with bread crumbs, herbs and seasoning, or, like our cockles, preserved in vinegar prior to consumption. We are not aware of its now being eaten within our District.

An old English name for the Pholas was "Piddock," and "Pittick" is still a colloquial at Folkestone, though some of the men speak of them as small "clams." Its long united syphons may suggest resemblance to the clam, but the lengthened shape of the shell, its extreme delicacy, prickled surface, &c., point to its separation. It is generally admitted that, like the Limpet, the foot in Pholas is the active agent or boring tool, supplemented by the syphonal water currents. The empty shells of the White Pholas are now and again found in the shrimper's trawl, even as far as the Nore sands, and they are also met with up the Blackwater, but Kent chalk is their chief domicile.

Cuttle-Fish Tribe (*Cephalopods*).—(*g*) These make capital bait by reason of their tough, fleshy body holding on well to the hook. Our Kent and Essex deep-sea liners bait with them when available, whether fresh or salted, the former preferred. The inshore fishers, either in boat or from pier-head, equally patronise squid or octopus as bait. The former specially are found to be a taking bait for cod, whiting, bass, conger and pollack. The various kinds of Cephalopods are preyed upon by several kinds of fishes, &c.,[*] whilst in their turn they as

---

[*] We have referred to the Hyperoodon and the Cachalot among the Whales as Cuttlefish eaters, *antea* p. 31 and p. 33.

greedily devour species of fish, mollusks and crustaceans. For instance, the common Octopus (*O. vulgaris*) is well known ruthlessly to destroy the crab tribe, and the lobster pots are their fair game, besides shell fish, such as species of *Tapes* and *Psammobia*, &c. Flocks of the little *Sepiolæ* mingle with the hordes of young shrimps, and play havoc among the brood and accompanying lower marine forms.

Little attention has hitherto been paid to the Cephalopods of our District, hence their distribution and frequency of visitation are but imperfectly known. Some, however, appear but rarely, others are more regular in their advent. We know only of two instances of the large, arrow-shaped FLYING SQUID (*Ommastrephes* sagittatus*) ; one captured near Folkestone, the other, a great-sized specimen,† found by Mr. Fitch stranded on the causeway leading to Northey Island (Blackwater), end of November, 1901. We have identified the northern Octopod, the CURLY ELEDONE (*E. cirrosa*), in the Thames estuary, and among some Octopods got by the trawlers (1899) (most probably the same species), one is said to have "nearly filled a bucket, and grasped dangerously with its arms ere being thrown overboard." The COMMON OCTOPUS (*O. vulgaris*), a more southern channel form, is recorded from Ramsgate, Dover and Folkestone.‡

FIG. 25.

Sepiola Rondeleti.

The diminutive *Sepiola Rondeleti*, regularly in midsummer and early autumn frequents the Essex coast and up the

---

* Hoyle, "Catalogue of Recent Cephalopoda," Edinb. 1886, places this under the genus *Todarodes* of Steenstrup.

† Its total length, tentacles inclusive, was 2 feet 5 inches, the body 1 foot 3 inches, and with head 1 foot 10 inches.

‡ "A plague of Octopus" occurred in 1899-00 on the South Devon and Cornish coasts, and the fisheries for edible crabs and lobsters were most seriously affected; even the small swimming crabs were almost exterminated by them. This excess of octopus was attributed to previous hot summers and migration from the French coast. As a remedial measure, empty longish-necked pitcher pots were recommended to be lowered and buoyed, wherein octopus entering would be secured in numbers.—Garstang in Jour. Mar. Biol. Assoc., Nov., 1900.

FIG. 26.

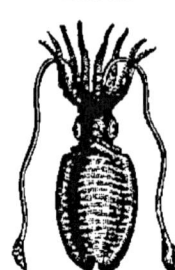

Common Cuttle-fish.
(*Sepia officinalis.*)

estuaries, whither they are taken in great numbers by the shrimpers in their trawls. They are of both sexes, and the females are then in gravid condition. The CUTTLE-FISH (*Sepia officinalis*) is more irregular in its visits, but has been obtained in both Kent and Essex seaboard, and we have obtained small fair-sized examples in the Thames estuary. Of the SQUIDS (*Loligo*), three species are more or less of frequent occurrence round both counties, viz., the COMMON SQUID (*L. vulgaris*), the smaller sized *L. media* and FORBES SQUID (*L. Forbesii*). In November, 1891, a large specimen of the last-mentioned was taken by spratters off the mouth of the Crouch river. It measured close on 2½ feet, body and arms included, its pen (cuttle-bone) being some 15 inches long.[*]

The fishermen usually discriminate between the long-shaped, arrow-tailed Squids and the flask-shaped suckers octopods, without further differentiation. At Folkestone, though, Cuttle-fish are familiarly known as "Ink-spewers," "Tortoises" (from hunching up their backs) and "Man-suckers."[†]

SHRIMP, CRAB AND LOBSTER KIND (= CRUSTACEA).

Around Kent and Essex is famous ground for certain kinds of stalk-eyed crustaceans, the shrimp being of the greatest mercantile value; whereas lobster and edible crab are sparse in comparison, and thus their fisheries are of less importance, commercially. There are, however, immense swarms of diminutive sessile-eyed (without stalks) crustaceans which, on account of their very small dimensions, are of no utility as

---

[*] *See* "Notes of two days' Trawling and Dredging in the River Crouch, Oct. 10th and 15th, 1891." Essex Nat. VI., 1892.

[†] Buckland, "Curiosities of Natural History," 2nd Ser., 1860.

market product. They, nevertheless, constitute an unfailing supply of food for fish, &c., and consequently are most advantageous to the well-being of our fisheries in general. To this richness in minor crustacean life may be attributed much of the abundance of immature fishes in our flats and estuaries.

The Shrimp and Prawn Families (*Crangonidae* and *Palæmonidae*).—To the ordinary person and trade requirements shrimps are of two kinds, viz., the Brown and the Pink Shrimp. The first (*Crangon*) typifies the true shrimp, which, off-hand, may be distinguished by its brownish grey colour (when alive), not boiling red, and its short flat nose or prow. The second (*Pandalus*), more nearly allied to the prawn (*Palæmon*), is of a whitish, pinkey tint (when alive), boils to a bright reddish hue, and has a prominent, long, toothed beak or rostrum. There are other intermediate so-called shrimps (*Hippolyte*), to be noticed in due course. Separate species of all three sorts haunt our shores.

The Family Crangonidæ, equivalent to the true shrimps.— (1) The BANDED SHRIMP (*C. fasciatus*). Only on one occasion, 10th May, 1898, have we been fortunate in obtaining a couple of specimens, and these between the W. Girdler Buoy and the Gilman, at 4 to 5 fathoms depth. It is a small, insignificant-looking shrimp, $\frac{1}{2}$ to $\frac{3}{4}$ inch long, and therefore easily overlooked. Its most readily distinguishing feature is a purple brown band about where the body bends behind. Patterson,[*] of Yarmouth, notes its rarity there, only having had a few brought him by the shrimpers in April and May.

(2) The YELLOW SHRIMP (locally "Yellow Hammer") of the Harwich shrimpers. We presume this is the Three-spined Shrimp (*C. trispinosus* ?), inasmuch as this species at Yarmouth gets the name of "Yellow Shrimp," and has been identified by Patterson ("Zool.," *l.c.*). We ourselves did not meet with them when accompanying the shrimpers from Harwich some years ago. Our informant, Robert Johnson, sen., is so reliable and

---

[*] Stalk-eyed crustacea of Great Yarmouth, "Zool.," April, 1898.

close an observer that we have no hesitation in accepting his statement, corroborated by fellow shrimpers. He says it is of a buff tint, slightly smaller than the pink shrimp, and at times is taken along with them in the proportion of about one-third the numbers. When it appears there is usually a falling off of the pink shrimps. He thinks they migrate from the north, at least he has never met with them south of the Tongue or Queen's Channel, seeming, like the pink shrimp, to prefer hard ground. Messrs. Lynn and Gibson, of Billingsgate, assure us that at times among their consignments from Brightlingsea many examples of the Yellow Shrimp turn up. Patterson (*l.c.*) has found them "commonest in August" at Yarmouth. He considers it superior in flavour to the pink or brown shrimp, but Johnson is of an opposite opinion. White names it "Hailstone's Shrimp," first described from Hastings, where they are known as "pug shrimps."* It is said to carry spawn in March (Hailstone), July at Plymouth (Weldon). The eggs are of a "light red green" colour (Thompson).

(3) The CHANNEL-TAILED SHRIMP (*Crangon Allmanni*), of Kinahan†, is not easily noticed among a heap of the Common Shrimps, whether alive or cooked, so like are the two in general appearance. Closer examination, however, shows the former, otherwise Allman's Shrimp, to possess a characteristic grooving on the upper side of its sixth tail-piece and other less pronounced differences (Fig. 27). We have only had a few 1½ and 1¾ inch specimens under observation. These were got in mid-October in the neighbourhood of the Nore, and detected as

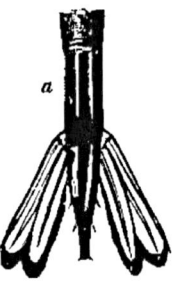

FIG. 27.

Upper view tail of Allman's Shrimp, showing grooving of 6th segment (*a*) (after Kinahan).

---

* *See* Yarrell, "Brit. Stalk-eyed Crust.," 1853, and Adam White, "Popular Hist. Brit. Crustacea," 1857.

† Proc. Roy. Irish Acad., Vol. VIII., 1864, and Trans. R.I. Acad. Vol. XXIV., Sci., 1871.

unusual by the quick eye of R. Johnson, jun. They may be commoner than suspected, though passing current as brown shrimps.* The three preceding shrimps have not previously been recorded from our District.

(4) The COMMON or BROWN SHRIMP (*Crangon vulgaris*). *Distribution.*—This species is met with all round the coasts of Kent and Essex, from Sussex nigh to South Suffolk, and it ascends the estuaries to almost beyond the brackish water. Possibly in the neighbourhood of the South Foreland it is less frequent than elsewhere. At least, "Dover is one of the very few seaside resorts where shrimping does not commend itself as a livelihood to any of its inhabitants"—the shrimps sold there being imported (Webb and Horsnaill). Along the great sandy bay from Dymchurch to Romney we have seen the shove-netters (hand or push-nets) at work getting fair catches. Pegwell Bay, with its sands, is another noted locality during summer for fine brown shrimps. But from Ramsgate round the North Foreland it gets scarcer. Thereabouts, seemingly, on the harder ground, the pink shrimp (*Pandalus*) replaces it.

Our information, derived from the elder and most experienced Leigh shrimpers, leads to the following conclusion. That taking a line from the neighbourhood of the Naze or Harwich southwards, cutting the Gunfleet, Middle Sunk and Shingles, thence onwards towards the Herne Bay direction, all westward of this to the Lower Hope and Gravesend Reach may be regarded (likewise in the other Essex estuaries) as brown shrimp ground. Everywhere within said area, whether in mid-channel's deeper water, or among the shallow sand-banks, or on the shores of sand or mud irrespectively, there they are to be found, few or many, according to circumstances. To the eastward of the above-mentioned line is the chief area of the pink shrimp. There is, however, no such hard and fast line as above indicated, for here and there the brown shrimp juts

---

* In the Trans. Liverpool Biol. Soc. for 1891 (Shrimp Enquiry), Mr. Ascroft, of Lytham, Lancashire, states that there are great numbers of *Crangon Allmanni* taken amongst the other shrimps thereabouts.

eastward on occasions, and at certain seasons the pink shrimp comes westward to beyond the Nore. Concerning both forms more explicit data is given hereafter under Fishing Grounds (Sect. V.), and Shrimp-trawling (Sect. VI.).

Size.—The catch as it is tumbled out of the trawl on to the deck, so far as shrimps are concerned, varies according to season and the ground fished. At special times there are numbers of small sized ones of an inch and $1\frac{1}{4}$ inches in length. Those of half an inch are very seldom indeed got in the trawl, and $\frac{3}{4}$ inch ones are not frequent. This, however, is not invariably the case, for at irregular intervals, chiefly climax of breeding season, the shrimpers will unexpectedly make a great haul of "dust" or "smig," their expressions for the undersized brood. Whether the meshes of the net allow the diminutive shrimps to escape, or the young mostly keep well down among the sea-weed, mud and sand, or that they perchance trend towards the shallows in their early stage, must be left to surmise.

Practically $\frac{3}{4}$ inch is the smallest size the net ever brings up, and 3-inch examples are the current limit of length seen by us. Yet this is not essentially their utmost limits of growth. When with shrimper near the West Oaze Buoy, 16th June, 1899, we took note of two most exceptionally large specimens, relatively giants among shrimps. Both aged females, one $3\frac{1}{2}$ the other $3\frac{3}{4}$ inches long, the former full berried. Moreover, we have been told of an extraordinary shrimp —over 4 inches— caught near the Spile some years ago. Measurements, it is to be understood, are from the eye to tail-end (telson), thus excluding the foot jaws and the short and the long antennae (feelers).

The general size of the cooked brown shrimps sent to the London market may be put down as ranging from $1\frac{1}{2}$ to $2\frac{1}{2}$ inches. In good samples those of 2 inches upwards are in excess, there may even be a fair proportion of $2\frac{1}{4}$ inches and others of $2\frac{1}{2}$ inches, besides relatively fewer of extra large old females, $2\frac{3}{4}$ inches, still more rarely a 3-inch one. If the sample is poor, and been hastily or carelessly culled, then smaller shrimps of an inch and $1\frac{1}{4}$ inch, as a matter of course, will be found among them. According to the predominance of small, middle or large sizes, or a moderate uniformity in appearance, so will the lot be regarded favourably or otherwise. As product of market value, size goes a long way, though colour, freshness and flavour of flesh are all to be taken into account, which the practised buyer recognises at once.

Numbers.—The abundance, nay vast armies of the brown shrimp, is best attested by the fleets of Essex and Kent beam-trawlers kept pretty constantly at work throughout the year. Besides, take into account the many individuals who use shove-nets during the season on the E. and S. Kent shores. *Crangon* cannot be considered scarce or declining in numbers when quite recently, as in years past, not only average catches of 30 to 50, but on red-letter days 80 to 100 gallons have sometimes rewarded a Leigh boat's trip. Nor do the Pegwell Bay, &c., shrimps seem to decrease. Of course there are times of pronounced glut and unforeseen scarcity. Doubtless (among others) meteorological conditions are a pressing factor, for shrimps it is well known are very sensitive to depression of temperature—with a frost few are to be got. An old shrimper recalls one year (about 1868 ?) when there was quite a dearth until July. The catch then was only from 1 to 2 gallons daily. His expression was "they were drove to bed somewhere."

With the view of ascertaining how many shrimps there are to the gallon, we measured half a gallon, and, accurately counting these, doubled the same. The results are given below.

Brown shrimps.— Smallest, below the usual market size, with an average of about $1\frac{1}{2}$ inches (some over) = 426. Of market size: smalls, $1\frac{3}{4}$ to 2 inches = 683; mediums, $2\frac{1}{4}$ inches average = 84; bigs, $2\frac{1}{2}$ and $2\frac{3}{4}$ inches = 56. Total of browns = 1,249.

Pink shrimps.—Smalls, $1\frac{1}{2}$ to $1\frac{3}{4}$ inches = 186; mediums, $1\frac{3}{4}$ to 2 inches = 19; bigs, $2\frac{1}{4}$ inches average = 15. Total of pinks = 220. The whole of both sorts in half a gallon = 1,469, or equivalent to 2,938 per gallon.

We chose mid-November, when the winter gauge of the sieve, $\frac{3}{10}$ inch wire to wire, is in use. With the summer sieve of $\frac{4}{16}$ ($=\frac{1}{4}$ inch) considerably fewer of the smallest size would be obtained. The shrimps enumerated above were measured in their fresh condition. After being roughly culled by hand from the heap on deck they were put into the sieve, washed and given the usual first riddling. We ascertained also that specimens in the fresh state adjust themselves so that they take up less room in the measure than do those in the cooked condition. Half a gallon boiled and again put into the measure were $\frac{1}{2}$ pint overplus—otherwise occupy more space by 1 pint to the gallon. This is to be accounted for by their bent condition, which leaves spaces; in other words, they do not pack so closely. On the other hand, a number of the smallest sized cooked shrimps get through the sieve during the second riddling.

Taking all circumstances into consideration, if the summer shrimps as a rule are larger in bulk, and cooking decreases numbers as measured, then as counter effect there may be hurried sifting, during night or rough weather, and smalls be more than usual. To be within rather than above bounds we may allow 2,700 to 2,800 shrimps to the gallon on an average throughout the year. Patterson, of Yarmouth, counted 400 shrimps to the pint in a March catch. This would yield 3,200 to the gallon. But he admits "they run larger in the finer months." Hence our estimate possibly is more likely to be nearer the facts for statistical purposes. The quantities in numbers of gallons landed at Leigh for several years are given in tabular form in Sect. X., General Returns for Fisheries; here we need only cursorily refer in abstract to a dozen annual results (brown and pink shrimps all told).

1889. Good. (Poor spring.)

1890. Fairly good. (Bad up river.)

1891. Very good. (Generally.)

1892. Very good. (Moderate up [river.)

1893. Moderate. (Very good up [river.)

1894. Very good. (Catch above [Grays.)

1895. Moderate,· severe spring. (Oct. big catch.)

1896. Good. (July heavy, Nov. [& Dec. scarce.)

1897. Very good for first 9 months.

1898. Very good. (Moderate parts [of Essex.)

1899. Good. (Bad spring, very [good fall.)

1900. Good summer, poor spring and fall.

The above brings out the fact that shrimps are not diminishing in numbers in the Thames estuary, notwithstanding their enormous fishery. Some seasons have bad beginning and good ending or *vice versâ*. Occasionally there is predominance, or a scarcity up river or seawards, as the case may be. Bad weather may affect numbers caught for one, two or three months, yet the annual quantity stand high.

Local Name and Habits.—(a) In the Thames estuary area the Common Shrimp (*Crangon vulgaris*) is constantly spoken of as the Brown Shrimp, and only on a chance occasion have we heard it referred to as "Sand-shrimp." Yet this latter is that by which it is best known on the Dorset coast, while in Ireland "Gray Shrimp" is its local name. "Dust" and "Smig" are general terms applied by our estuary fishermen to small brood of whatever species. At Leigh certain supposed young shrimps have another colloquial, viz., "Jerry's Donkeys"; but these in reality belong to another group of diminutive crustacea (*see* Mysidæ).

(b) Concerning their habits generally, parties of the young brown shrimps, when about $\frac{1}{2}$ inch to $\frac{3}{4}$ inch long or over, frequent the sandy and muddy shores within low tide mark. In the spring, as the weather begins to get warm, and during the long summer days, they are seen darting about in the shallow and weedy pools left by the retiring tide. Or they hunt up and down the shallow guts, keenly hanging about such drainage runlets as carry sludge or garbage of any sort. In the pools they so assimilate in colour to the ground that their presence is not perceptible until their quick zigzag jerks betray them. When disturbed, in a second they flash about, are hidden in the mud or sand, and only a cloud of particles left, obscuring their whereabouts. As autumn merges into colder winter, and having increased in size, the brood shrimps gather together in companies and gradually progress towards the deeper water.* Ultimately the recruits swell the ranks of some of the main bodies of the roving adult shrimps.

---

* Among several places, Hadleigh Ray and Egypt Bay, &c., form good muster-grounds.

In so far as the trawl discloses, in an ordinary haul there is a mixture of shrimps of different ages. The middle moderate-sized adults usually form the great majority, and the aged big ones, or the growing adolescent small ones, may vary in proportion to make up the minority. It is patent though that youth and age of the brown shrimp (along with pink shrimps at certain seasons) freely associate, and constitute their every-day assemblages. But in early spring, late autumn or winter, should cold weather or frost set in, most suddenly there is a great diminution, often an entire disappearance, of the larger shrimps, which are not seen again until a cessation of the severe weather.

Meantime the shrimper chiefly catches undersized ones. It matters little whether fishing is pursued in the shallower, up river, brackish reaches or in the more seaward, deeper, salt water. Our Thames cocklers also find, chiefly large sized, shrimps sunk among the sands of the Maplins and other places, when at their vocation, winter time or after a spell of cold weather. Hence most reasonably it is believed that the older prime shrimps "bed" or "go to ground" in the mud or sand* in the neighbourhood, instead of retiring to distant deeps, as Buckland has stated†.

On other occasions, with fair weather, say near the Oaze or Girdler, two boats may be fishing in proximity (say a cable's length apart), one's catch will be chiefly big sized, the other small sized shrimps. This points out that shrimps at certain times, do grade off in lots, according to age. Everyday experience shows that the gregarious shrimps, as a rule, sojourn among the zoophyte clumps, sea-weeds and objects on or close to the bottom. Howsoever, instances are known to us of exuberant catches in stow-net in deepish water midway between surface and the ground. (*See below*—Migration.)

---

* The Lancashire shrimpers also aver that during cold, stormy weather they bury themselves; the cocklers in that District raking them up nigh a foot deep in the sand. Herdman, " Fauna of Liverpool Bay," Vol. III. (1892). "Shrimp Enquiry."

† Commissioners Sea-Fisheries Report, 1879; Appendix II., Shrimps.

The rapidity and burrowing powers of the shrimps in moist sand are surprising. Several eminent naturalists affirm that there is a reciprocal relation of colour to habitat—light where sandy, darker where muddy. Some of our Thames shrimpers hold that this is not the case. On the contrary, they find that the shrimps taken on muddy grounds (*e.g.*, the Blyth, &c.) are more often pale or somewhat blanched in colour, and they cook of a still paler hue. Whereas on sandy ground (say Oaze or Warp) the shrimps caught are more highly coloured, both when fresh and cooked. We are inclined to think moreover that in the aged there is an accession of pigment irrespective of the nature of the bottom.

Their Food.—As to this, we find the juvenile shore shrimps are busy scavengers in their way. Odds and ends come not amiss, so be it that they contain fleshy morsels to their taste. Perchance brown diatomaceous frustules, atoms of sea-weed and fine sand with traces of mud-worms, &c. The older shrimps appear to have a more comprehensive dietary, its nature somewhat depending on the time of year and in what locality they are feeding. The bulk of their food is quite fragmentary and microscopic. There is a pretty constant presence of infinitesimal sand-granules, and when on some grounds occasionally a tendency to muddy particles or shreds of extraneous plant-tissues, &c., all which foreign matter evidently are swallowed at random with their true provender.

Like most Crustaceans, animal substance predominates in their fare. Still Diatoms, threadlike algæ and comminuted pickings of seaweeds are present at times. We have detected Foraminifera, even scraps of sponges (judging from triradiate spicules, &c.), likewise Hydroid structures. Where the tube-forming worms *Pectinaria** (*see* Fig. 30) is numerous, there shrimps congregate and greedily feed on them. Several species of Annelids, the Nereids particularly, can be identified, and are

---

* Lovett mentions his finding a shrimp which had backed into a Pectinaria tube, and there got stuck fast ("Zool.," Dec., 1885).

quite an attractive aliment. Another nutrient source seems to be early and passing stages of minute Crustaceans; for fragmentary portions of their hairy-clad appendages, &c., denote presence of Mysidæ, Amphipods, Copepods and allied Entomostraca. Delicate morsels of the soft parts of shell-fish are not uncommon.

The Leighmen have long known that where brood mussels and cockle-"trayle" are, thereabouts shrimps abound.* On those flats (dry at low ebb), tenanted by *Tellina* and *Scrobicularia*, shrimps thrive on their fry and such fragments of the adults' flesh as plaice, dab and flounder scatter about. Herdman has recorded finding *Donax* eaten by shrimps on the Lancashire coast, even parts of young shrimps and crabs, spines of minute starfish and fish-brood remains.†

Migration.—Authorities ‡ have promulgated the idea that there is a regular annual migration of the common shrimp at breeding time from the sea up the estuaries and rivers, with a corresponding return in due course. This seems questionable, so far as our information goes, or rather we ought to receive the statement with extenuating circumstances. Possibly there has been a tendency to interweave part history of the pink with that of the brown shrimps? It must be acknowledged that information concerning the movements of the latter on the outer sea-boards of our District requires further investigation. Still, there is no pronounced evidence of immense shoals of the common shrimp passing along the coasts to reach the estuaries, or the reverse movement. On the contrary, there is so to some extent in the case of the pink and yellow shrimps.

It is undeniable that under ordinary conditions brown shrimps are found spread broadcast over a great part of the

---

* *See* Buckland, Commiss. Rep., 1879, Append. II., Shrimps. He also notes that the heads of sardines are used for shrimp bait in their hoop-barrel nets by the French fishermen.

† Lancashire Sea-Fish. Labor. Reps. for 1892–94.

‡ Yarrell says "In the breeding season the shrimps approach the estuaries and even ascend the rivers." Buckland (in Rep. *l.c.*) refers to M. Delidon as stating that when migrating they swim ⋙ fashion in mid-water and follow the sinuosities of the coast wherever there is sand.

Thames estuary habitat every day in the year. They may be scattered about or many together in droves; the shrimps being either small or of moderate size, according to locality and other circumstances. Withal there is among them what may be termed a partial local to and fro movement of the family groups, impelled by several contingencies. For instance, seeing that the crustacean section of their prey roam about, there is a necessity to follow them. Then the various species of worms and shell-fish multiply at different periods and places intermittingly, so shrimp visits to this or that bed in the course of things result periodically. Sexual impulse, again, doubtless brings shrimps together, though special spawning grounds are quite unknown. There is an absolute necessity at times to shift ground and avoid a crowd of enemies always hovering in pursuit. The weather influences we have already mentioned. Besides, tidal currents have a potent effect. With powerful spring tides the shrimps seem driven from their usual haunts; during neaps they cling more to the main estuarine channels.

Again, we know of an instance where spratters at work with stow-net in early winter opposite the Garrison Point, Sheerness, in fourteen fathoms water, have taken a shoal of shrimps in their net. Whitebaiters, also, on the Essex shore below Southend pier have had similar experience. It shows that shrimps on occasions do leave their bottom haunts and travel about in mid-water. Whether this is of the nature of a limited migration, or, as we suspect, sexual congregations, we can only hazard a guess.

To sum up, everything known points to the inference that the brown shrimp remains pretty much within estuarine limits. Its local shifting about though, other things being equal, is comparable, and indeed is analogous to the longer distance journeys of the pink shrimp. Notwithstanding, *Crangon vulgaris* is not migratory in the sense of the anadromous fishes (*e.g.* salmon tribe), which ascend rivers solely to deposit their eggs, and then return to the deep sea to recuperate.

With regard to the brown shrimp sea-coast dwellers, these have been got on clean sandy ground up to twenty-five fathoms, but only old and large sized specimens.   The younger shrimps and brood keep well to the sand-flats.   With these sea shrimps it may be surmised that there is a limited to and fro movement, viz., from the shores to deeper water, and conversely, though not necessarily a special shoaling to the estuaries.   But data thereon is yet too limited to establish a sound conclusion.

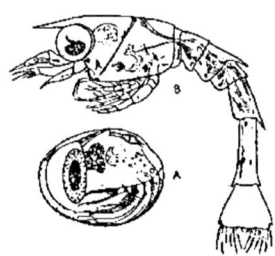

FIG. 28.

A Egg of Brown Shrimp (*Crangon vulgaris*),   containing embryo in an advanced stage. B Shrimp as hatched, in the minute   surface - swimming Zöea stage ; no swimmerets and tail end (telson) a broad shovel-shaped organ. Slightly modified after Kingsley. Bull, Essex Inst. (U.S.), Vol. XXI., 1889.

Breeding and Development.—What the precise proportion of the two sexes to one another are in the common shrimp is uncertain.   Though this much can be said, viz., that during the height of the spring spawning, occasionally more than half a catch in the trawl will carry berry.   Moreover, those without eggs, undersized shrimps, are not necessarily all males, some being tardy breeding or young unripe females.   The males, even when fully mature, are small sized.   Within our District there is, so far as we are aware, but feeble indication of separation of the sexes into distinct squads at any season.   Females may be reckoned then as preponderating considerably over the males.[*]

[*] Referring to sexual characteristics, Herdman (Labor. Rep. for 1892), does not coincide with Ehrenbaum's representations in his "Naturgeschichte von *Crangon vulgaris*," 1890.   The latter important contribution we searched for in vain among the London scientific libraries.   Since then we managed to procure a copy direct from Berlin. Ehrenbaum we find has investigated the relation of the sexes.   At stations apart and different months his results were conflicting—the numbers of males varying from 1% to 43%, and even in one instance (July) = 70% males. The percentage of females carrying abdominal eggs is quite as inconstant a factor, though there is a certain regularity of breeding time.   Ehrenbaum's extensive researches seem to endorse the view that there are periods when each sex congregates in numbers apart from the other.

As to the period of spawning, the fishermen's stock phrase runs: "we gets them in berry all the year round." Strictly speaking there is an underlying truth in this assertion. Though when cross-questioned they admit that during the three autumn months merging into beginning of winter very few indeed are berried. This we find is the actual state of things, based on our examination of series of specimens at different times.

The subjoined gives an approximate idea of the relative per centage numbers carrying eggs on their swimmerets, during different months in the Thames estuary.

Jan.	...	12%—20%	May	...	60%—70%	Sept.	...	8%—10%
Feb.	...	——?	June	...	50%	Oct.	...	1%— 2%
March	...	51%	July	...	27%—30%	Nov.	...	3%— 5%
April	...	54%—65%	Aug.	...	15%—18%	Dec.	...	7%—10%

These figures demonstrate that March, April, May and June are the months when the great majority of the brown shrimps are berried. In July and August there is a considerable drop in numbers. Still more so in September, and in October the minimum is reached. By November there is an apparent increase, though still the per centage is very low. From December to February there is a steady rise, and a leap up in March if the weather is favourable.

We qualify the preceding by adding that the observations (as tabulated) were not made consecutively throughout a single year. For example, as a rule April and May are the culminating months; but in one May trip a sample of the catch showed no more than half the ordinary run. On some occasions samples were merely hand picked roughly from the catch without being riddled. Others were the residue of one sifting, fresh condition. Still others cooked, that is those retained after being sieved twice. It consequently follows that the more the sifting and elimination of the immature, the higher becomes the ratio of spawn carriers. Whichever the month, a touch of cold weather reduces the numbers of large mature shrimps, with decrease of their ratio. Hence with seasonal variation, the apparent number of spawners notably fluctuates, and otherwise per centage data cannot be strictly relied on.

Herdman records* that on the Lancashire coast, in December and February, "most of the shrimps examined had spawn." In March there were 60 per cent., in April 75 per cent. to 85 per cent., and in May 60 per cent. to 80 per cent. Furthermore, he observes, in said neighbourhood there seems to be two chief spawning periods in the year—November, and April and May. He remarks that Ehrenbaum has found the same thing on the German coast.† All we can say, from old shrimpers' experience and our observations, is that in the Kent and Essex District these conditions do not obtain. Irrespective of varying monthly and annual per centages of spawners, or defective observations, or errors of method or calculations, certain broad facts remain regarding the Brown Shrimp. They are that March, April, May, sometimes June, are the maximum months when the eggs fully ripen and hatch out; October and November the minimum. Further, that every day of the year a few or many are to be found in a berried condition. We are thus led to inquire, what length of time does it take to hatch out the eggs carried on the abdomen of each shrimp? and are the eggs shed all at once or by degrees? We are not prepared to give decisive answers to these queries.‡ From what occurs in other crustacea—the lobster, the edible and the shore crab, for example—there is every reason to believe that the Common Shrimp likewise carries its spawn for several months, and that the eggs ripen gradually, or, so to say, do not all liberate their embryo-brood at one sharp effort. This applies more particularly to the big, old female Brown Shrimps with large numbers of

---

* In Lanc. Sea-Fish Labor. Reports for 1893 and 1894; also Trans. Livpl. Biol. Soc. 4th Ann. Rep., 1890.

† On this head we find Ehrenbaum in his memoir does enunciate two maximum periods—mid April to beginning of June and October and November. Howsoever, from his tabular data and context, we are inclined to take a modified view of the case. Egg-bearing in shrimps (both *Crangon* and *Pandalus*) does not necessarily mean immediate expulsion of embryo from the egg. Temperature is an important factor in advancing or retarding incubation, as Ehrenbaum himself accentuates; and even age of animal influences an early or later breeding tendency. Within the Thames area the autumn months seem those of sexual congress, this being accelerated or delayed according to nature of season and concomitant circumstances. The October and November egg-bearers are only the forward product. Moreover, too much stress must not be laid on per centage numbers in spawn, for the reasons given above.

‡ Ehrenbaum says that in the summer time in his aquarium eggs hatched in four to five weeks, though in winter he believes they take as many months to ripen.

abdominal eggs, found at the end of the year. These, we apprehend, are the advance breeders of the beginning of following year. As spring arrives, younger females, bearing fewer eggs, seem to ripen in a shorter time. They form the bulk of the maximum spawning season, and the few later breeders succeed in due course.

From another point of view it may be assumed that the Brown Shrimp has but a single long ripe spawning season—the first six or eight months of the year. The few late summer breeders are overlapped by those seniors which begin to bear abdominal eggs in autumn and carry them throughout the winter season. Thus does it come about that the Brown Shrimp appears as if actively breeding throughout the entire year; whereas there are several months of its cessation. Meanwhile the egg-bearers or incubators give a defective semblance of continuity of brood.

Buckland remarks that the shrimp has comparatively a small number of eggs—a few hundreds only. Whereas Herdman mentions about 5,000 in a fully mature shrimp. We counted the eggs deposited on the abdomen in several Brown Shrimps. Among them in one 2 inches long there were in round numbers 300; in a second specimen of $2\frac{1}{8}$ inches some 850; and in a third = $2\frac{3}{4}$ inches long, about 3,550 eggs.* In each case there were some ovarian eggs not yet extruded. What looks like a discrepancy of statement, therefore, rectifies itself, for the older and bigger the shrimp, so is the plenitude of its spawn. This equally applies to crabs and lobsters. The newly extruded eggs are translucent, by degrees assuming a faint amber tinge, ultimately becoming opaque and gradually darkening as they advance in ripeness. They are attached to the abdominal segments and swimmerets by a gluey-like secretion. Here they are freely bathed and oxygenated by the sea water while incubation goes on.

---

* In good-sized females Ehrenbaum has calculated the presence of 4,000 abdominal eggs; and he suggests some shrimps may breed twice a year, and thus produce from 6,000 to 7,000 eggs annually. We have grave doubts of the shrimp's ripening its eggs and producing young twice within twelve months. Doubtless the same shrimp may carry two separate batches of eggs on the abdomen in the same year; but only one set of these hatches out young during the twelve months.

When the process is completed and the young shrimp escapes from the egg, it is then only about $\frac{1}{20}$ to $\frac{1}{16}$ of an inch long. Its combined head and body (cephalothorax) are relatively biggish; as yet there are no swimmerets; and the tail ends in a broad, shovel-shaped expansion. It is now in the so-called Zoëa-stage of naturalists. These diminutive and larval shrimps, little more than pin-heads in size, are active, free-swimming creatures, which seek and dwell on the surface of the water. (*See* fig. 28, p. 236, and fig. 29 *infra.*)

Development meantime proceeds very rapidly. But it is only after several skin moultings in quick succession, together with outgrowths of appendages and other modifications or metamorphoses, that the little shrimp acquires the adult form.*

---

* Ehrenbaum in his researches has minutely described five larval stages, and a sixth when it enters into the complete young shrimp form. His figures, though bearing the stamp of accuracy, unfortunately, are not well adapted for unscientific readers. Since our report has been in the printer's hands, Williamson, of the Aberdeen Laboratory, Scotch Fishing Board, in the 19th Ann. Rep. for 1900 (1901) has given further additions to, and confirmatory of Ehrenbaum's work. He traces with elaborate detail the development of the several head, body and tail appendages, and copiously illustrates the same. For our purpose we limit notice to those figures exhibiting the general aspect of the temporary surface resident larvæ and early ground residents. Williamson's delineations being irregularly dispersed in his plates may fail to attract the attention they deserve. We here reproduce them about half the size of his drawings, and rearranged in the manner subjoined, for more ready comparison of changes incident to each moulting stage.

FIG. 29.

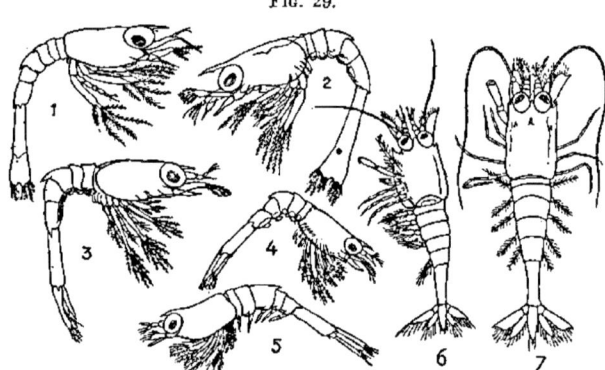

Brown Shrimp (*Crangon vulgaris*). Figs. 1 to 5 (inclusive). Magnified representations of the five larval stages, when minute habitants of top water. They show the progressive changes in head, body and tail appendages after each larval moult.

Fig. 6. In this, the sixth stage, when the creature takes to a bottom life, the adult characters are obvious, though the appendages are scarcely fully formed.

Fig. 7. With increase of size and further development of parts, the complete young shrimp condition of the shallows is reached. (*Note* that Williamson's figs. 1 to 3 were drawn to scale × 30, whereas figs. 4 to 7 were only × 12.)

It is then somewhere about a quarter of an inch long; later on it begins to change its habits, moves towards the shores and shallows, where it becomes a ground feeder. Whilst in the Zoëa, and immediately succeeding larval stages they can be obtained numerously in the surface tow-net. After an interval we find the young shrimps of half an inch upwards among the pools on our muddy flats, as has already been described. We get them from early spring, all during summer till late autumn. During winter, or with an early spell of sharp, frosty weather, their presence descends to zero. Their summer growth is manifest, and they attain 1 inch to $1\frac{1}{2}$ inches ere shoaling off to deeper water.

The smallest size of females with abdominal eggs that we have noticed have been $1\frac{3}{4}$ inches in length ; at 2 inches they are quite numerous. Taking progressive growth into consideration, it may be inferred these are not less than 12, say, rather, 15 months old ; though maturity and eggs within the ovary necessarily have been earlier. The large females presumably have attained several years of age ; but how long they may ultimately live would be haphazard guess.*

Exuviation.—This, otherwise casting of the skin or moulting, is common to the crustacea, and the shrimp is no exception. In former years, when the smacks had wells, it was a regular occurrence for the men when cleaning them out to get almost a shovelful of the shrimps' skins, the residue of their moultings. These were found more particularly in the spring—never in the height of summer—but a fair amount occasionally towards the autumn season.

In absence of wells, their moulting deceptively appears less pronounced, only because, the shrimps coming on deck in a heap, those with soft carapace are quickly passed over, almost unnoticed. As soon as the rough hand-culling is finished the

---

* Ehrenbaum holds that the N. German shrimps are productive at a year old, and those at 2-2½ inches he reckons are 15 to 18 months of age. He expresses doubts whether they ever attain more than three years, though the 2½ 3-inch sized females may be three years. We are inclined to think the 3½-3¾ inch specimens obtained by us must have been nigh four years old or over.

decks are washed down and all "rubbish" thrown overboard.
Still, we have repeatedly detected fragmentary castings with
empty egg shells adherent among the heaps, and found many
shrimps in varied stages of moulting. As this process generally
takes place in the mature shrimp[*] after the young are hatched
out, it points to the above periods as the decline or close of the
true spawning seasons.

Enemies.—Within the Thames estuary, as likewise mouths
of the Stour, Medway, Crouch, Blackwater and Colne, fishes
and crabs are the worst enemies of shrimps young and old.
Among the former we have found the flounder, dab,
brill, sole, codling, whiting, rockling, weever, smelt, bass,
gurnards, bullheads, eel pout, goby (species), dragonet
("fox"), common tope (the "rigs" and "dogs" of Kent and
Essex fishermen), skate and thornback all more or less to feed
on shrimps. Perhaps their direst foes are members of the cod
family, followed by the gurnards, bullheads, skate and thornback. The destruction and havoc that the vast shoals of
whitings and codlings commit annually among the shrimp
tribe must be something enormous, judging from the crammed
stomachfuls of them in the many which we have examined.

Nor are the Common Shore Crabs (*Carcinus mœnas*) far
behind, if we take into account that, at all seasons, they are
spread about everywhere, be it mud-flat, shallow shore or
deeper water. On occasions on some grounds the trawl will
bring up an astonishing multitude of crabs in proportion to
shrimps, &c. Then there are the edible and the swimming
crabs, &c., which play their part as well; hence (unless
fecundity) it becomes a problem how our estuarine shrimps
survive their persistent decimation by man and marine
enemies.

Variations.—Regarding albino and parti-coloured or piebald
shrimps, these we have found are not altogether uncommon in

---

[*] Moulting, as a matter of fact, is not restricted to the adults, for, as already
hinted (*supra*), when almost of microscopic size, the process is undergone frequently
within a brief interval.

the Thames estuary.*   A Yarmouth specimen, with a brown
body and milk-white tail, is figured by Patterson in the
Zoologist, 1898.

The Family Palæmonidae comprises the Prawn-like Shrimps
and the True or Common Prawn.   Their notable features are:
long saw-like beak, flattened or laterally compressed body
and humpy after-bend.

The genus *Hippolyte* has two representatives of no significance in our fisheries.

(1) SOWERBY'S SHRIMP (*Hippolyte spinus*), which is of a
buff tint, is quite a small stumpy creature with prominent
tail-bend.   It is rather a northern form, though got sparingly
on the East Coast.   We only know of it from off Harwich
when taken in shrimpers' nets (Lovett).

(2) CRANCH'S SHRIMP (*H. Cranchii*). — This diminutive
species has rather an English Channel distribution, but has
been recorded from Harwich (Lovett) and once at Yarmouth
(Patterson); length, $\frac{1}{2}$ to $\frac{3}{4}$ inch; colour, pale or drab above and
light purple below.

The PINK SHRIMP (*Pandalus annulicornis*) has several
cognomens, being known as Red Shrimp, Soldier Shrimp,
Rock Shrimp, Sea Shrimp, Æsop's Prawn, Ring-horned Prawn,
and, lastly, as the Shank on the Lancashire Coast.   Within our
District, Pink Shrimp is the more common appellation.

Concerning distribution, its southern range may be
regarded as the most north-easterly part of Kent, and
thence north among the channels, and deeps, towards the
Suffolk and Norfolk seaboard.   The brown or sand shrimp
clings shorewards to the flats and estuaries, whilst the pink
shrimp usually keeps more outwards.   Thus, from the stony
nature of the ground and their deep water habitat, the latter
derive the names of rock shrimp and sea shrimp.

---

* Tame shrimps would seem an anomaly, nevertheless W. H. Congreve tells of a
pair kept in a bell glass aquarium, which became so tame that they would take bits of
beef from the fingers.   One began to shed its coat, and its mate seemed to help in the
act of moulting (Sci. Gossip, 1886, p. 278).

The pink shrimp has decidedly a migratory habit. In early spring great shoals make their appearance, seemingly from the Norfolk and Suffolk coasts, or possibly approach landwards from the deep sea. The latter supposition seems the more feasible one, and receives strong support from the statements of the Ramsgate deep sea trawlers and Margate fishermen. The former affirm that during their winter fishing it is of common occurrence to find pink shrimps in the stomachs of the cod, and even at times a host of shrimps will be found in the trawl net itself. The ground frequented may be said to extend from the Shipwash to the Gabbards, towards the Galloper Sand and North Falls, thence to the neighbourhood of the Kentish Knock. At all events, in spring the shrimps appear to steer from opposite Orfordness towards the Wallet and make shorewards and southwards among the various deeps and channels to Prince's and Queen's Channel, where they are plentiful for weeks together. Thereafter they seem to push drove after drove chiefly towards the Girdler, Gilman and Red Sand. Later on more straggling bands head up the Thames estuary, and, becoming more scattered, mingle with the brown shrimps, to and even beyond the Nore. Later on they are still found here and there, usually diminishing in numbers as autumn wanes. But still a few are about up to the end of November—some seasons even later—especially if the weather keeps moderate. By mid-winter to all intents and purposes they have fled back to the deep sea waters, again to return the following spring season.

The wherefore of this wandering of *Pandalus*, so far as we can judge, seems to be search for food and procreative instinct. As our East Coast shrimpers have long known, the principal diet of the pink shrimp is what goes by the local name of "ross." Substantially this is but the honeycomb-work and sand-aggregated tubing of a species of worm, *Sabellaria alveolata*. The worm exists in enormous numbers among the sands and rough ground in certain localities within the great sea-bight from Orfordness to N. Kent as aforesaid. Its presence more particularly, and of another allied form of tube-building worm, *Pectinaria belgica* ("pipes" of fishers), are great sources of attraction to the prawn shrimps. Their other food is similar to that of the brown shrimp. Again, though we cannot pitch on any special locality as breeding ground of the latter, yet we have reasons for believing that around the long parallel sandbanks girding the outer arch facing Essex, there the pink shrimps flock in early spring and throw off their winter-hatched brood. Thereabouts the young shrimp's safety and food are secured in the abundance of marine vegetation and proximate zoophytes (*Sertularia, Plumularia,* &c.), with Foraminifera, minute Annelids, Mollusca and Crustacea to boot.

Whether pink or brown is the most superabundant shrimp within the Committee's District is probably conjectural. According to given locality, so does one or other exhibit excess in numbers. Nor can size be rigidly compared, for in the case of the pink shrimp, its abrupt bend rearwards and flattened sides give it a somewhat short and thin appearance. The largest passing through our hands have been $2\frac{1}{2}$ inches to $2\frac{3}{4}$ inches eye to point of telson; the smallest $\frac{1}{2}$ inch to $\frac{3}{4}$ inch. Two inches are about the medium market size of those sent from Leigh and Southend; but during the summer season the Harwich shrimpers' average catch yield a better result. Altogether, taking length, breadth and girth into consideration, the pink shrimp never attains the dimensions of the burly, vigorous brown one. Compare measurements of latter already given.

The females of *Pandalus* seem to preponderate, but in what ratio to the males we are not prepared to answer. When the female "pinks" begin to have a "hard head" (shrimpers' parlance), *i.e.*, the carapace bulges atop; this the men are sharp enough to detect as signifying the approach of, or is a premonitory sign of the berried stage. The physiological explanation is that the rigid horny carapace, unable to contain the augmentation of ova, the latter are gradually transferred to the abdominal region, there to undergo the process of incubation.

The numbers of eggs in the pink shrimp are relatively somewhat fewer than in the brown species. Their pale, emerald-green colour, when ripe, is in marked contrast to the amber tint of the latter's abdominal eggs. Moreover, in the "pinks" they are carried more in a shorter, deepish, but laterally compressed bunch than is the case in the wider-bodied "browns." On escape from the egg, the young undergo changes or metamorphoses, and an after-development in most respects resembling that of the common shrimp already adverted to.

From his long experience, R. Johnson, sen., arrives at the conclusion that the Pink Shrimp (*P. annulicornis*) has only one continuous spawning season, terminating somewhat abruptly in the spring. This, according to him, commences about November or December, and continues on to March and April. Scarcely any or none are berried during the summer months, when the brown shrimp is then at its maximum breeding season. Our own observations confirm the above. With moderate seasons even towards mid-October we have failed to find the Pink Shrimps with eggs on the swimmerets, though the ovary has shown ample signs of advancement. By mid-November or after, a small per centage would be berried, such shrimps being only of medium size; as often, with a depression of temperature, the older ones with incubating eggs hasten off to sea. Usually in December, January and early February "pinks" are conspicuous by their absence. Their condition in North Sea residence is problematical until their influx, nearly ripe-egged, at the close of February and early March. Then quickly follows escape of brood, and May sees the end of the hatching process until the November following.

A Summary and Comparison.

(*a*) The Pink (Red or Shank) Shrimp (*Pandalus*) is with us decidedly a North Sea or off-shore form, of wandering habit, seldom passing beyond salt-water range in estuaries, with partiality for hummocky sand, rough boulder or rocky grounds, showing a preference for worm diet, commonly resident where seaweeds and zoophytes abound, and with a relatively limited breeding season, terminating somewhat abruptly.

(b) The Brown (Common or Sand) Shrimp (*Crangon*) is an all-round coast, inshore form, frequenting shallow, sandy and muddy grounds; less migratory, widespread yet peculiarly estuarine in habit, at times resident in most brackish waters; predisposed to an omnivorous diet, and with a nearly continuous or only partly intermittent breeding season. In both species amatory congregations we take for granted are autumnal.

These differences, though slight and not sharply defined in all particulars, nevertheless give rise to certain variations in their mode of fishery, of which more anon.

The COMMON PRAWN (*Palæmon Serratus*).—This species may be reckoned as fairly abundant during the summer months and fall on the Kentish shores. It appears to be somewhat scarcer or more irregularly distributed within the Thames estuary, thins away in numbers on the Essex coast northwards, and becomes quite a rarity towards Yarmouth.* The Harwich shrimpers affirm that as a rule it is only on chance occasions that they bring up a few among the contents in their trawl. Various individuals tell the same tale of their luck in obtaining an odd half or whole gallon either in the East Swin or in the neighbourhood of roughish ground, east of the Naze.

Prawns do not form any special fishery among the Leigh-men, nor from Southend. During every summer and autumn, however, a scattered few occasionally are caught in their trawl-nets among the shrimps, with which evidently they associate. It is asserted by the older fishermen that in former times prawns were somewhat more abundant in the upper estuary of the Thames than they are at present. Over 30 years ago, when the Leighmen used freely to fish in the Medway, almost every autumn they would by chance have a good haul of prawns, but the men did not make a constant practice of going out for them alone. The greatest quantity, it seems, was obtained in the Medway, somewhere between Cockle Shell

---

* Patterson in " Zool.," April, 1898, says: "The news of the capture of one by a shrimper becomes quite an item of conversation amongst the fraternity."

House and the entrance of Colemouth Creek. At such times from 3 to 5 gallons would be taken at a single haul. But this could not be repeated the same day, for on being disturbed the prawns quickly dispersed, and temporarily left the locality. When the fishermen were fortunate in a catch of prawns they sent them off to the London market by the Tilbury rail from Leigh. It has been conjectured that since the formation of Port Victoria (a terminal branch of N. Kent rail) the prawns do not frequent the above Medway shore. This is very likely, as change of shore line and rooting up of a weedy bank there have materially altered the said place, at one time most attractive in its prawn food.

At Broadstairs prawns are taken along with shrimps by the shove-netters.* The recess at St. Margaret's Bay (South Fore-land) is another spot where they are annually taken. But the chief centre of prawn-fishing in our District is at Folkestone. There it is regularly pursued as a calling from May to September; some dozen to eighteen small boats being thus engaged.† Thereabouts, as also along Dymchurch sands, shove-nets are in use; but the locally so-called "lock-nets" (veritable hoop-nets or prawn-nets of West of England) are the recognised instruments of catch at Folkestone. These hoop-nets are simply conical bag-nets rove on a ring—in many respects similar to the Leigh dab-net, described later on and figured hereafter in the Plate "Thames Fishing Nets." A cord crosses the mouth, whereon pieces of fish, crabs or offal are strung as bait.‡ A 3-rayed bridle is affixed to the hoop, to which a line is hitched, this terminating in a bung-shaped cork. The float-ing corks are covered with white cloth to render them more visible at night time. By a long stick, forked at the extremity, the cork buoy is jerked up and the net run home by line from the bottom, where it lay with the prawns (and often crabs) feasting on the bait. These nets are either used among rocks or worked from a boat.

---

* These nets likewise go by the name of " push-nets " and " strand-nets " else-where.
† According to the Government Inspector's Reports of successive years.
‡ Buckland says "a fresh sheep's head" is the best bait for prawns (Curios Nat. Hist.).

The prawn's migratory and other habits are rather akin perhaps to the " pinks " more than to the " brown shrimps." So far as we learn their winter residence is the deep water off shore in the English Channel. During spring they approach inshore among the shallows and rock-pools along the coast, particularly Hants, Sussex and Kent. Squadrons of them even wander right round the S. and N. Foreland, scattering broadcast in the estuaries, &c., of the Essex bight as aforesaid. As autumn closes or cold weather creeps in they retire from the estuary, presumably returning Channelwards. At least, they then gather in large congregations on the South Kentish coast, prior to their winter's disappearance. The inference to be drawn points to the prawn's being a Channel or southern form, with a limited migration northwards ; the pink shrimp reversely comes S.W. from the North Sea and retires N. Easterly. The two species commingle, or cross and re-cross each other's usual boundaries at the entrance to the Thames, and here temporarily mix with the brown shrimp.* It may be gathered from the above, and what precedes concerning distribution, how it is that prawning is distinctly a Kentish industry, whilst pink shrimping obtains in N. Kent and Essex. Moreover, though fishery for brown shrimps is common to both, Essex inclines to have the advantage, for its capacious estuaries, mudflats, and food-yielding brackish waters apparently are those which *Crangon* prefer.

Prime market prawns from the English Channel and W. coast of Ireland occasionally are over 4 inches in length (eye to end of tail), but the current medium market size is about $3\frac{1}{4}$ inches, the smallest about $2\frac{1}{2}$ inches. Those obtained by us from the Nore sands to the Oaze and Girdler, the very largest of them have rarely exceeded 3 inches. Such as are taken more towards Harwich are said to be seldom larger. The smallest estuarine ones coming under our observation have resembled pink shrimps in dimensions.

---

* Whether the diverse tidal phenomena at the Straits of Dover, to which attention has been drawn in Chap. II., pp. 8 to 16, has an influence on shrimp and prawn areas, as derivative of former times, is quite conjectural.

Within our District prawn is the only local name, though Bell (Brit. Stalk-eyed Crust.) mentions that at Poole diminutive common prawns and allied forms are there sold as " cup-shrimps." Such as we have examined in the fresh condition contained food similar in kind to the shrimps with which they were keeping company.

Of the ratio of the sexes and their Kent and Essex spawn-ing grounds we have no reliable information. As regards breeding period, this to some extent appears to agree with that of the brown shrimp. In our estuaries they are met with bearing nearly ripe eggs on their swimmerets during May and June. On the Devonshire coast they are got with spawn on the swimmerets from November till June. Hence late autumn may be their time of congress, and the extruded eggs borne on the abdominal region throughout winter and spring, as in the case of the shrimp.

We have observed that in the prawn there appears to be a relation between size and age to the numbers of eggs carried ; a counterpart to what obtains in the true shrimp. For instance, in $2\frac{1}{2}$ inches long specimens we have counted 1,500, and in $3\frac{1}{4}$ inches examples more than twice that number. According to Thompson,[*] the eggs primarily are somewhat oval-shaped, becoming rounder as they enlarge. They change from yellowish to reddish-brown, ultimately acquiring a transparent flesh-colour. He traced the several stages after escaping from the egg ; its larval development resembling that of the shrimp, and with successive early moultings. Warrington[†] kept some in an aquarium, and observed that they moulted from the end of May till beginning of September. They ceased to feed before the operation, and afterwards devoured their castings. The period of moulting varied from 12 to 24 days in different cases. He remarks that the prawn's eyes are very brilliant at night and shine out like bull's-eye lamps.

---

[*] Edinb. New Philos. Journ., XXI. (1838), Pl. 1.
[†] Ann. and Mag. Nat. Hist., 1855, Ser. 2, IV., p. 247.

Lightning Source UK Ltd.
Milton Keynes UK
UKOW032123261112

202822UK00001B/244/P